ALSO BY STEPHEN DIXON

No Relief (1976)

Work (1977)

Too Late (1978)

Quite Contrary (1979)

14 Stories (1980)

Movies (1983)

Time to Go (1984)

Fall & Rise (1985)

Garbage (1988)

Love and Will (1989)

The Play (1989)

All Gone (1990)

Friends (1990)

Frog (1991)

Long Made Short (1993)

The Stories of Stephen Dixon (1994)

Interstate (1995)

Gould

a novel in two novels

STEPHEN DIXON

Henry Holt and Company
New York

Henry Holt and Company, Inc.
Publishers since 1866
115 West 18th Street
New York, New York 10011

Henry Holt® is a registered
trademark of Henry Holt and Company, Inc.

Published in Canada by Fitzhenry & Whiteside Ltd.,
195 Allstate Parkway, Markham, Ontario L3R 4T8.

Library of Congress Cataloging-in-Publication Data
Dixon, Stephen
Gould: a novel in two novels/Stephen Dixon.—1st ed.
        p.   cm.
        I. Title.
PS3554.I92G68   1997   96-19778
813'.54—dc20   CIP

ISBN 0-8050-4424-8

Henry Holt books are available for special promotions and
premiums. For details contact: Director, Special Markets.

Excerpts from *Gould* have been published in *Bakunin, Cups,
CutBank, Literary Review, Sonora Review,* and *Two Girls Review.*

First Edition—1997

Designed by Michelle McMillian

Printed in the United States of America
All first editions are printed on acid-free paper. ∞

1   3   5   7   9   10   8   6   4   2

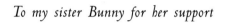

To my sister Bunny for her support

CONTENTS

Abortions

The first was when he was seventeen and just a freshman in college and she was a couple of years older. She originally told him she was eighteen because she didn't think he'd want to go out with someone almost two and a half years older than he. But he looked through her wallet and found out her real age and later told her "I'm sorry, I went into your wallet, I won't pretend I was looking for anything but to find out how old you are, because I didn't think you were eighteen—you don't act it and that you're almost a junior and your looks and clothes. And I found one of your IDs with your age on it, and so what?—for what's wrong with you being that

3

much older than me? We seem suited together, don't we?—no big deal like where you experienced World War Two and knew what be-bop was and I didn't. And it's not that you act younger than you are but maybe I act older and if that seems like bragging then just that two and a half years isn't much difference at our age, or at least not between us." Later he thought, Maybe her being almost twenty and so far along in college is the reason she let him go so far with her so quickly or let him get in her at all: third date, her folks not home, first one they kissed, second she let him rub her behind through her skirt, they'd intended to see a movie but she said while he stood by the door waiting for her to get her coat "I don't really feel like going out, it isn't that I'm feeling unwell or my period or anything like that, would it be all right if we just watched something on TV and maybe later go out for a snack?" and he said he hates TV, it's for idiots, and Saturday night?—nothing's on but dopey comedy shows; he would never own one if he had his own place, he never watches it, his father insists they do at dinner—the news; the news is important, his father says; it's the world, it's what's around us, you learn things; you're a smart boy but afraid to learn things or think the world today is unimportant?—and it always leads to arguments like that and sometimes him leaving the table before dinner's finished. *I Love Lucy*—oh wonderful; Arthur Godfrey, Sid Caesar, George whatever-his-name-is, with the crewcut and checkered jacket and overstuffed shoulder pads and always a bow tie and horselaugh—what morons, and she said "Fine, we won't watch TV, but why do you have to get so virulent about it? Maybe we should go to a movie after all, though I looked in the paper and there's nothing in walking distance that I want to see and I really don't want to take a subway or bus back and forth." "We can stay here and talk," and she said "All right, hang up your talk and let's coat," and he said "Did you mean that?" and she said "What?" and he said "You reversed a couple of words; it was pretty clever," and she said "I can't take credit for it. I have a brain problem, nothing fatal, and sometimes do that and also with my reading. But what do you want to talk about?" and he said "Can't we discuss this in a more comfortable spot?"—already maneuvering her, not so much to score but to kiss again, this time with the tongue, feel her breasts, maybe get his finger in her cunt, but that'll probably come the next date or one or two after that—"You have a living room with chairs and a couch here, don't you?" and she said "Nope, we read, talk and play chess on the floor. Well, chess I sometimes do play with my father there, but you're so smart, Mr. Thinkpants," and they went into the living room, and she said "Would you like something to drink? My father has a liquor cabinet stuffed with things, and they won't be home till past midnight, so I'll have plenty of time to wash your glass out and put water in whatever bottle you choose so it doesn't seem poured from," and he said "Boy, did I once say we were suited?—even down to our fathers. Mine's also a cheapskate with his booze," and she said "It's not that; he doesn't like the boys dating me getting tipsy on his whiskey and then getting frisky with me—it's like giving them a gun to shoot me, he's said, Freud not intended," and he said "I know Freud but not what he says, except for that double-meaning thing. But sure, I'll have something hard—what's he got?" and she said "He likes scotch, so probably lots of scotches," and he said "That's for old men, not that your father's old, but you know . . . do you have anything else? Canadian Club, that Royal something . . . a good rye?" and she looked and he drank two highballs and she had one but hardly touched it and they talked about their parents and people they'd dated and where they both were on several historical occasions to see if their paths had ever crossed—he was walking to school on D-Day when he'd heard about it, her parents told her about it at breakfast and "then went into almost like a history lesson as to what it meant"; he was in summer camp in New Jersey when World War Two ended; she was lying in a hammock at a friend's summer cottage near Peekskill when she first learned of it, "Peekskill," he said, "my folks took a bungalow there for a month when I was four or five," and she said "That was the only time I was near there—her family felt sorry I had to spend the summer in the city"; Roosevelt's death: they both walked into their apartments to find people crying and the radio blaring, but in different boroughs; Stalin's: he found out from newspaper headlines on a newsstand in the Garment Center ("Corner of 36th or 37th and Eighth Avenue to be exact") when he was delivering belts for a belt company, she was a block or two away between Seventh and Eighth and maybe around the same hour—it was after school—applying for a showroom modeling job with a coat and suit house—and he touched her hand, said "This little piggy—ah, that's silly, isn't it?" and felt himself getting high and said "Drink all yours down, catch up with me—or as you might say: 'Drink all yours down and catch down with me,' though that makes no sense, and no sense is good sense—nah, that makes no sense too. But I'm about twice your weight or a little less, so two of mine is one of yours, and you gotta be equal and fair," and she finished her drink and said "I believe you're trying to compromise me through the use of my father's booze, just as he said," and he said "That's right, I'd never lie to you," and she said "That's a lie, the last part," and he said "Oh, so what," and smiled and she did and squeezed his hand and he moved closer and said "Now I'm going to be piggy," and she said "We'll see—better than wolf, I guess, but that's a bad pun," and he thought "Pun"? What's she mean?, and she moved closer—he let her; he could have moved even closer than he was when he first started to but wanted to see if he moved a little closer whether she would too—and she put her head on his shoulder and shut her eyes and looked so satisfied and peaceful that for a moment he thought he should leave her like that—they were sitting on the couch—but he took her chin between his thumb and forefinger and said in a fake European accent he'd heard in a few movies "Mine darlink," and kissed her and she kissed back and they kissed and while they were kissing with their eyes closed he touched her breast through her blouse and she pulled her head away and said "I don't know if I want you touching me there," and he said "Then where can I?" and she said "I don't think anywhere," and he said "You let me touch your tushie last time and now you're sitting on it so I can't," and she said "If you did touch my behind then I didn't feel it so I wasn't aware you were touching it," and he said "Come off it, you don't lie, I don't lie," and she said "So maybe I did feel it but I thought that was a love tap you were doing," and he said "No, a sex tap," and she said *"Touché,"* and he said "Yes, *mucho touché,* if what I know of the word's right, *mucho* tushie *touché,"* and she said "Too much *touché,* but what I meant by 'love' was 'playful'—you were fooling around—*kidding*—and I let you because I thought it was harmless," and he said "Oh brother, was I fooling around and harmless," and she said "Don't suddenly get immature," and he said "Sorry, lady," and slid over to the end of the couch and looked at his feet and pouted and she said "What's wrong now?" and still looking at his feet he said "You know, darnit," and she said "Are you trying to manipulate me again?" and he said "I know what manual labor is," and she said "What's that supposed to mean?" and he said "It isn't the name of a Mexican worker," and she said "You sound stupid now— excuse me: just a touch silly then, for I hate that, when an intelligent sensible man intentionally acts dumb, as much as I hate an operator," and he looked at her and smiled and said "Okay, I'm wrong, I admit it, I'm sorry, very sorry, if I could apologize a hundred times without sounding redundant, I'd do it," and she smiled and he slid over to her and said "But you know, getting back to the other subject, we do know each other," and she said "We hardly do—three times plus when we first met and before that seeing each other on campus," and he said "You know me now, all about me, my ups and downs, my bads and goods, my bumps and humps—no, not that," and she said "Great time for puns," and he said "You used that word before, and now you'll see how honest and stupid I am—I mean, when you weren't looking I could have written it down and looked it up later—but what's a pun?" and she gave her definition of it and he said "How come I didn't know it?" and she said "Some people know, others do—that's a pun, almost, but more just a joke," and he said "And funny, but anyway, to end what I was saying about knowing me, you do, and I feel I know you, and I really like you," and she said "And I like you," and he said "Then, settled?" and she said "To an extent," and he said "Good," and they kissed and after about a minute of kissing he touched her breast and kept his hand there and after another minute of kissing he started unbuttoning her blouse and she tried to rebutton it and he pulled her hand away and unbuttoned the rest and rubbed her nipple with his finger and then unhooked her bra, all while they were kissing, and pulled her bra up and got her breast out from under her blouse and kissed it and while he was kissing it in different places he put her hand on his pants where his penis was and she squeezed it once and moved her hand away and he said "Come on, please, just a little more," and put her hand back and she squeezed it a few times and then left her hand on top of it and he unzipped his fly and pulled his penis out and put her hand around it and she began jerking it and then faster and he said "Easy, not so hard, I'll mess up the couch," and she said "We should stop, then, my parents will see the stain and they'll know what it is and go crazy," and he said "Wait a second, I've an idea," and kissed her and put his hand up her skirt and scratched her hair through the panties and then curled his pinky underneath the panties and felt around and got the tip of it inside her vagina and while they were kissing and two of his fingers were inside her vagina he stretched his other hand to the side table lamp behind her and she said "What are you doing?" still jerking his penis and he said "Shutting the light or making it lower—does it have two bulbs?" and she said "That one, three," and he said "I'll shut off two, all right?—it's hurting my eyes," and she said "Why? Your eyes are mostly closed," and he said "It still comes through, or it's just nicer all around that way, softer," and felt around the socket for a switch but felt light chains and pulled two of them and the room went dark and she said "Why'd you turn them all off?" and he said "I only pulled two, so that must have been all that was on," and she said "Oh well, now you don't have to look at me," and he said "Yeah, very tough to do, looking at you—you're a beauty," and she said "Sure," and he said "You are, you are—kees me, you chrazy mixed-up beauty," and kissed her and she pushed his face away and said "What do I do if the phone rings?" and he said "I don't know—where's the phone? You can't find it in the dark?" and she said "I mean, do I answer it?" and he said "No-o-o," and started pulling her panties down and she said "Suppose it was something important?" and he said "How could it be? Your parents are out. Why don't I just take it off the hook—where is it?" and she said "There's one in the kitchen," and he said "Ah, let's just let it ring," and pulled her panties down farther and she didn't stop him and he pulled them off and felt her legs and behind and inside her behind and she said "Not that place, it could be dirty," and he said "It isn't dirty—it's part of fooling around when you're doing it," and she said "Dirty as in feces, okay?"

and he said "I understand," and felt her legs around her crotch and her hair there and started pulling his pants off and she said "What are you doing?" and he said "My pants, off, they're uncomfortable, the belt buckle thing's sticking me," and thought Say "Help me, will you?" and said "Help me with them, will ya please?" and she said "I'm not sure," and he said "Don't worry, anything you don't want to do, we won't—we can just stay close to each other, rubbing and hugging but that's all," and felt her vagina and inside it and she jerked him back and forth and they were kissing and then he pulled off his pants and then shorts and shirt off and her blouse off and bra from around her arm where it was hanging and he said "Our shoes and socks," and he pulled their shoes off and his socks for she didn't have anything like that on and then he was on top of her and she said "I don't know if we should continue, this could be dangerous. Suppose my folks come back early and we do mess up the couch?" and he said "Why would they and if you want I can put my hanky or something under you or we can go to a bed," and she said "No bed," and he said "Then here, we won't be messy and nothing might come of it," and she said "One of them could get sick—my mother, one drink, and they drink a lot at those dinner affairs," and he said "Is that where they went?—where, way downtown?" feeling her body all around, and she said "Some political club event—once a year, I think it's at a big midtown hotel, with lots of speeches. They never miss it and she's a terrible drinker if they don't serve her lots of appetizers before; my father can hold his though," and he said "Don't worry, they left, what, an hour ago?—so they're just starting, and we can do anything, if we do it, quickly," and she said "I don't want to do it any kind of way," and he said "Have you ever?" and she said "Once, with a guy I liked, a few times, when I was much younger—it was a big mistake. And you?" and he said "Yes, but I have to admit it, only with women I paid—I don't like that, I'm sorry," and she said "That's all right," and he said "So what do you think?" and she said "I really don't think we should," and he said "Okay," and kissed her neck and face and breasts and belly and said "I think we should," and vagina and stuck his tongue in and turned his body around, and she said "I've never done this—I didn't with the other guy, though he wanted me to," and he said "Just try, if it's no good, not something you like, don't then, really," and she did and continued to and he did and then he felt himself coming and pushed her face away and said "You don't want to be swallowing the stuff, do you?" and she said "No, never, though I think I tasted it now," and he turned around again and kissed her and put his tongue in her mouth because he thought she'd wanted to be kissed like that after, for that would make her think he didn't think her mouth was dirty from doing it, and then he tried putting his penis in her and she said "The whole thing doesn't feel good like this, the couch isn't wide enough and my shoulder's pressed—let's get on the floor," and he thought "Good, it's done, I'm in," and said "Why not your room?" and she said "The floor's easier," and he said "How could it be?—the bed's softer," and she said "My room's a mess," and he said "Who cares about that?" and she said "I just don't want us to be there, I share it with my sister when she

12

comes home from college, and this is a good thick carpet and please don't argue," and he said "Okay," because she just might get so upset at him that she'd stop now and they got on the floor and she got on her back and spread her legs and patted her thighs, he saw all this from the light in the kitchen, and said "I'm not wearing anything, I haven't got one yet, did you bring something?" and he said yes and got up to get his wallet out of his pants and she said "Actually, I've already started my period a little, if you don't mind that—I never should have let you do what you did," and he said "By the way, when I said I had one, it wasn't for this time particularly, I just happen to have it in my wallet for a while—and before, when you shouldn't have let me do what I did, did you mean with my mouth?" and it seemed she was nodding and he said "You're nodding?" and she said yes, and he said "I didn't taste anything unusual, so maybe it had stopped before I was there—but you sure you can't get pregnant by us doing this without anything?" and she said "Positive, it's biologically impossible, though if you want to put on something, just to be extra safe, go ahead," and he said he'd rather not and got down on the floor and inside her and flattened himself on top and she said "That can't be the way, I'm not the most experienced at it, but what you're doing would squash anyone," and he said "Sorry," and raised his rear a little and after a few moves by both of them, came. They did it again a short time later and then almost every weekend someplace, sometimes both weekend nights and occasionally on a weekday, when his parents weren't home, hers, couple of times at the apartment of a friend of hers when the friend's parents were out and she left them alone for an hour, and used condoms for a while and then a diaphragm when she got fitted for one or didn't use anything around the time of her period and some-times right at the height of it—he didn't really like to do it then, all the blood on him after and the thought of her bleeding while they were doing it, the slippery stuff not so much theirs but her blood, but it didn't seem to bother her much, she'd just pull the tampon out and roll it in a tissue or napkin and drop it on the floor and once even said, lying back flat on the bed, "Why don't you do the honors this time—it's only a little string," and he told her lots of times he loved her though he only liked her a lot but loved making love with her and just knowing he had someone steady to make love with and that his friends knew, that was important too, and she said she loved him more than she had anyone before, "even if there haven't been that many guys in my life I felt deeply about: two, you're the third, and one of those two when I was so young I never let him touch me or do anything but kiss, but that was exciting enough then," and they met on campus the days they both had classes and had lunch there and sat outside when it was nice and talked and sometimes she took the subway downtown with him when he had to go to work after school, just to be another hour with him, she said. He wished he could really love her and felt bad and troubled that he didn't and sometimes thought he was wasting his time going with someone and doing such serious things with her whom he didn't think he'd ever love so much as to say it *and* mean it, and he also felt at times he was only going with her for the sex and that if she suddenly said "No more for a while" and the "while" meant a few weeks or a month or more he'd stop seeing her, cut her off quick, and he wondered what it was stopping him from loving her—her intelligence, he finally decided, she just wasn't smart enough or didn't have the kind of artistic and creative brains he liked, someone intensely interested, or just more interested than she was, in all kinds of art and could see it with a certain clearness and talk about it right, and she was also at times so bourgeois—that was the word he used to himself, for he knew it sounded so condescending— even if she was sleeping with him and enjoying it and even initiating lots of the little things when they had sex, and not just in music and books and that she thought all sorts of opera was funny—just the mention of it made her laugh—but in furniture and clothes and cars, that she really did like certain kinds of women's magazines and TV, that when they walked out of a movie he'd hated for its stupidity and obviousness she'd say it was very good if not great—this happened several times—and also what she wanted out of life: to be an elementary school teacher; he said "Outside of the long summer vacation, which I think every job should have, how could you go to the same classroom day after day with kids?" and she said "Because I'd love to and feel it's the most hard-working rewarding professional profession of all the teaching fields," and he said she ought to at least try to be a college teacher—"longer vacations and you only get to be with adults"—and she said "Why, if I love kids better and think teaching them is a much more important job?" and he said "Because it's deeper work intellectually and you'll get challenged—your brains will—more, and you'll have more time to do research and with the longer vacations and fewer classroom hours you might even eventually have more time to spend with me," and she said "Oh, you're saying we're going to last forever and ever till death do one of us part? and I'm certainly not in the least—*most* remote way—talking of marriage here; Jesus, no! but just that we're going to go on for a long time?" and he said "Why not, what's to stop us? but we'll see—one year at a time for the time being, but you also become, by being an education professor, if that's the field you want to go in to, an expert on one thing and more well read, and I'd think your conversations would also be better—who wants to hear all the things that go on with kids?" and she said "You don't like what I read now or our conversations?" and he said "I'm talking about the future; our conversations are fine, you're very bright, much brighter than me," and she said "No I'm not and you know it," and he said "We're equal then with you holding a little lead," and she said "You don't believe that either; and if you don't like the way I am or think or what I want to do with my life, then the hell with you, mister, you can take a flying leap right now," and he said "Wait, hold it, I didn't mean it that way," and she was crying and they were sitting at the kitchen table in her parents' apartment, having cake and a special mint tea she bought and he thought here's a chance to get out of it for good; just say "Well, that's it then as you said, I've had enough of this," and leave and never call again and if she called him, to just say "I'm sorry, I don't mean to hurt your feelings or anything but that last time told me everything that was wrong with us and was the finish and that's all I'm going to say," but he looked at her and her mouth and her pretty face, beautiful really, though not the smartest-looking, and her small nose and long hair in a thickly corded braid and those greenish though sometimes pale-bluish eyes he loved looking at but were now behind the closed crying lids and her mouth again, lips which he once told her, or twice, three times, she could model for cigarettes, which he'd hate for her to do because then it might mean she'd have to smoke, or lipstick or straws or ice cream pops, they were so perfectly shaped and he got an erection and looked at her breasts but her arms covered them and at her legs and bulge in the calf where it crossed over the knee making it look even more muscular and thought when she squeezes his waist with those it actually can hurt and then that if he goes now that'll be the end of their sex for the day, which they'd planned on without saying so for her folks were away for the weekend at some resort upstate and for the second time in six months he was going to stay the night here, and still seated he edged his chair up to hers and touched her face with his hand and thought what she'd like for him to do, since this is what finally stopped her crying the only other time which was over nothing he did or said but something she'd remembered from her past, someone dead, is hold her and he held her and said "Tears tears tears, who needs them and why do I incite them, right?" and without opening her eyes she said "I don't know," and he said "But I'm right about my being wrong, right?" and she said "Right, if you say so," and he said "I'm right: I'm wrong, wrong, really wrong," and kissed one lid and she opened it and smiled and he said "Your face looks crooked that way," and she opened the other eye and smiled and kissed his hand now back on her cheek and they kissed and hugged and then made love. Then she called one night and said "I have to talk to you tonight and it's not something I want to say on the phone, can we meet?" and he said "It's Wednesday and I've got an important German exam tomorrow plus my job after and I'll probably be working there late," and she said "So what are you saying?—one night, if I say it means so much to me, you can come up here even if it's that inconvenient for you, do part of your studying on the subway, and it won't take long," and he said "It has nothing to do with anything like your being very sick, something you just found out about?" and she said no and he said "Then that's a relief, but I think I know what it is," and she said "Don't say it; I've said enough already and people around here got big ears," and he said "Where're you calling from?" and she said "The candystore on Jerome, but just come up now," and they met at a coffee shop in her neighborhood and she said she was pregnant and he said "That's what I thought it was, even before I thought it might be that you're sick," and she said "You're a genius, is that what you wanted to hear?—well, you are," and he said "It's not that, it was your voice," and she said "Listen, stop it, we have things to discuss, and whatever you say next, don't ask how it happened or if there was even a possibility of another guy or I'll go crazy—I'm already crazy enough over it, what a thing!" and he said "All right, take it easy, I wasn't going to ask, but it is kind of perplexing how it could have happened, for we were very careful, weren't we?" and she said " 'He won't, he won't'—you won't, you sure about that? What a joke. Of course, you ninny, but we did it a lot when we were doing it, so maybe my protection can only hold so much or for so long—overnight, I'm saying—once, remember? Or when we were using yours you squirted a lot into it and some of it spilled over, but I don't know—accidents in the making of these things at the place they're made at. Or it could be that one day when I was so sure I didn't need protection because I'd started bleeding, I did, and it was just nature that gave me a wrong signal," and he said "You did 'what'?" and she said "It needs explaining? I did *need*, I did *need*, but I'm only speculating with all these," and he said "You've had a test?" and she said "I'm a woman, I know the signs, and yes, I've seen a doctor," and he said "Okay, then what do we do?" and she said "If you don't know, I have a solution. Through a cousin of his—" and he said "Who?" and she said "Someone, I'll tell you later, I have the name of an a.b. man on Burnside," and he said "That's in the Bronx?" and she said "Yes, it's a big avenue, cutting clear across it, almost—east and west; this one's on west," and he said "What's 'a.b.'?" and she said " 'A.b.' for you know what—to get rid of it, the a.b. man does—he performs them. He's a real doctor, licensed, but does this on the side and we need three hundred dollars," and he said "Where're we going to come up with that?" and she said "You've told me you have some money saved," and he said "I do, I forgot about that, a little," and she said "How much?" and he said "A hundred twenty-five, maybe a hundred thirty-five—I haven't had my interest posted in a long time, but no more than that, even with it," when he had about four hundred, and she said "You take your hundred twenty-five or more, if there's more—you'll have to close your account, that's all. And I'll get my hundred and a few dollars and have to scrape together another fifty, and we'll do it even-Steven: if I contribute more than you, then you owe me. But you'll come with me for it, won't you? Because if you don't I'll be afraid and mad, very mad, and you should be with me there and to take me home and this has never happened to me, so I'll need someone like you," and he said "Sure, what do you think?" but didn't want to but would because if he didn't she'd stop speaking to him, he was almost sure of that, or just stop sleeping with him, and he really was mostly going out with her to get laid, and if he did what she wanted she'd feel even better to him after that, not that she could do any more for him than she was or he'd even want her to. So she made the appointment, they went to the doctor's office, the doctor said "Good, right on time," and told him to go out for two hours and come back. He said "I thought I was supposed to stay—she wanted me to," and then to her, since he really would rather be away from her during it, "Is it okay with you?" and she said "I don't know, I don't like it," and the doctor said "Whether it's okay with her or she likes it or not, it's what you have to do, I don't want any other person here during the procedures, for our own safety," and he said "How do you mean, we in any danger?" and he said "Please, young man, valuable time's wasting and if a minute more of it does I'll have to ask the both of you to go," so he left, said before he did "You'll be all right?" and she said "I'm sure I will," and gave him a scared, or maybe for his sake, a reassuring smile—he couldn't tell which—went to a movie theater a few blocks away which he'd seen when they'd climbed out of the subway station, left in half an hour because he couldn't sit there when he was feeling he wasn't sure what, jittery, unhappy, guilty, not only worried for her but that they'd be caught by the police, sick in the stomach a little at what she was probably going through now, that she was there, legs strapped in, she'd told him what it'd probably be like and on something like an operating table, while he was watching a so-called serious art movie with people, when he looked around, looking at the screen so intently, walked around the neighborhood for about an hour and went back to the doctor's building, knew he'd come back too soon but wanted to be there if just sitting in the waiting room while she was being finished up, buzzed the office from the lobby and the doctor said on the intercom "Yes?" and he said "It's me, I'd like to be rung in, please," and the doctor said "I'll be done with my work in half an hour, sir, have a coffee someplace," so he walked around some more, had a soda at a coffee shop, bought a paperback and read a few pages, went back; "Your friend is resting in the next room," the doctor said, "but not to worry; she's been there long enough and I think we can disturb her now," and went into a room, came out with her with his hand supporting her elbow, she looked as if she'd been crying and said "I hurt so down there, but the doctor said it'll all pass. I wasn't out during it— not even a painkiller. He said the medical problems might really begin if he did one of those and he wanted me alert when I left and also so I'd be attentive to any bad symptoms. So I was altogether awake and it felt like I was having my guts scooped out," and the doctor said "If it felt like that, young lady, it could only have been momentarily. I didn't touch anything that didn't need to be touched. You'll be sore for a while, but that's all," and told her what to look out for: blood, hemorrhaging, severe cramps, and where to go if anything went wrong—"Not here but to a hospital, and just say you did it yourselves," and Gould said at the door "Just one question, Doctor. When do you think, meaning in how long, we'll be able to have sex again?—I'm only asking so she doesn't take any chances with her body healing," and she said "What a question.—Forget he asked that," to the doctor, and to him "How could you, Gould? I'll know myself when I feel better, if I'll ever even want to do it again after what I went through," and he looked at her sharply, they'd given phony names and here she was using his real one, and she said "What's the look for? Okay, okay, so I used your last name, I'm sorry," and the doctor said "Not to worry, dear. Nobody gives me his right name and I could care less about it. And to me this 'Gould' could be yet another alias in a carefully concocted collaboration between the two of you to steer me away from your real names, and that could be par for the course too. Believe me, though: once you're out of here I don't know you and have never seen you and same, as far as it can be done, the other way around. As to your question, young man, it's a legitimate one and something I should have addressed. Don't have intercourse where there's genital penetration till after her next period, even if that takes a month.—So, that wasn't too bad, was it, young lady? Now good-bye," and they left, he helped her downstairs and on the street as they headed for the subway he thought over what he was thinking of saying to her and then said to himself "Ah, go on and say it, what's the harm?" and he said "I can see how you're not feeling good and what I'm going to say has nothing to do with anything today or tomorrow and so on, but I don't know if I'll be able to hold out on the intercourse for as long as the doctor said," and she said "Oh, such urgency; such sensitivity; he even takes my current distress into consideration; what a man! As I already told you, sex is the last thing on my mind now, the absolute last, and if you mention it once more this week you're guaranteed it never happening again between us and not as any punishment either but because you're such a conceited heel." They saw each other every weekend till summer; then she got a counselor job at a sleepaway camp, wanted him to come with her and he applied but the camp had nothing for him and he said he'd write her a lot and try visiting her on one of her days off. She wrote him less and less after the first two weeks and her letters had become kind of cold. She's found someone else, he thought. Well, that's okay, for he was seeing someone at the Catskill resort he got a waiter's job at, though not anyone he felt deeply about; a waitress who covered his station and helped him set up when he was behind and put out for him whenever he wanted and was pretty and his age and fairly smart and who one day he might even get to like a lot; she was bubbly, compared to the other one, and not as dark about life and liked having fun more. He called his girlfriend at camp and she said "What is it? I'm only supposed to be taken away from my kids for an emergency and you must have said it was, else they never would have dragged me up here," and he said "So I lied to speak to you; so big deal, my terrible sin, that I wanted to hear your voice so much after six weeks. So tell me, how come you hardly write anymore and when you do your words are just bursting with warmth, that's all I want to know," and she said "You asked, but you really want an answer?" and he said "Why else?" and she said "Okay. I've been seeing this man—the head counselor, if you want to know—and I felt bad about it because of you and didn't know how to say it. But let's face it: you never really loved me. You only said you did when I asked, but you loved my body more and only liked and appreciated the rest of me a little, maybe, isn't that true?" and he said "If he's the head counselor, why would they give you any crap about going to a phone?" and she said "You know that has nothing to do with what I was saying. I was talking about what I was to you before the summer, but by now that's a moot point," and he said "Oh, moot is it, moot? What the hell's that, something you put on a trombone?" and she said "Are we going to start arguing again, and you extra stupidly, after not seeing each other for so long?" and he said "No. Anyway, before the summer, you were saying that you think you meant little to me. Well, not so, you were more than that, much more, and I'll be honest and say I miss you a lot and you never know what can happen in the future too. My feelings to you could get much better, three times, four times, go sky high," for he thought who's he going to screw in New York when he gets back? Not the waitress. She comes from Hartford and will be in college near Boston and who wants to go up there every weekend or every other one or any time, no matter how much he might get to like her, since she'll be with thirty girls and a house mother in a sorority house, so where will he even stay? Not in a hotel, on what he makes, and just the bus or train fare . . . But she said "Gould, there's not going to be any future for us, I'm no seer but I see that and I'm sorry. And this fellow I'm seeing is serious about me and I think I'm in love with him too, so he looks like a much better prospect for the future than you," and he said "Does he live in New York?" and she said "Close. Jersey; Trenton," and he said "Do you know how far Trenton is from New York? How will you ever get to see him?" and she said "It's at the most an hour and a half away by train and he said he'll come in as often as I want. And he has his own apartment, so I can stay with him when I'm there," and he said "Have you ever seen Trenton? I have, from the train. It's a dump—seedy, ugly; maybe you'll end up living there. Well, good, go on, but it'll be the end of your intellectual or just spiritual life for good—shitholes like that tear an intelligent person down," and she said "What would you know about what cities do? You've lived in *one*, New York. And I don't plan to settle there and neither does he. He's a law student and can get a job anywhere after, so long as he takes that state's bar," and he said "How old's this guy?" and she said "Twenty-four, why?" and he said "Oh boy, older men, real experienced, I bet he's had lots of girls—lots of counselors—it's probably even why he took the job. Mr. Head Authority, lording it over his slaves; tells them to go down on him or they lose their puny jobs, and they do, the imbeciles, they're too young and dumb not to. But good, you finally got someone who can teach you something about life, though whether you'll like the lesson after a while—" and she said "You're being asinine again. And about him teaching me anything, I'm not sure what you're referring to, but if it's what I think it is then you're not only a big schmo but," and she whispered this, "a pathetic jerk," and hung up. He called right back and the man who answered said she was already halfway down the hill and he said "Well get her back right away. It's about her father, something new," and she came back and said "Yes?" and he said "It's me again," and she said "No kidding. What is it, though? I had to come back, just so they wouldn't think I was having an argument with someone—this is the camp office, you know—or that I'd ignore something about my father being ill," and he said "I called back, well, to apologize; seriously, I do. I'm sorry, I am a big schmo and jerk and probably even worse," and she said "Fine, you know it, and I accept your apology. But oh gosh, you can be awful when you get mean," and he said "You're right, thoroughly and incontrovertibly, and I won't get that way anymore, I swear not to, but we will get back together again, if just a little, when we're back in the city— we'll at least give it a shot, won't we?" and she said "No, and that's final," and he said "All right, it was nice and you were great and we really went through something with that a.b.— you, most of it—and which I'll never forget and I think it linked us in some way forever," thinking maybe at hearing all that she'll think of what they did go through and how he went to the doctor's with her and paid half and everything and change her mind about not seeing him again, and she said "Yes, me too," and hung up. He called her in New York a couple of times, her mother said she wasn't home and she'd give her the message, but she never called back.

The second time was also in New York. He met her at a party she came to with a friend of his, she seemed to be interested in him just by her occasional glances his way, he signaled her to meet him in the kitchen and said there "Look, I'd love to get your number and call you up sometime but you go out with a guy I know, or at least you came in with him, so that's a problem, isn't it?" and she said "We're really just good friends," and he said "You don't sleep with him?" and she said "Who said that's your business? And if we did we could still just be good friends, couldn't we? but like to sleep with each other, even though I'm not saying that's the situation with Tim and me," and he said "So then maybe we could see each other one time," and she said "It's okay with me and I don't think Tim will mind too much; I'll ask him," and he said "Maybe I should," and she said "Better if I do; he might get mad at you for horning in and then there could be a row; I'll put it in a way you wouldn't be able to," and he said "How's that?" and she said "I'll say 'I flashed on this guy, Tim, and he happens to be someone you know. He doesn't want to have anything to do with me because of that, but that's not what I want, so what do you say, Tim, will you mind very much if I see him while seeing you too?'" and he said "I don't know how I like that arrangement, you seeing him one day, me the next, maybe even some other guy you flash on being a third, and so on," and she said "What's the matter, you want everything? You don't even know me, so you have no hold. And Tim's my friend and if it happened where I started sleeping with you, what'll be the harm that I also sometimes sleep with him? I knew him first and who's to say I won't always like him more than you and also like

27

sleeping with him more? But, you know, if it turned out that you're the only guy I want to sleep with, then that's how it'll be. That is, if we do end up sleeping together, for that's not why I'm interested in you, I want you to know," and he said "I won't ask why; that'd be too self-serving, I suppose," and she said "I already told you: we flashed on each other and the outlook appears bright," and he said "Then good, I'm glad; I also realize that isn't all there is, what you said," and she said "I was wondering, for a moment." She came back with Tim about ten minutes later and Tim looked angry and said "What the hell you think you're doing, Gould?" and he said "I'm sorry, and I told her I didn't want to have anything to do with it, so what are you talking about?" and Tim said "Don't hand me that; trying to steal my girl away," and he said "I wasn't trying to steal. We were talking, didn't she tell you?—and then, I don't know what, but nothing's happened, and you don't even want me talking to her, well, so I won't, she's all yours," and the girl said "Oh look at you two: 'Here, you take her'; 'Yeah, I'll take her,' as if I was a big slab of prize beef you got cheap," and Tim laughed and said "Only joking, you fool," and to Gould "She flashed on you, she said; way to go, you're getting a great babe, or *woman,* I'm afraid," bowing gallantly to her with his hand sweeping in front of him as if he had an eighteenth-century hat in it, "and there's nothing between us, right?" to her, and she said "Right," and Gould said "Even better," and Tim said "Not that I want you leaving with her tonight; I came with her, I escort her home," and she said "Excuse me, I'll decide," and Tim said "Okay, decide," and she said "I choose to go with . . ." and Tim said

"Oh, go with Gould; I understand he has a shlong a mile long," and she punched his arm and said "You beast," and Tim said "Only joking again; he's got a matchstick that's all wet, so don't expect much for a number of reasons," and left, and she said "What a drip he can be sometimes," and then "Ah, now we're alone and free," and Gould said "This is making me dizzy," and she said "I got the cure; shut your eyes and pucker-thee-up," and he said "Right, we haven't done anything like that yet," and she said "So? What about it?" and he put his arms around her and they kissed and kissed again and she said "Umm, you taste sweet; Tim tasted from ugly pipe tobacco," and after some more kissing they went inside and sat on the couch and held hands and she leaned her head back on his arm around her shoulders and kissed the fingers near her cheek once and Tim said "Look at those goofy lovebirds; so, fuck already, fuck or fly away," and she said "Did I ask you?" and the host said "Tim, your language, will ya?" and Tim said "Ah, screw it, it's my way of grieving," and she said "You dodo—c'mere," and kissed him on the lips and Tim said "I guess that's the best I'm gonna get, eh?" and Gould wished it were so, wanted to love a woman he was sleeping with, but what the hell, this was second best; no, sitting here and holding her was third best; first was the whole thing, arm around her at a party and kissing and sex, and second just sleeping with a girl he liked but there was no chance of his being in love with, and she shared an apartment with another girl and was a beauty all right, the face, the neck, when he first saw her he thought she was a dancer, which had always been an attraction, and she turned out to be, with a great body, long legs, the works, hard rear and from what he could see from the bulge they made against her shirt and what he'd felt against his chest, solid breasts, but she was Negro and that was a problem but he didn't think it'd be much of one. He'd never had sex with a Negro except a whore in Harlem when he was in high school and drove up with an older friend in his friend's father's car and picked up a hooker on the street and she didn't want to drive with them to the park or somewhere because you never know, girls have got killed that way and they were afraid of going to one of the local hotels so they each in turn did it with her standing up in a little area under the stairs on the ground floor of a rundown brownstone and a few times during it people leaving or entering the building said as they went up or down the stairs "What're you doing back there? Kids live here. Do your filthy, scummy business some other place." They went to her apartment and she said to her roommate "This is Gould; you know, I don't even remember his last name. But a nice guy I met at the party tonight. If you're up at eight tomorrow and I'm not wake me and don't take a no; I have early rehearsal," and they went to her room, she said "You want to wash up now, because I'm tired and want to get to bed quickly," and he said "I don't have a toothbrush and I'd seriously like to use one," and she said use hers, it's the pink one and told him where the bathroom was and as he went to it he passed her roommate's door, it was open a little and he could smell cigarette smoke and hear soft music, chamber, Vivaldi or Bach or one of those from the Baroque, she was a dancer and good-looking too and he thought maybe one day she might want to do a threesome with them; he'd never done it, but these two, they seem so free or unconcerned or something like that about sex and men sleeping over, so who knows if they might not go for it—it's been a fantasy of his for a while; he'll be sure to be extra nice and polite to the roommate and also but in a subtle way do what he can to be physically attractive to her and after a while hint at it to the girl. She was naked when he got back to the room and she said "Any special preference to which side of the bed you want?" and he said "Either," and she said "Then take the left one; traditionally, I'm a smack-dab-in-the-center sleeper, but with a guy I like to be on the right," and went to the bathroom without putting anything on. When she came back he was on top of the bed with his clothes on and she said "What are you waiting for? Oh, itty baby wants momma to undress him?" and he said "That wouldn't be so bad, though it's not essential; but first time, it would've been nice to remove each other's clothes and, you know, gradually reveal what's underneath," and she said "That's hogwash; as you can see, what I've got underneath every girl's got—boobs, bush and cracks—unless she has one of those third nipples or something, which I don't have. Look, you just want to screw and so do I, but if you insist—next time, if there'll be one, the slow shedding of clothes and striptease, all right? To-night, let's just get it over with, if you're not too tired—I am, almost—because I do have that early rehearsal call tomorrow, which means neither of us sleeps late." She helped him take off his shirt, only because it got stuck around his ears, he took off his pants and shorts and they got under the covers and made love. He wanted to make love in the morning and she started to but looked at the clock and said "Oh my gosh, sorry, gotta catch a bus," and took his hand away from her vagina and got out of bed. He saw her a couple of times a week for months and she had a number of boyfriends, she said, but she liked him most and he was her best lover too, and he said "I don't believe a word you say about that," and she said "Really, you are, for two of the other three guys are demi-fags so they sometimes want to do it to me as if I'm a man, and that I want no part of, none. All I need is a ruptured rectum or torn sphincter, if that's what you get. Not just that it'll hurt like the devil, but try and dance with it." Sometimes he felt self-conscious with her on the street or in a restaurant, for some reason never on movie lines or in theaters or bars or at talks. People occasionally stared, pointed them out, more like touching someone's arm and saying "Don't look to your left too quickly but there's something there I want you to see," sometimes he's sure because she was so beautiful, and her height and figure, and she talked so dramatically, her gestures and big voice, but he knew the looks from others were also angry at times, though some people smiled at them in a way which said "Good, white and Negro can go together, they can even fall in love, it's healthy and right and important and time for that and this couple proves it can work." But he's getting away from the point. The point's abortion. He held hands with her on the street, put his arm around her at bars, kissed in those places, did everything anywhere he would with any girl he was seeing, though he was never in love with her; they had a good time, got along well, made each other laugh, saw other partners during all this time, and then they broke up. She said she wanted something more stable, just wanted to see one man now, maybe even think of eventually marrying and having a kid or two and she for sure knew it wasn't going to be with him. She had fun with him, the sex was great, he was smart, nice-looking enough, pleasant and witty most times though too often a bit removed and cold or grim, but she didn't feel anything—what should she call it? help her out with this, he's good with words, which was another thing she liked about him and that he didn't parade it—anyway, nothing deep or just really emotional toward him, and don't kid her, he didn't for her either, so she thinks they ought to break up and without any fuss. Not "ought," they have to, that's all; some things you don't want to take beyond their natural life spans and maybe even some things you should end while they're still pretty good so before their natural life spans are up. He said okay, he likes her but as she said he doesn't love her, though he thinks he did a few times and sometimes for days, but enough about that, and they were silent, not looking at each other, or at least he wasn't to her, as they walked to her building from the bar they'd had this talk at, and he said goodnight at the door and she said "Look, one last time won't kill us and it'll be interesting too, knowing that unless there's this tremendous sexual emergency of some kind in the future that the other one can quickly relieve, this is the last for all time," and he said "You think there's a chance for some future thing like that, because I wouldn't mind?" and she said "No, I was really just talking, but so what." They went to bed and in the morning he wanted to do it again and she said "Last night's was fine as a fond fare-thee-well-my-undarlinged—how do you like that one? better than even you've made—but now I'm not in the mood and don't see myself getting in it, so I wouldn't want this time to be the one I remember as the last," and he said "Last, fast, we both have no clothes on and we're all greased up for it from last night so let's just do it, and you can get into it for a few minutes," and she said "I mean it, don't make me think I made a mistake by suggesting the one last night, and I would have to put more gook in the diaphragm when what I want to do most is take the damn thing out." She called him a few months later and said "How are you?" and he said "Fine, but surprised to hear from you after so long," and she said "Uh-oh, your voice, it's so unwelcoming—so I should probably get right to it, why I called, right?" and he said "It'd be appreciated," and she said "Well, guess what? I've gone and got myself pregnant by you, how's that for openers?" and he said "What're you talking about? I haven't seen you for three months," and she said "That's exactly how many months pregnant I am, and I have to get an abortion now unless I want it to be an induced miscarriage or worse," and he said "Why do you think . . . no, this once got me into trouble, not with you, but—oh, I'll ask it anyway, for it fits here: Why are you so sure it's mine? You were always seeing three to four other guys," and she said "No more than three others, and because I know who I sleep with and at the time I hadn't slept with anyone for about three weeks before you. Not those fags, if that's what you're about to say; we just petted or did other things but no penetration—and nobody the weeks after you or till I skipped my regular period. It's you," and he said "Also, which makes me curious, why'd you wait so long in telling me, if it is me who you say did it?" and she said "I thought I could take care of it myself, but I put it off too long, for reasons of my own making but which have nothing to do with you, and I now see where I need the money for the operation," and he said "What reasons that don't have to do with me—the whole thing seems to have to do with me, am I wrong?" and she said "Boy, you're stubborn. Reasons, I'm saying; stupidity on my part, I'm saying. I don't know; that I thought I was smarter and cleverer and more capable than I am and also maybe believing that some cheap home remedies, as someone told me, would work, and which I never even got around to try, I'm so lazy—okay?" and he said "I'm still a little skeptical about this," and she said "Does that mean you're not going to help me?" and he said "Let me think about it," and she said "I've arranged an abortion in two days and I need help fast if you're going to help—that means money right away and it also means, if you really want to be helpful, coming with me when I go in for it," and he said "I still have to think about it first; I'll call you tomorrow," and she said "You were never like this, that I remember—so what happened?" and he said "We've been split up for a while, you know, so I don't have the right to be skeptical?" and she said "I don't see where the two equate. No, I'll say, you don't have the right, because haven't I always been straight-out and open with you, holding nothing back?" and he said "Yeah, I guess, but I also think I do have a reason for being at least somewhat skeptical, for who knows what could have happened with you the last three months; but I'll call tomorrow, I swear," and she said

"Fuck you then, you shithead; call nobody tomorrow as I never want to talk to your ugly snake face again," and hung up. He didn't call and a month later got a letter from her saying "Don't ask me why I'm being so conciliatory to you in relating all this, but here goes: the good news. Everything worked out A-OK. If you want to contribute to the fund that made it this way, you can send whatever you want, although $200 would be fine and rock-bottom and quite fair. No matter what, papa is off the hook, even if he contributes zero. How's that for gracious pardons, and I don't mean the excusez-me kind. Best and much luck. Yours sincerely and honestly." He thought why should he send her anything? It probably was some other guy who was responsible, or easily could have been. Sure, she was usually honest and direct to him, or seemed to be, but sometimes he didn't think she was telling the truth. Even with the two homosexuals. He bets both those guys, or has a sneaky suspicion, were straight and she just said they weren't . . . for what? So his ego wouldn't be bruised, or something? Or so he wouldn't feel he was one of four guys sticking it in her, and all the images that brings up, and maybe sometimes the four of them in a week, or five guys, even, or six—because how would he know for sure? As for the contribution, he didn't know what to do. Maybe a hundred, or more like fifty, which was about what he could afford. Either would help out a little and shut her up—for sure a hundred would—and cut him off from her for good. Well, maybe, but a hundred the max. He sent nothing. He never heard from her again. About a year later he was at a friend's apartment for dinner, a married couple, and while the woman was washing the dishes and he was drying them she said "You know, of course, that Lynette Taylor died," and he said "What? What're you saying? Lynette? The dancer?" and she was nodding and he said "But what do you mean? What could've happened?" and felt faint, at least his legs got weak, and he had to sit and was still holding the dish and towel and the woman took the dish out of his hand and said "Why are you so white? What's wrong? You look sick," and he said "Don't you know?" and she said "Know what? That you went out with her a couple of times and more than likely shtupped her?—for she was a free bird if there ever was one. But what of it? So did a lot of men," and he said "I went out with her for months; maybe a half year. Two to three times a week. She wanted to marry me. I was very close to her. She was pregnant with my baby once and had an abortion—a year ago, or sometime around that," and she said "That I also didn't know.—Monty, come in here, Gould's not feeling well," and her husband came into the room and said "What's wrong, your stomach?" and he said "Anna just told me Lynette, the dancer, died," and Monty said "And you didn't know? I thought everyone who knew her had at least heard about it. Overdose, at a party; got sick, went into the bedroom to rest and she never woke up. What, a month ago?" to Anna and she said "I think so; no more than that," and Monty said to him "She wasn't an addict; it might have been the first time she took the stuff. Cocaine with the booze, they said. But she just stopped breathing," and Anna said "He took it so badly before I thought he was going to have a stroke himself. Did you know they were so close?" and Monty said "I knew they saw each

37

other sometimes, and that Tim Rudd was pissed, someone said, because Gould took her away from him at a party—or something like that happened, anyway—but that's about it," and she said "That's what I remember too, except for the Tim thing. Once at a party I saw Gould and Lynette, is all, though I don't recall any incandescence between them, do you?" and Monty said "Never, which is why we're both so surprised, Gould. What were you doing, hiding it?" and he said "What do you mean, because of her color?" and Monty said "Yes, if you want me to be honest about it," and he said "But it's not so; I came to a few parties with her that you two were at, you don't remember?" and Anna said "Just that one that I can recall," and he said "Well, I haven't been invited to many for the past year or so, so maybe that's why," and she said "To be frank with you, I think that's because you were usually telling people off at parties—getting drunk, maybe, to do it—and they were getting bugged by your attitude," and he said "Well, I don't know, people we know have become so freaking . . . middle class or something, lately, and it got to me—long ago—and their minds like compression machines, so old before their time when before they were so lively, talked about writing, thought about art, were going to chip away at walls in whatever field we went in, were freer and didn't just think advancement and money. But I still can't believe it about her—Lynette, her dying. There wasn't a funeral? Or there was and you went and never thought to tell me?" and Anna said "What did they do with her, honey?" and Monty said "Her family came up and brought her back to Raleigh to be buried and there wasn't even a memorial here for her, that I'm aware of. Was there and we just missed it?" and she said "We would have known, and gone to it, of that I'm positive," and Monty said "True, we would have known, but why would we have gone to it? She wasn't, to be perfectly honest, anything particularly special in our lives, though really a nice, beautiful girl, I thought, and from everything I heard, a terrific modern dancer," and he said "Poor Lynette," and Anna said "She was beautiful—gorgeous, is more like it. Those cheeks, and with a gorgeous figure, which is to be expected. I can see why you were drawn to her—I think Monty, by what he said, was too—but I'd think she'd be too wild for you after a few times . . . for almost anybody. Unlike Monty, I wasn't surprised when I heard about it; nor do I believe . . . what I'm saying is I'm almost positive she was involved with hard drugs for a while, or she was heading for it. She seemed to want to try anything; you could see it in her gaze and by what she said. That wasn't the time I saw her with you, Gould, but—Tim, for instance; I forget if that was before or after you—and with others, I think, or alone. But you said she was pregnant with your baby?" and Monty said "She was? I never heard that," and Anna said "Don't believe it, Gould, just don't, or have very strong doubts. It could have been no baby or one from any number of men, because someone as wild as she was could also be an imaginative and, all right, I'll say it, a conniving liar too," and he said "She said she was pregnant and that I was the father, and when a woman says that you have to believe it unqualifiedly and help her out," and she said "You went to the doctor with her and everything—I mean, the abortionist too?" and he said "She said I didn't need to and that she in fact didn't want me there—this was after we broke up, you understand. That she was plenty independent enough to do all of it herself—her words, almost verbatim," and Monty said "She told you she got pregnant *after* you broke up?" and he said "That she got pregnant before, but told me after we broke up," and Monty said "I was wondering, but it still smells a bit fishy to me. Listen, no disrespect meant to that lovely creature, but I wouldn't run around telling people you got even that close to being a father, though it was certainly the more than decent thing to do to help her out with the abortion, I assume you were talking about," and he said yes, and Anna said "What do they go for these days? You might not know this, but I had one— Monty and I—right when we were starting grad school, and before it turned out we couldn't have children, and it cost us a then-walloping two hundred," and he said "No, I didn't know; I'm sorry. She didn't give me the exact figure, but I managed to scrounge up three-fifty for her, which I think covered it completely and with maybe a few bucks to spare," and she said "Wow, unbelievable, *unbelievable*; can you imagine that, Monty?" and Monty said "If she had one, then at that price I suspect it was done by a real physician," and he said "I believe so." He called her roommate when he got home and she said "It's late, my new roommate has super hearing so can hear my talking through the walls, but besides all that I don't want to talk about it on the phone. It's too disturbing. If you want to discuss it, come here," and he went to see her the next night. She said "I was devastated; she was my closest friend. There's nothing I can tell you to add to anything, nor do I want to; you have no right to know," and he said "So thanks, but why'd I come down here then?" and she said "I asked you here so I could say to your face what I've been hoping to since even before she died and that's that you're a rotten stinking scumbag. She was in trouble and asked you for help and you wouldn't give it. You even hung up on her," and he said "I didn't hang up. I told her I'd call the next day with my decision and I thought it over and decided to help her as much as I could, financially and every other way—personally—but your line was busy and busy and busy, and same for the next day and the one after that. I gave up, thinking something was wrong with your phone—the operator didn't think so; I called one and she checked your line—and that Lynette would call me, knowing something might be wrong with the phone, but she didn't. When that happened I thought 'Well, she wants to do it all herself; so let her.' And then I got a letter from her a few weeks later saying everything was okay and the abortion a success and she had no bad feelings toward me anymore, and that was it, so why are you letting me have it like this?" and she said "Lynette never lied and I'm sure our phone was fine then. And that when you hung up on her you in effect kissed her off. And she was right, because you never came through with a red cent, not then nor when she later asked you in a letter to help cover it. It hurt her tremendously. To the point where I thought she was even thinking of harming herself because of it," and he said "Oh, come on. What are you going to accuse me of next, the overdose?" and she said "I'm not. She was foolish that way, took too many chances. But I also know she was broken up over having to lose the fetus the way she did, and your fetus, for she told me it was yours. And also that she had to borrow from her parents to pay for it, and all that didn't help her to not take chances at parties the months after or not to carry out her experiments on herself, I'll call them, too far. But that's all I wanted to say to you." She closed her eyes, for a few seconds was silent in thought it seemed, and then said "Yes, that's all. I don't want to tell you anything else; you don't deserve it. What she felt about you—she felt a lot. How you hurt her by taking her to certain places and not others and only seeing her in the evening or here, and so on, because she wasn't the right color. I couldn't understand why she continued dating you once she knew all this, and sleeping with you too?—she must have been out of her mind. But that was another problem she had, a psychological one with white guys—the fascination with the Other, and taking their shit, and all that crap, and the more egotistical and callous they were, the harder she fell for them. But get out of here, you bastard. Get out now," and he said "Hold it, just hear me out, because she fell for who?—she didn't fall for me," and she said "Now, out, now, or I'll yell for Janice in there to call the cops," and he left. Who knows? he thought on the way home. She could have lied to her roommate too. Or who knows, the baby could have been his. Let's say it was; well, he still shouldn't feel responsible in any way for her death. Did he try to keep her under wraps? Okay, he did a little, but not that much and he did feel, and she must have seen this, more and more comfortable being with her—on the street, anyplace—the longer he knew her, and she could have said something if any of it bothered her, no? They just weren't right for each other, that's the main thing; for a long-term commitment or short-term romance or anything except an overnight fling, and maybe you don't even want to start with something like that, and she should have been able to take care of herself. She said she could and he believed her, so why's he being blamed by that neurotic witch and why was he before by Lynette? She gave off the presence, and this is what she wanted to give off, of someone able to look after every aspect of herself, so why wasn't she? It couldn't have been all a goddamn farce on her part, could it? And she knew as well as he they only went with each other for the sex and to have a good time other ways, and to see someone fairly steadily but not to be tied down, and things like that and maybe, just maybe there was a little more to it for both of them—some feeling—he even said that to her once about himself, and sometimes when he was with her he did feel it, for a moment, for a night, but he did—but that was about it, all they wanted at the time and all there was. Does he have it right? He thinks he does. Is he being straight with himself? He thinks so, or as much as he can when he hasn't thought much about it before, and if he isn't being straight, then only by a little. She liked his looks, he loved hers and her wildness most times and boldness and outspokenness and unconventionalness and the profession she was in and so forth, and same she for him with two or three of those and his intelligence, or at least his book knowledge—his critical abilities when it came to artistic things, she said—and they liked—for him it was nearly "worshipped"—each other's bodies. They used to talk about it: "I've never seen such a hard perfectly shaped ass"—he; "I love your fat brawny neck; you look like you could jack up cars with it"—she; "Your biceps and popping veins in your forearms [she meant from the muscles] and large high-arched feet"; "Your endless legs and, solid as they are, the modeling clay–like way they curl around me"—he; "Your big dick with the beauty mark on it"; "Your every-single-time ready-to-go hole"—nothing brainy, nothing serious or new, except maybe for them; this is how they talked when they were alone in his flat or her room or on their bed, and if she missed a period a week or two after they last had sex—he can picture her right now lying in bed when she said that about his dick; he was sitting in a chair opposite her putting on his briefs; she still had the sheet over her shoulders and was sort of peeping out from behind it—why didn't she call him then? Did he ask her that? He thinks he did. But if she said anything, right now he forgets. And same with her ass: he was in bed, she was standing nude in front of her bedroom's long door mirror, leaning forward a little to inspect something on her face when he said that about its shape. He would have believed her if she'd called then. Be honest, would he have? More than her calling him three months later, and what she said then, he now remembers, is that she thought she could take care of it herself. What did she mean—a coat hanger, special pills, something like that? Did he ask her? He thinks he did, but now he can't remember it. No, once she stopped seeing him—once they stopped seeing each other, for he doesn't remember doing much to prevent it—she probably picked other guys up the way she did him or let other guys pick her up that way. In other words, the same way they'd met: at a party (or a bar), a little talk, eye contact, or lots of eye contact first and then talk, or asking someone to make the introduction, then necking in the kitchen (or at the bar)—even if she came to whatever she came to with someone else; all that mattered was if she was immediately taken with the new guy—and then to her home or his and the bed and up early next day for a dance rehearsal or class or the new thing she was thinking of starting to do: drama school. Or no new guys but just the old ones, some she had even discarded from the past. Or maybe even one of her homosexuals—for something different this time or to really give her a bang—decided, or she convinced him, to put it in. Oh, he'll never know, so leave it at that. At what? At his not ever finally knowing for sure if the baby was really his and how responsible he should feel over it and so on. "So on" what? Her color and if he did mostly want it to be night and not day when he was with her outside and the rest of the things. "Rest of the things" what? Everything, all of it, too many and too much to think about right now, what's he expect of himself? One thing leading to the other, from his baby to his not giving money to get rid of the baby, to her death—how much he should feel involved in it, "responsible" was the word he used. If he can never know, what can he do? Nothing, so for now forget it. He drank a lot at home that night, sat in the big easy chair and read yesterday's and today's *Times* while he drank and ate sliced carrots and pieces of cheese, and passed out. Her poor parents, he thought while he was drinking; Christ, what it must be like to lose such a beautiful high-spirited talented daughter in her twenties. To lose one anytime, any child, but this one in her early twenties at the most, right? He knows: they even celebrated her twenty-third birthday with a champagne split and two eclairs he brought to her apartment. "Here's to you, Miss Twenty-three; not a significant number or earthshaking passage, like twenty-one, fifty, but just the right one perhaps for big things to open up for you. So here's to ya, Linny La-la," and they drank up, saved the pastry for later, saw a movie, came back, ate the eclairs and made love. Her younger sister, slightly older brother, or maybe he has them reversed, but such a live wire she was, how stupid could she have been to go screwing around with drugs or just using them in strange combinations? "Here's to you, lovely Lynette," he said from the chair, raising his glass of vodka and ice, standing up, newspapers and plate of carrots sliding off his lap to the floor, and holding the glass out, shooting the drink down, sitting down and from the chair pouring another. "What a phony I am, a fake, washout, drain— take take take, that's all I do, can't help a fucking soul and all I want is to get laid, right? Yes, I think so. Right? Yes, it's goddamn true. Even now I want to go through my phone list to see who to call, but I won't because I'm too sloshed to even move from this chair." And such a gorgeous body. There you go again. But those legs, breasts, backside, cunt that was always ready for him and never stunk. Just shut up about it, stop, everything you're thinking's wrong. Then he passed out.

Met her when they were both grad students in the same university. She was in the theater department and because she didn't have as good a fellowship as he, worked in the town's Woolworth's. Met her in the school's main cafeteria. Wasn't going with anyone then, wanted to talk to someone now, walked over, had seen her before at the same big round empty table, or one of the ones right around it, eating from a bagged lunch and Thermos, liked her looks, not just her intelligent face but the long thick braid and dark sensible clothes and even her frayed canvas bookbag and the two serious modern novels and book of plays on the table the last time and what seemed like different books this time, had never seen her standing up so didn't know how tall she was and what her legs and waist and rear end were like, told himself to be bold, sit down beside her and start talking, however inane the first things he says are, it'll be okay, if she's attracted to him, sat down and said "I don't know, you were sitting alone. I was, I mean, and you too, of course, and excuse me for sitting down without being asked, if you were reading and not just eating I wouldn't have, but I thought it'd be nice on such a nice day to talk to someone for a few minutes, do you mind?—though I don't see what the nice day has to do with it. Probably a rainy or cloudy or very cold day, not that you're going to get many very cold ones around here in winter. But one that draws you into yourself and where you'd be less likely to want to look out these enormous dirty windows, would even be a better reason to want to talk to someone and that person to want to talk to you, even if for both of you it's someone you don't know. I'm sorry, that couldn't have made much sense, but I'll get around to what I want to say eventually. Anyway, if you do—*mind*—just say the word and I'll go," and she said "No, fine, sit here, free country and so forth, and I'm not reserving or preserving," and he said " 'Reserving' I understand, but 'preserving'?" and she said "If you want to talk, you can't do all the talking—those are the basic conversational rules, agreed?" and he said "Deal," and stared at her and she said "Yes, so, what?" and he said "Well, I already talked too much, you said so and I agree with it, but if you don't want to say anything just this moment, I'll go on?" and she said "No, I have things to say, except my mouth takes a few more seconds than yours to start up," and talked and he did and the conversation was fast, stimulating, lively and they laughed and after about a half-hour of it he wanted to see her standing up before he went any further with her and he said "Like a coffee or tea?" and she said "I brought some, hot cider," tapping the Thermos, and he said "But you also wouldn't like a coffee or tea?" and she said "I don't want to seem health-nutty, but I don't drink stimulants and I abhor all those decontaminated alternates," and he said "Then something else?—here," standing up, "come with me to the food line and choose whatever you want—my treat, since I've been chewing your head off—but not anything lavish, of course," and she said "What could they have lavish in that kitchen midden? . . . but honestly, right now I wouldn't walk very well," and he said "What's wrong?" and she said "I have a limp," and he said "Something really wrong with one of your legs, or just temporary?" and she said "Let's simply say you're anatomically close and there was and what I have is a relic of what existed and that right now that foot wants to recess," and he said "So, your foot, not a leg, okay," and got coffee and they talked more and later walked to the parking lot and she did have a bad limp and kept having to stop because she said "My relic's rebelling, but you go on, though I won't be able to catch up with you and you don't know which one's my car and I'm not sure where it is," and she drove him home and he got her phone number and after she drove away he realized he'd forgotten to look at, or maybe for her sake with the limp he just wanted to keep his eyes off of, the bottom half of her, but from what he thinks he fleetingly saw when she got into the car, nothing was out of the ordinary there. She had a hole in her foot, wide as a quarter and deep as, well, a quarter standing on its edge. Maybe not that deep. The first time they made love, which was on the first night they went out—drove to San Francisco, had a fish dinner, walked around a block of elegant food and clothes shops in a building that had recently been a chocolate factory but was now called a square—she took off her sock while they were undressing—"You mind if I get right under the covers," she said when he started kissing and fondling her, "I'm cold?"—and pointed out the hole to him and said "This is my limp *raison* for baying . . . excuse me, I thought that'd be funnier than it came out sounding. Anyhow, I thought you wouldn't, when you glided your lips up and down my body, which I hope you'll do, want to discover it on your own and possibly get frightened. You did show unusual restraint or disinterest in not further pursuing the question of its existence. I got my foot trampled by a truck and this little crater is where they had to operate to save it." At first her hole mortified her, she said, but she showed how used to it she got by sticking her forefinger in about half an inch and he said "Stop, take it out, and please don't ever do that when I'm here or you might never see me again," and she said she'll cover it with a Band-Aid in bed or always keep a sock on if it really repulses him so much and he said "One or the other, but maybe you should. Blood, shit, gore, I don't know why, but nothing like that makes me squeamish when it's on someone, and I can probably stick my hands in all of it. Just holes like what's left in the neck after a tracheotomy and the ones where someone's skull's been drilled to get at the brain or the two or three I've seen where all that's left of the eye is the socket it was in." She was conventionally pretty, didn't do anything it seemed to take care of her body so it was kind of flabby, wasn't a good lovemaker. She wanted lots of things done to her she'd read in *Kama Sutra*–type books but wouldn't do anything to him except suck his earlobe halfheartedly for a few seconds or massage his shoulders, not even hold his penis. She berated him if he came before she did and he was through for the time being. "Hey, you have obligations," and he'd say "Not when nature says no, for look at my fucking prick." "Bastard," she'd say, and he'd say "The only time you curse or are anything but gentle and understanding is when this happens; well, it shuts me down completely, so I'm going to sleep," and she'd say "Go on, sleep, you motherfucker, and if it so happens, don't wake up," and he'd think if it wasn't so late and he wasn't so tired and he had a car to drive back to his place he'd get the hell out of there pronto and never come back, but in the morning she'd apologize, say something like "I must be hormonally out of joint or just sex-crazed when I get so close to liftoff and then have to abruptly stop, not that I'm blaming you—as you say, 'nature,'" and be nice again and stroke his arm and say "If you want to, make love

to me any way you wish and complete it when it's most sponta-
neous or pleasurable for you to, but I'll never act that way
again." But the abortion. He lived in a single room in a professor's home with his own private entryway that couldn't because
of some fire regulation be locked and she'd show up lots of
times, knock on his locked door—it could be two in the morning, once it was four—and say something like "I've been driving
around for hours listening to radio music and late-night shows
from as far away as Chicago—it must be almost daybreak
there—and suddenly I felt lonely, do you mind?" or "Excuse
me, Gould, don't come to the door if you're too sleepy to or
you have a woman in there, but can you tolerate some company?
Because of something scary [or 'disturbingly erotic'] I read I
wanted to be nestled in bed with someone and you're the only
man I'm balling these days. I know I must sound pathetic, even
the use of that uncharacteristic 'balling,' which only hip simple-
tons say, so if you want just tell me 'go away.' " They drove to
San Jose for cheap Mexican dinners, San Francisco for cheap
Japanese and Chinese dinners, over the mountain to Pescadero
Beach to read and look for polished stones and grill hot dogs or
hamburger steaks, did a number of things together for about
three months, all in her car—he totaled his a month before he
met her and was now riding a borrowed one-speed bike—and
then he said, he'd thought of saying it for weeks, then thought
Hell, why not, this is how I think she expects me to be, up-front
and on the level: "This thing between us, it's not working, don't
you agree?" and she said "It is for me; we should give it some
more time," and he said "Well, it isn't for me, that's a fact," and

she looked sad and said "What is it, you're not attracted to me?" and he said "It's not that so much; in fact, not at all," and she said "It's not only my looks you don't like but my body," and he said "No, you're quite pretty and exceptionally smart; it's true—but whose is?—your body's not that of an acrobat's or ballerina's, but you're not heavy or flat-chested or with enormous thighs, and even if you were—" and she said "You also don't like that I limp so badly," and he said "Now that I can tell you doesn't bother me one bit; in fact, I find how fast and much you get around courageous, or maybe that's a word you hate, and if it is, I—" and she said "You would never touch or even look at my foot," and he said "Why should I touch it—I mean, what's that supposed to prove? And I've looked at it plenty, I think, the few times you left it uncovered—in the shower once, or twice, but not to stare at it; simply because it was in front of my puss so I looked, and so what?" and she said "Have you noticed, or the water could have been spraying too fast, that the hole closed?" and he said "Good, that's wonderful, and I haven't noticed, I'm sorry," and she said "It hasn't, but that just shows how much you've looked, though one day it might," and he said "I hope so, I know how much the whole thing disturbs you," and she said "You're not spiritually or physically involved with me—forget intellect; that never counts for much after the first few minutes. But that's what you're saying—and emotionally too—that you don't feel at all deeply toward me," and he said "Maybe something like that," and she said "Then why didn't you come out with it months ago and we could have cut the whole stinking thing off from the beginning?" and he said

"Because I didn't know then and I'm still not precisely sure what it is that isn't working and maybe never did," and she said "So what am I to do? I'm precisely attracted and involved with you in all the ways you say you aren't, even your intellect—that's supposed to be for laughing, but you're not—and perhaps enough for us both," and he said "You know it doesn't work that way," and she said "Then this is the last time?" and he said "Though I hate to be, and I never was before, the one to say it to anyone, and maybe that's the wrong thing to say, but yes, I think it's best, if it's okay with you, since the last thing I want to do is hurt you in any—" and she said "It isn't okay, and you *are* hurting, and what you said before was not only the wrong thing but a rotten thing to say, so what do you say to all of that?" and he said "You know what I mean," and she said "I not only know but I knew and correct me if I'm wrong, but it's that there's nothing I can say or do to stop it, isn't that true?" and he said "I guess so," and she said "Then okay, it's over, I don't feel the relief yet but I suspect that'll come in due time; but you know, I'd hate going home alone, especially when I'd expected to stay, and worse, sleeping alone after hearing this, so would you object very much if I spent just one more night here?" and he said "It's not a good idea," and she said "Good idea, no idea—please, a prisoner's last request—laugh laugh—and I won't be asking for a last meal," and he said "Good, that's funny, and if staying here's really what you want, all right. Though it's very un-likely—I'm not sure, but is that what you meant by your last meal?—that we won't make love," and she said "That's not what I want. And listen, I think my fondest memory of us—I can't recall it exactly, but I think one of us was sick, so it must have been you, since I was the one who really enjoyed it—is when we just held each other through the entire night. I kept waking up and we were still face-to-face holding each other," and he said "I don't remember that," and she said "I have it in my journals and will gladly show it to you if you want," and he said "I believe you." They made love. She always slept with no clothes, he too, and just being near her in bed—she'd made no move to him, seemed to be on her back with her eyes closed— gave him an erection. He didn't think it was a good idea to make love and stuck it between his thighs, but it sprung out and hit her leg and she grabbed it for maybe the second or third time since he'd known her, said something he didn't get all of but with "baby bonnet" and "smooth lil' doll" in it, and so on. Then she got on top and said "I'm a-gonna abuse you, Señor Phallus, make you weep chili peppers, you bastardo, for the future rather than the past—how's that for hopelessly imitation swagger?—but do new things to you I've never done, since this one's supposed to be the finale and there are many things we pathetically haven't tried," and rode up and down on him a few minutes, he was sure they'd done that before, but his stomach began to ache so he grabbed her waist and started to slide her off and she flattened herself out on him, spread her legs and arms out as if she was going to do a belly flop off a high dive and he thought "Goddamn, what now?" for he'd popped out of her and she didn't put him back, and scratched his shoulders and buttocks and legs and he said "Evelyn, that hurts," but then thought it doesn't hurt that much but let her think it did, maybe it'll help her later in some way, and he said "Yes, this is memorable sex," and she said "You've never talked once during it, but I'm glad, frivolous as what you said is." Then she jiggled a bit and came, he was still out of her and he thinks not even semi-erect, and she said "Want me to minister to it in some way, I've still lots of kick and hot wind left," and he said "No, I'm just sleepy and have been practically all day, that's the only reason. Nothing to do with you—it was great." He let her hold him as she fell asleep and then he turned over on his side. In the morning he pretended to sleep while she got out of bed and washed and dressed, then said "Oh, you up?" and got dressed and made the bed and put on his jacket and she said "Can't I have a cup of coffee—for the road?" and he said "I'm sorry, thought you wanted to get out of here," and made it, they read yesterday's newspaper while they had coffee and toast, then he walked her to her car. She started crying the moment she got in it and he said "Don't, please," and indicated with his hand for her to wipe the tears away and she opened the window and said "I bet if I had a normal foot and no limp and hole we'd still be seeing each other or this wouldn't be the last time—maybe only the penultimate one; say, how about it being that, Gould— please?" and he said "You really put me in a position," and to himself, She's probably right, he wouldn't give her up till something better came along or till he saw it was getting too risky sticking with her and that when he finally had to break it off it would hurt her even worse than it has today, and she would be a different person too without that limp and hole, not so sullen and abject and self-pitying and whatever else, for her whole psyche seems to be postulated on that foot, and the sex last night was the best he's had with her so far, even if he didn't ejaculate—at least she was up there and trying out things and acting free, but he said "Look, sometimes the guy leaves, sometimes the girl, that's the way it is, so I'm saying I've been deep in the dumps about it too," and she said "With me, it's always the guy, though there haven't been a whole lot of them," and he said "Funny, because with me—well, not always and I'm sure, by a much wider margin and not just because you're a woman, not always with you too," and she said "That's true. Though of course I could be lying there because I don't want you to think I'm an utter loser and thus reduce my chances of ever getting together with you again, but you'll never know unless you call me," and she started the car and he walked away. When he heard it pulling out of the spot he turned around and waved but couldn't tell if she saw him. She called two months later and he said "Hi, how are you?" and she said "Not so great. I aborted our fetus two days ago," and he said "Oh my goodness, God, I'm sorry, why didn't you tell me before this?" and she said "You wouldn't have cared," and he said "Not so, I would have done something," and she asked what, and he said "I don't know, helped you with the abortion—money if you needed it— taken you to the doctor to have it, things like that," and she said "You wouldn't have wanted me to keep the baby and then married me, right?" and he said "Marriage? Why would you want to be married to me? I have almost no money; I don't really know where I'm going after this year. I'm not ready for it by any measure, and a kid?—oh come on," and she said "You're a nice guy, intelligent, personable, have decent looks and in good clothes you'd be very presentable, and plenty of other things, and for me personally, particularly how I feel about you. I felt a lot, and it's obvious I believe in you a lot too, and for some reason it also seemed you'd be a terrific father, loving, caring—" and he said "Maybe I would. They say good uncles make for good fathers, though I have no nieces or nephews, so why'd I say that?" and she said "You're being clever, trying to take me out of my misery, and it *was* funny," and he said "No, I said it seriously, so I must, as another one of my paternal virtues, be losing my marbles," and she said "Anyhow, it wasn't a real abortion, so there was no money involved, unless you want to help me make up for the three hours' work I missed; I would have missed more but I stuck it out on the floor for as long as I could. Can I come over and talk?" and he said "Not right now; and there's no one here, that's not why. But 'on the floor' where?" and she said "Woolworth's. I first found out I was pregnant when my period was late," and he said "You mean you got suspicious," and she said "So I got a test at a pharmacist's— after other signs had appeared—and when it turned out positive I took something someone gave me—a drink to induce the abortion or miscarriage or anything you want to call it," and he said "And it worked like that?" and she said "Not the first time. So I took it again and then realized—it's supposed to take a day or so—that I had to be at work behind the counter, so like an idiot I went. I needed the money," and he said "You should have called me," and she said "And then it started happening— terrific cramps—maybe from the first time I took it, or the second, or both, but I had to go to the bathroom real bad and was also discharging," and he said "Blood?" and she said "When I later looked in my underpants, everything. So I went, I was a mess before I even sat on the toilet, and the rest of it just swooshed out of me there. I tried to check what sex it was, didn't have a clue from what I could observe of it, and flushed it down. An ignominious way to go, wouldn't you say? Now I wish I had saved it, given it a backyard burial, but that wouldn't be so good. Dog might dig it up and eat it, or worse, walk around with it and drop it at my feet as if he'd caught and killed it," and he said "It's no joke; it must have been terrible and physically painful for you; I'm sorry," and she said "I felt sick after but told myself I wasn't going to let this send me home— why should I lose good pay? *Good?* The lousy cheapskates . . . but after a few hours I told them I had the flu, and left. I hope that won't be the last time I get pregnant," and he said "Why should it be? Look how easily you conceived this time? We went out for how long, a couple of months?" and she said "More than three, but it's not as if we did it just once," and he said "Anyway, you're fertile. You took precautions and you still got pregnant, which either means, and I doubt you'd do this— you're too much of a perfectionist—" and she said "Me? Not me. Miss Unperfectnik. But regarding what?" and he said "Your IUD device. About putting it in right," and she said "The 'D' is for 'device,' and the device is always in, didn't you know?" and he said "Sort of. But my point is that you had to have put it in right originally, being what I think you are—" and she said "The doctor does that, and then takes it out if you need a new one or it expels on its own or it's irritating you," and he said "But it didn't expel, did it?" and she said "No, it's still in there and feels fine," and he said "But anyway, that you're so fertile that you got pregnant despite the device. So at least you now know you can conceive, and against one of the most uncompromising obstacles, which has to be of some relief to you, unless it's happened before," and she said "It hasn't, this was a first, and the good you see in it with that relief thing is too premeditatedly positive a notion for me—think right and ye shall be all right, and that sort of baloney—and I'd think for you too. Because you, do you feel any relief in knowing you can help conceive? Nah, you've probably got a chorus line of knocked-up women behind you," and he said "Not that I know of," and she said "So I'm your first, huh? Well, that's something; you'll always remember me. But some women I've heard of, and in their twenties, have had just one conception disruption like mine and were never able to conceive again. Doctors couldn't explain it. It's as though all their repro organs went down the toilet too, or wherever their predelivery took place—doctors' offices' waste containers, in trash bags out the window or in the incinerator. It would be horrible to imagine that this little guy of mine I flushed down was it, the very last of my unilluminated lonely line, since, I think I told you, I'm siblingless and so are my parents on both sides," and he said "I'm sure it wasn't," and she asked why and he said "Just, I'm sure, because you'll be at your procreative peak for years—why wouldn't you be? you're just that age. Meanwhile, if you're not feeling well, anything I can do for you?" and she said "You won't like this, I'm *positive,* but could you come see me? You can even sleep with me if you wish, not to make me pregnant. I'm not about to do one of those predictable bits: immediately after losing it, try to make up for it by getting another. No, it's simply that I'm feeling extra sad today over losing it—" and he said "You wouldn't have kept it, would you?" and she said "Probably yes; I'm hypocritically opposed to abortion, in addition to my fears that this was my last huzza. I also don't have any present company to speak of—not even to speak to—so you'd be welcome," and he said "You know that wouldn't be any good," and she said "You have another steady already?" and he said "If you must know, I haven't had sex or, to be vulgar, even a handjob with anyone since you, and not because I haven't wanted to. Just haven't met anyone or anyone where it went that far." She said "I could always come to your room if you still haven't a car and it'd just be one last shot. I'm not exciting you with this chatter? It's not doing a thing to you?—be honest," and he said "No; I've got an erection, but what's that? I don't want to say I also get them when cats jump in my lap or I'm holding a particularly heavy book there for a few minutes. I'm sorry for what happened to you, I wish I could have done better by you, I don't know what the hell didn't happen with me in relation to you, but it didn't and that's all I can say," and she said "Okay, I like that honesty, and I thought you'd want to know about baby Gil—they have gills, you know; and about our getting together a final time, I felt I ought to at least give it a whirl. I wish you felt the same for me as I do for you," and he said "I wish that was so too," and she said "But you don't," and he said "I suppose not," and she said "No supposing, schmozo, either you do or you don't," and he said "Then 'don't,' I'm sorry," and they were silent and he thought "What's she thinking? Probably 'What's he thinking?' " and then she said "Oh well, good-bye," and he said good-bye and waited for her to say something else or hang up, but she didn't so he said good-bye again and hung up. He thought right after he couldn't believe he really did that, because it was the truth his having no sex since he last saw her, but he would have got stuck badly if he slept with her today and he doesn't know how easy that would be to get out of, since he for sure wouldn't want to do it again soon. He maybe would have done differently—he probably almost certainly would have—if this was a couple of months from now and he still hadn't had any sex and she had been a great beauty and lay. Maybe even without the great beauty and lay part—just that she was willing, asking for it—and he wouldn't have to use any line or contrivance to get her to do it—for that's how horny he can get. He saw her on campus a number of times the next few months, said hello or waved but that was all and always kept moving. He avoided the main cafeteria the hours he thought she might be there, then realized they were well into the new semester so her school hours had probably mostly changed. Once, he looked up from his table and saw her sitting with some people a few tables away, but she didn't see him or pretended not to and he didn't do anything to get her attention. He did think while he was sitting there, what if she came up to him now, said something like "Hi, how are you, I only have a minute to speak—I'm with friends— but would you want to come to my place later or me to come to yours?" He still hadn't had sex since he was last with her, but he'd reject the offer, tactfully, saying "No, thank you, I'm all tied up with work these days, but that's very kind of you." And if she pleaded? How would she plead? "Please, cut the bull, I just want to get fucked, it has nothing to do with you except you're the only guy I know around here that way—wear a mask, even, what do I care?—all I want is your goddamn penis in me and then you can buzz off and never come by or call again, and I won't contact you again either." Or nicer, politer, but he'd reject it no matter what, and she'd never plead and he doubts she'd ask. But here's something: what if she had come up to him last November right around the time of the abortion and said "I want to have your baby I'm pregnant with, will you go along with me?" He would have asked, what does she specifically mean will he go along with her, and she would have explained, and he would have said "No, because the truth is I don't want to live with anyone I might have to support or take care of in any way and I also don't want to be responsible for a child—I don't have the money or time." Suppose she'd then have said "All right, then I want to have the baby but not with you; you don't have to see me again or the baby ever, not even in the hospital after it's born. But will you at least give me your moral support—your financial support I promise never to ask you for and will even sign an affidavit regarding that—and say you don't mind my having it? I just want the child to know its father wasn't against its birth, even if he wasn't strongly for it either, and then just leave it to the future for you two to work that little issue out." He would have said "Okay, sure, have it, I don't see any problem—I'll in fact come see you and it sometime, and maybe even in the hospital, if I'm still in the area and you wouldn't mind. And if I ever make any money beyond what keeps me bordering on poverty, and again if you don't mind, I'll contribute to its upkeep." Because he was beginning to want children, two of them, though not necessarily by the same woman. In fact, probably by two women, since he feels the courts would go after him for child support quicker if he had two by the same woman in one state. But he just wanted to say, or this was mostly it, "Yes, I'm a father," and doesn't think he'd be embarrassed at saying "And no, I was never a husband," for he was already twenty-eight and the way he was going he didn't think he'd have enough income in the next ten years to have kids any other way and he didn't want to wait till he was forty or so to have his first one, if he'd be able to afford to have it even then. She sent him two tickets in May to the graduate theater department play she did the lighting for and had a small role in—"In case you want to bring a friend, gal or guy, but I'd love for you to see what I've done stagewise and am pretty proud of—not my acting: that's always been bad."—but he didn't go. About a year later he got a letter from her mailed to his graduate department and forwarded to him. She'd left school, never got her masters, was back in Mass., had given up theater altogether and was now working as a housekeeper and applying to the American Studies programs of several grad schools, none in Cal., and rest assured: not because, as she's heard, he's still there. "After you didn't attend the play I lit and acted passably in I tried out on myself lots of times what I'd say if we bumped into each other: 'You're not interested in what I do, then you're not interested in me, and no doubt vice v. for both of us (after all, it was a big mirror I was doing this to, though it actually doesn't hold true from me to you, but anyway), so nice knowing ya, Bucko, and take a flying leap!' so then why'm I writing? Not to knock you. Probably to say that if I had bumped into you I never would have said those things: no guts, flair or bravado and I simply ain't the censorious type. I also thought you might want to know why you never bump into me anymore or see me thermosing in the main caf, perhaps to give you additional liberty if you've been trying to steer clear of me the past year. As for Cal., I've had my fill of that empty self-absorbed state and don't know how anyone can go through four nominal seasons without wearing an overcoat and galoshes or their equivalents and still call himself a healthy-headed human being." She hoped he was well, and despite everything she's said here she still thinks of him fondly, "Believe me. The only person I bear a grudge against is myself." He wrote back saying he'd left grad school too but wasn't planning to apply to any other kind of program no matter how enticing another fat stipend seemed—he just wasn't a student, something he knew since first-year grade school, so he'd continue to work at what he was persistently pursuing so unsuccessfully and see if he got lucky enough and also a miracle occurred, where it eventually came out half okay. As for housekeeping, he was doing lots of it these days, as he was living with an extremely indolent, indefatigably sybaritic woman—"picture the most famous odalisque picture you can picture and you'll picture her, except she has pigtails and bangs—and her rambunctious, untidy son from her first husband. Did that sound as if I'm her current one? I'm not, nor does she plan to remarry or rekid by anyone, so who knows how long, considering my ballooning penchant for pahood and dandling and so on, I'll be living with her and grooming her sumptuous home. You'll also be surprised, since I don't think you ever thought of me as hardworking and resourceful, that for dough I have three jobs, as this woman and boy are essentially living off me and the monthly pittance her ex sends for the kid every other month: artist model around ten clockwatching hours a week, substitute teacher in several high schools till the state board boots me out when it learns I haven't the ed credits I said I did, and my main labor: thirty working hours a week at a Woolworth's in the area but not the one you slaved at, and mostly doing stock, and I didn't mention that place to bring back bad memories for you. I'm tremendously sorry for what you had to go through alone a year ago and how terribly I behaved and I hope you've forgiven me or will sometime soon." She didn't answer his letter and he never wrote her address down, thinking she'd write back and he'd get it then, and a few years later he tried recalling her last name when he met someone her age from the same town she grew up in, but couldn't. He tried describing her, it didn't work, so he said "Maybe this will help you remember her. She had a large open hole in her left foot, I think, or maybe it was the right, from an accident in childhood, she said—a car or truck ran over it. It was about the size of a quarter and was on the top part of her foot—what do you call it? the instep—a hole so wide and deep I swear you could almost see flesh and bone in it, so something you would have noticed if she wore sandals with thin straps or was barefoot," but this woman, who looked as if she was getting sick because of his description, kept shaking her head no.

He was living with a woman in California, was called to New York when his father had a life-threatening massive heart attack, or that's the way it was put to him on the phone by his mother: "Fly in quick, you might not even have time if you got on the plane this minute; they're all saying, or you can see and hear it in the way they're wavering, that he might die." His father pulled through easily, and while there Gould met a woman at a party. Nice face, intelligent and attractive, dressed simply, tall with a slim figure, quiet wry smile, pleasant educated voice, the look of someone with a good disposition and no affectation, seemed to have a young son with her and to have come with another woman, since she was always standing beside or moving around the apartment with her and occasionally stopping the boy to tend to him—"You want something more to eat? . . . This will be dinner, so perhaps you ought to have a second walk around the food table with me. . . . Did you see there's another boy here around your age? He looks nice."—and there didn't seem to be a man she signaled across the room to periodically and met up with every fifteen minutes or so and things like that—what he always does when he goes to a party like this with a woman—and he went over to her and said, pointing to the boy, "He yours?" and she looked warily at him and nodded and he said "Excuse me, the introductions, very rude of me to you two—Gould Bookbinder," and held out his hand to her and she shook it and he shook her friend's hand and the friend said "Miriam," and he said "How do you do, Miriam, Gould Bookbinder, but I said that," and then to the boy, while he was thinking should he ask the woman her name? Ah, she doesn't want to offer it now, let her, "Rude to all three of you I should've said, right there, kid?" and put out his hand and the boy looked at it and he said "Really, and I hate using this word, but he's adorable, and I'm not going to steal him so don't be leery," and the woman said "Who even said?" and he said "Of course, but you see, I just look at him and realize how much I miss the little kid I live with in California—towhead too and same height and haircut—in fact, they almost all have the same cut today, people of a certain . . . well, just so many people with kids this age, I mean his age with people like that—got popular with the president's son, if I'm not wrong, and before that the elite prep schools and Prince Valiant, though I think Valiant's was a little longer and he was older," and Miriam said "Who's he?" and he said "A comic strip, which might not be around anymore and I never read it . . . and after the president got shot and the son got older, it just kept on with boys that age . . . and he's not biologically mine either, I should have right away said, but I think acts like he is, whatever that's supposed to mean—relies on me a lot, hangs on me a little— and I guess I feel like his father too after so long, as I also hang on to and rely on him for different emotional things. But what's yours, five in a couple of months?" and she said "Three, in one, and he's not tall for his age, far as I know—is your boy unusually short? But where in California? That's where I'm from originally," and said she grew up in the county just south of the one he now lived in, Miriam and she had gone to the university he'd been a grad student at, which wasn't a coincidence, since the couple giving the party had been in their undergraduate class and he'd first met them when the man came back after a few years for a master's in his department—but to get to it: they talked, Miriam stepped away and then called the boy to the window to see a sliver of one of the new World Trade Center towers they could just about make out through two buildings, his grad student friend came over and said "So you two need no introducing?" and he wanted to say "I still don't know her name yet" but they both said "Yes," and he said "Jinx," and held up two joined fingers and she said "What's that supposed to mean?" and he said "An East Coast thing kids used to and still might do, and maybe on the West Coast too, when two people say the same word or phrase synchronously: 'What comes out of a chimney?'" and she said "What?" and he said "You're supposed to say 'smoke,'" and the host said "I don't know it either," and left, and he said "And then I say 'What color is it?'—the chimney smoke. There are four to five quick questions: ladies' pocketbooks, coins, gray and gold, and then you do the—I mean I do, the questioner—though you're certainly questioning me now—'Do not speak till you are spoken to.' That's right, it's not my fingers joined together but both parties' in this, the index fingers at the tips, and when it's all over, questions answered correctly, one of us breaks the fingertip conjunction with a gentle chop of his hand. You want to go through with it?—though if we go by the rules it's already too late," and she said "Please, no games. What am I, a child?" and he said "Sorry, it all just suddenly came back, but only having fun." Married for five years, lived in Madison where her husband taught law at the university, only here a week to be with her best friend from college "who apparently thinks I should be talking to you alone—I must have told her last night more about my life than I should have, and which I've already disclosed to you, in just saying that, more than enough too," and he said "So you're saying I should be diplomatic, untactical and gallant," driving back in two days with her son and he said "Why so soon?" and she said "Because I've been here five," and he said "Oh jeez, what a pity, because I don't know, I'd love seeing you again, maybe that's it," and she said "Excuse me, and I'm not trying to prompt you with this query nor induce you into a clumsy confession you'll regret later, but whatever for? You have yours, I have mine, there are children involved, I'm leaving in less than two days and you'll never see me again unless by accident and then we probably won't recognize each other or remember this party, and we've only just met and spoken a few minutes together," and she looked at her watch and said "My watch must have stopped, what time is it?" and he said "I don't wear one," and she said "Well, I know I have to be out of here in less than half an hour to take John to a birthday party another college chum's having for her girl—we all seemed to have had our first babies around the same time," and he said " 'John,' like the president's son with the prep cut if not even the prez himself," and she said "Yes, it's the boy's father's and grandfather's name too, though he's not the third," and he said "He's not?" and she said "After his name." "Excuse me, but this isn't right what I'm about to say," and she said "Please now, I can sense what's coming, so don't," and he said "Ya gonna let me continue, lady?" and she shut her eyes as if she'd just stay that way tolerating what he was going to say and then walk away and he thought Should I say it then? and said "To say it then, and this isn't a line I'm giving you—" and she looked at him and said "You've used that one before," and he said "Never— but low, though, so nobody else hears, and maybe the most important words of my life," and she said "Jesus Christ," and he said "I wish, and this after only ten minutes alone with you— even more than ten, but good conversation, time flew, so another solid sigh—*sign*, but I won't bring that up to add to my argument," and she said "Ha-ha, all right, enough? you got your laugh," and he said "And I didn't trip over that sigh-sign thing intentionally—but that you were—this is the continument; that's not a word, I don't think, but seemed apt—the woman I was now living with," and tears, really just a couple of drops popped out, one from each eye, and he wiped them and said "Talk about silliness?" and she said "What are you doing?—are you a professional actor?" and looked at him in a way where he thought I think I'm winning her over, and said "No, I told you, or maybe I didn't, but that'd be strange, since you told me what you do, but I'm in something—" and she was shaking her head and started to move off and he said "Don't go, and notice I'm not grabbing your hand or touching your cheek or using any of those restraining actions or physical and facial tricks—moving closer, looking straight into your eyes soulfully of sorts in an attempt to engender more sympathy from you if that's what it was and employing to me grandiloquent words like 'engender,' 'employing' and 'grandiloquent' to impress you and strengthen my *présentation,* and French *aussi* or *aussi français* and that drippy stuff with the eye sacs before which I swear I had nothing to do with except to furnish the liquid; they just sprouted, little there was, naturally, but you seem, and here it it comes, despite our respective homelife situations—I couldn't come up with a better term for it . . . you know: spouses, kids and place—like at last my ideal mate: mind, body and face, soft voice and ways, interest in lit and involvement in music . . . that you play the viola and are in a quartet no less . . . for godsakes, the six Mozart quintets I bet when you add another violinist," and she said "Violist—don't take away one of the few breaks our underappreciated instrument gets," and he said "Humor, skin, everything, sense of this and irony of that plus straightforwardness, the entire corpus, litany and library, that I'm panting in the pants for you, pardon me pa, he does not know what he brays, and even look at our sizes and physiques—we were cut from two different bolts for each other," and she said "Done?" and looked miffed, and he said "I really overdid it too much, serious as I—" and she said "Please, be done, done, because whether anyone heard you or not I still feel humiliated and embarrassed—why do you think you have to b.s. so? And who knows, if you stopped slinging it I might even be a little interested," and he said "I stopped, though it wasn't slinging, at least I don't think so, but I'm so relieved I haven't killed it off completely, which your remark implied, and I haven't with what I just said after I said I was done and had stopped, have I?" and she said "It shouldn't be but it's okay and I'll accept all heretofore as an anomaly, your getting carried away for so indeterminate an end," and he didn't quite understand what she meant but let it pass because he knew it wasn't too critical and she was still standing beside him and he said "I won't say a thing; can we sit down?" and she said "I don't know why we should; I must be lonelier than I am nuts. Uh-oh, said too much." Lunch the next day. After they arranged it and the place he said "Could we also meet later after the birthday party? Or I can pick you and John up at whatever the time—I just want to be with you," and she said "Tomorrow," and he said "And of course bring John along; really, I'd love it," and she said "I wouldn't, and we went over this: he's going to the shore with Miriam," and he looked puzzled and she said "The friend I came with and you spoke to and, honestly, the sole reason I'm here—I dislike parties and huge reunions," and he thought then the person he's indebted to but won't say it because she'll think that's just more coming-on. "One priviso though," she said. "When we do meet tomorrow promise to have toned down and tamed to subaudible and indistinct the words and approach, for you're much too gusty, rutty and fast," and he said "Check." Lunch. Kissed during it. Pushed the bud vase aside, leaned forward and she met him above the table. "Well," she said, "for half a kiss that wasn't half bad. But nip it; *people.*" Invited him back to Miriam's apartment. At lunch talked about her husband: brilliant, could be a U.S. attorney or solicitor general, everyone thinks so, clerked for a federal judge, first in his class everywhere, could make a quarter of a million a year in five years with some big city firm but chooses to teach, a skirtchaser from the word *gesundheit* but the most deplorable thing he does is sleep with his students. If he only did it with his colleagues or from the secretarial pool she'd say Well, that's what's going on today, everyone seems to have someone on the side, and the worst thing about it is they're not doing it out of power on his part or wanting to get ahead on theirs but for good old sheer sensual Circean fun, or so he tells her. Imagine, at their age and when she'd like another child before John becomes too old to play with it, they now have separate beds but in the same room for the once every month he wants to sleep with her and half those times he passes out from wine or drugs before he gets the pensum done. She had a lover she admired but he went to Japan last spring to design bridges that won't collapse during earthquakes. Before that a couple of one-night stands she met after out-of-town concerts, but she thought them too cheap and problematical with disease. Yet look at her now, in all problematicability another one to two-nighter or afternooner and he said not on her life. Did he tell her his head's reeling and heart's going whack whack whack whackety whack for her? She said resist that crap, she doesn't go for it and nothing quicker will turn her off and he said okay, his heart isn't pulsing thus, but he'd love riding back to Madison with her, she can drop him off at the airport there just before she goes the rest of the way to her place and she said that'd be too peculiar to John, even if she would relish the help with the driving, and though her husband wouldn't begrudge her a brief fling in New York he'd resent her bringing the beau so close to home, and he said then let him off in Michigan or Illinois if either's before she hits Wisconsin and she said what about his California woman, wouldn't she mind? and he said that little romance is definitely on the way out and has been for two years. Not his ideal mate or even a simulacrum of one and same in spades for her with him. She wants a rich businessman or professional with a P.A. who likes camping and horseback riding and outdoor barbecuing and cars and canoes. He needed a place to stay for a week, they got along okay for a month or two and then he got so taken with her kid and too lazy to move, he's been able to keep all her house bills paid or just a month behind, they have adequate to sometimes apotheosized sex when she's not busting his chops to the point where he doesn't even want to make love with her or suffering from one of her half-dozen imagined ailments or states of fatigue; the loss would be the boy; besides, she smokes. In bed after they undressed she said he should probably know beforehand she's never had an orgasm. Oh, perhaps once or twice when she was pubescent and did it to herself. But either she's lost that touch or something's happened to her nervous system since to make it a near physical impossibility. She's not saying she doesn't participate actively and at times avidly during the act, though occasionally fakes it as much as anyone, and does most of the things normal hetero-sexual couples do except anal sex, but to her regret he shouldn't expect any vociferous end-screams and yips and yaps and then postcoital sighs and later postorgasmic sleep from her, so she supposes she's saying he should, as every man she's been with has, after a reasonable period of time get what he can before she begins tiring of it and suddenly stops. He didn't bring a condom, assuming she'd take care of everything, and she hadn't brought her diaphragm to New York, having given up on one-night stands and also preferring to pack as little as she can, so they decided he'd pull out a few moments before his peak ones. He was about a minute away from ejaculation, he figured, starting that familiar climb, at least long enough away where he'd be able to hold it back if he had to and he said "I don't think I'll be able to pull out, nor do I really want to the first time, will it be okay?" and she said "I can be a little irregular but think I have my dates sufficiently straight where it'll be safe, but to reduce the chance of fertilization don't go in too deep when you discharge." When he was about fifteen seconds away, he figured, and knew that though he couldn't hold it back or even control the amount he ejected he could pull out in time, he thought but does he want to? He'd like getting her pregnant and having a hold on her like that and maybe even a child if she wanted it or he could persuade her to keep it or just something troublesome they went through like an abortion that would sort of seal something between them and where he could fly to Madison for it or the birth if she wanted him to and her husband didn't object, when he came, involuntarily shoving his hands under her and grabbing her buttocks so he could get in as far as he could get. "I asked you," she said after and he said "What?" and she said "And will you please?—I've been trying to get your big load off me for the past minute," pushing him and he rolled himself off and said "The depth?" and she said "Gee whiz, all of a sudden he's showing signs of life again—where do you go?

The depth, yes; you knew, don't tell me, even if you are sleepy and spent, so why did you? and it hurt besides. Simply so you could experience the experience of experiences fuller—well darnit, haven't you done it enough, and this isn't out of bitterness because I never arrive there, where when someone asks you earnestly not to and for extremely important reasons, you don't?" and he said "But you said it was okay to shoot in you," and she said "But not so far in and hard. Do you have a tissue or handkerchief, please?" and he reached over her to the floor and felt her skin as he did and wanted to rest across her and kiss her belly and belly button and things but knew she wasn't in the mood and got a hanky out of his pants pocket and gave it to her and said "It's clean, or maybe at the most I used it for one nose blow but folded it over," and she said "Where I'm putting it, who cares?" and wiped her vagina—"Even if I get fifty billion with this, there's another fifty billion I didn't. Probably I should flush the buggers out," and went to the bathroom; he watched her and thought beautiful ass too but won't say it, that's all he needs. When she was back in bed he said "Sorry about all that, but how much would it have reduced anyway?" and she said "If you ever read a manual on conception or spoken to a specialist about it, you'd know; but it would have even been worse if you'd done it that way from behind as you first wanted to," and he said "That helps it too?" and she said "Tell me, why are you trying so hard to be dense?" and he said "Now you're busting my balls too; what's going on, what'd I say?—ah, screw you and all women, at least the grown-up kind: how quick you switch," and turned over and she said "Who did?" and he thought

"Who did"? What's she mean, "switch" or my "balls"? And what did I get myself into now with my big mouth and how do I get out of it? and she said "Gould, please, not now when we've just done lovemaking, and I couldn't bear another over-super-sensitive when-there's-something-to-gain-from-it self-centered misogynous man—I've had my fill," and he said "Oh you have, huh? And 'misogynous'; why couldn't you have just said woman-hating? When I use them it's always for fun or self-mockery but you're serious about your ostentatious words." She didn't say anything, his back was still to her, and a few seconds later, while he was wondering if she was looking at him now, and then that he really did it this time; she'll never trust him again with his promises and she seemed so disappointed and pissed; well, the hell with her, who needs her? who needs any of them, just as he told her, she said "Oh no, it's happened, the same thing when I got pregnant with John; I know you don't want to talk to me or even look this way and think I'm nothing less than a pompous priss, but I just felt the tiniest kind of detonation inside me and several small aftershocks before it stopped; believe me, Gould, I've conceived," and she touched his back and he looked at her and saw she was serious and said "Now that's nuts, much more than anything you said or did before," and she said "Practically what Harry said when I told him it a few weeks later about John, but I'm sure it's happened with millions of other women and lots of them I bet even recognized what it was," and he said "Girl or boy?" and she said "You sneer but if there's a calculably different sensation for a girl, then it's a boy," and he said "Don't spare my feelings, I want to know now: Down's syndrome or completely free of it or anything like that?" and she said "That wouldn't be funny to a lot of people," and he said "That's true, nothing to laugh about, and we should talk later about what you just felt, this is serious, but I'm feeling dozey after our sex and for the next half hour would like to be good for nothing else but a nap," and she said "Just one or two more things if I'm right about this. As I already told you, John could use a sibling now more than later and if it's a boy then even better for him and I think easier for me and certainly fewer clothes to buy—I'm being facetious there—and I know I want another child some day so I might as well get it over with now. And you seem, other than for a few crank shortfalls, as if you have good genes and the chances are that between us we'd produce a healthy, reasonably nice-looking intelligent human being. Of course I'll have to tell Harry, something I'd do anyway about us—that's the agreement we have, not to keep it a secret for more than a month, though he's always gotten more incensed than I over the disclosure—but didn't think there'd be a fertilization to divulge too, and by then a moderately defined embryo. He's even said he wouldn't mind our having another child if it resulted by accident, and if it came to it he'd have no problem with it being from someone else. He's very fair that way," and he said "It sure isn't how I'd take it if you were my wife. I'd throw you the hell out," and she said "Maybe that's why if I were single again, something I'll never be unless Harry dies or leaves and doesn't return for several years or tells me he wants to remarry and actually does or suddenly begins to repeatedly beat on John or me, I wouldn't think of marrying you or even continuing with you for any extended length of time for fear it'd wreck my marriage," and he said "Well, that gets me off cheap, for here I was about to do the right thing, which I had no desire to, and that's to propose to you," and she said "Some funny joke?" They made up after he awoke. He said "I'm sorry but when I said I'd throw you the hell out I meant that if I were married to you I'd never cheat and would expect the same from you," and she said "How do you know? And you can see how my phlegmatism and dispassionate—but you don't want those sort of words, so my . . . the way I'm . . . look, I can't think of simpler ones this moment for what I usually am that can so easily nettle a man or make him feel he has the license to skirtchase and frig whomever he wants to. But since I don't want to battle after only a day as if we've been married several years and also because of this new complication that I for one believe we'll have to face eventually, I accept your apology. Now, if you want to make love again— the carnal kind—for I suspect that's what you're building up to and perhaps why you apologized so generously . . ."—"Not so though I wouldn't mind having sex."—". . . then okay, but if it's no hassle getting dressed I'd like you to go out and buy a packet of the most expensive unscented nonlubricated condoms to lessen the chances of conception in case I was wrong about what I felt before; this way will also make it easier, if you'd still like to, to come in deep as you want from behind." He came over the next morning soon after her friend had left for work and when she thought John would still be asleep in the guest room. John walked into the living room while he was on top of her on the couch and he quickly pulled out and rolled off her and said "Oh my gosh, excuse me, this is terrible," and tried covering his genitals with his hands and she said "What are you doing? don't panic, keep yourself exposed and your erection erect if you still have one till the normal time it'd take for it to go down and for you to put your underpants on. He's seen us so let him think what we're doing is entirely natural and not something to be hidden or feel guilty or discomposed about or he can be troubled by it for years and possibly into his own sex life. And it isn't as if he'll be telling his father anything Harry won't already know. I don't keep a journal of what takes place but I will remember the main events when I inform him." She drove to Madison the day after, he didn't hear from her or write, and two months later . . . but why didn't he? Thought if she wrote him first he'd have permission to write back or she'd tell him where to write if not to her home—he had her address—and perhaps even how he should address the envelope, maybe by some other name or care of a friend or something. Maybe she wouldn't tell her husband what happened in New York but if she did he didn't want to make it any harder for her with him. They'd talked about it before she left. He said he likes her a lot, probably loves her, anyway, he feels very good about her, loves being with her and doesn't want to stop seeing her, and she said "I won't reveal my feelings for you. Obviously, they're fairly good or I wouldn't have slept with you. If it was just sexual frustration that motivated it, I think that would have been the end of it after the first time, as I'm satisfied easily that way and one time can hold me for a week, even without the end-all punch. Let's see what develops in my belly before we make any plans. If nothing does then I don't see why we can't hook up someplace for a few days, and without John; Harry's done it several times with his girls and once for a month. Have you ever been to the Grand Canyon?" and he said he never had any desire to: "You get up to the edge and look into it and what do you see: an enormous ditch and trickle of water winding through it and ruddy rock and dry brush and stuff and maybe some Western-garbed people on donkeys lumbering down a narrow path, and I could never afford it," and she said "It's much more, yours is just travelogue, but all right, then I can drive east or even fly here, but let's wait and see. One day . . ." and two months later (he'd look for a letter from her almost every time he opened his mailbox) she wrote saying everything's been confirmed except the gender, she's already started to show but only a bump, and rather than risk never getting pregnant again and for all the other reasons she gave she's going to go through with it; "Harry's more than for it, he's delighted with the prospect and also that he isn't the biological father. He might be an egomaniac some ways but he doesn't think there's anything genetically useful, especially not his narcissism and cockiness, he can pass on except his intellect, and I told him you're his equal in that regard and you're substantially more creative and artistic than he, which he wants more of in his progeny. He said to convey his congratulations to you and that unlike me he hopes it's a girl," baby's due in March. He wrote back saying that, clubby as this insipid remark sounds, he sends his best wishes to Harry too and appreciates his temperance—how 'bout dat for a word? Thanx, Roget—in the matter and if there's anything he can do for them regarding the pregnancy and birth, to let him know. He doesn't have much cash socked away and Harry, only a teacher though he hears law professors do okay, must still be in a much better financial position than he, but he'd be willing to part with a little if they needed it, and please keep him informed. He thinks of her fondly and has missed her, he's sure she's not interested to hear, at least a few minutes of every day of every week since. A month later she sent him a photo of herself from the side, naked from the hips up and showing mostly her slightly swollen stomach, with her arms covering her breasts and the top half of her head cropped. In a note she said "If you wish I can send you one of these Polaroid shots every month though never with my face fully shown, for obvious reasons: 'Wife Disseminates Porno Photos, Law Prof Hubby Loses Job.' I shoot them myself with a delayed timer, but I'm sure that clicking and running into position will become increasingly strenuous with each succeeding month, so I don't know how long I'll be able to keep it up. But this will be as close as I can get you to the experience of my gravidity other than for reporting various particulars of it, e.g., I'm nauseated daily while at the same time pining for you a little a couple of times weekly (figure out the math of that yourself). Those two, nausea and nostalgia, aren't necessarily linked but were only written poorly here—your influence, I think, which seems to have continued with this sentence (can the father's genes be transferred to the mother via the fetus?). Harry sends his best and wishes you were rich." He wrote back saying he hoped her nausea had passed by now—he heard it usually lasts only a month—but if it hasn't he's including a recipe composed mainly of cranberries for an antidote he got out of his woman friend's book of natural self-healing remedies. He still thinks of her fondly, maybe a minute to two more a day than a month ago and about three minutes more than when he first started to—at this rate his mind will be totally consumed by her in twenty to thirty years—hopes his genes haven't been transferred via the route she said for that conjures up horrific incestuous possibilities that for health and moral reasons—anyway, she gets the point. Tell Harry he'd love to be better fixed but doesn't know anyone holding down more poor-paying jobs at one time for so long as he and little appreciation from the woman he's supporting, though for her dear son he'd work his butt off, with no thanks needed, till his father started to or he was twenty-one. He'd love a month-by-month Polaroidized pornographic account of her pregnancy—he had to go to the local university library's biggest dictionary for "gravidity"—if she's still up for it. "By the way, I thought you looked fine in the photo. I was going to say 'great' but I know how you hate compliments of any sort. By the way two, you never asked and I never said how the woman I live with reacted to my meeting you in N.Y. and your getting gravid—I hadn't planned on telling her but it all sort of came out in front of the washing machine when she saw the lipstick on my collar and smelled the perfume on my hanky. She said it was just what she expected from me: that my primary pursuit in life is not art nor scholarship nor the deepest things men think but 'to sniff out the vaginas of every well-stacked and/or beautiful woman' I meet, though if she and I are still together after the child's born (it isn't true about me and vaginas of any kind, by the way three, as I haven't bedded with anyone else but her and you in a few years, though my eyes have; maybe that's what she's saying but since she knows that, why did she refer to my nose?) she'd like—she's periodically fantasized having a second child but knows she'd abort the first real sign of one, since it'd put a few more wrinkles on her stomach and crimp in her noncareer—for it to spend half the year with us once it's around three or four. I'm just repeating her words, as she also said that probability's probably an impossibility or the opposite, because you wouldn't go for it—'What non-doped-up rational mother would?'—and I've also told her I love you more than I do her (I actually don't love her at all but how am I to say that?) and she wants me out of her house soon as I can cough up the next quarterly mortgage payment for it and leave enough money behind for that period's utility bills (she thinks she'll be ready by then to look for a job to support herself and her son). I know I sound as if I'm ridiculing her but please understand, we've been at the edge of that Grand Canyon's highest precipice for a year with each of us contemplating shoving the other off. I never should have stayed out there that long since she's much more vehement, vengeful and grievance-stricken than I. Cheers to Harry, love to you. How come, by the way four, you don't sign off with anything resembling a 'Ta ta,' 'See ya,' '¡vaya con Dios!' 'Happy landing' or 'Write soon'?" He didn't hear from her for a few months. By this time he was living alone in the city in a single room. He wrote asking how she was—wrote several times—wrote he was

84

getting worried she hadn't written back—wrote he was now even more worried she hadn't written back after his last letter about it—wrote he was thinking of calling her but thought that'd be intrusive, was he right?—wrote that for the last time, answer him if everything's okay, Harry, her boy, she, and yes, is the baby okay?—wrote saying he's sure everything's okay, as she can see from his last letter he just gets worried that way, but please write and tell him a little of what's going on . . . if she in fact doesn't want him writing her anymore . . . and he forgot to tell her in any of his letters the last two months, though assumed she guessed by his change of address, that he and the woman split up before either of them pushed the other off that canyon cliff or jumped or did both but he takes her son once a week for a night and day, something the kid's beginning to shrink from as he'd rather be free all weekend for his friends—and she finally wrote back saying she had a miscarriage and, to be honest, Harry and she are relieved, as the baby was putting a strain on their marriage much worse than any affair or love involvement would. "Harry wanted the child to know as soon as it was able to (a year? two? for one not so comprehending, three?) the identity of its biological father (or so out of it: four? five? Though I took a new kind of amniotic-fluid prenatal test and it was a girl who was destined to be, unless there were delivery snags, healthy and learned) and, if possible, for you to see it once or twice a week for—I mean 'twice a year for a week' (that unpremeditated slip should in no way be interpreted as to how I occasionally feel about you, if you'll excuse). He said you could even stay with us and, if you also liked, sleep with me but not every night, or not the ones he wanted to. I wouldn't have gone for that, thank you, being passed around like a felt hat—'Orgasms for the needy and poor!'—but I know what was on his mind: he wanted to continue to putter around outside, especially those nights you and I were supposed to be doing it here: maybe he believed it'd make his own sex more exciting or it was part of his misguided ideas of husbandly liberation. As for me, I wanted my children to grow up as bonded same-parents siblings and for the new one never to see or speak to you and surely not to know what you are to it. I thought it would have a disadvantage, being both a bastard and genetically connected to the family only by half, besides what Harry might say to it in one of his drug- or booze- or rage-induced stupors and that its brother would also from time to time make sure it knew of its liability too. If I got my way it'd mean I'd have to lie to this second child about its origins which is antithetical to the only life rule I have (and then, of course, by my husband or son, be refuted), or the only one I regard high enough to want to pass on to my children: Never lie, cheat or steal ('cheat' in money, swindle, defraud, violate rules deliberately, gull, betray, double-cross). And I thought it would have to eventually find out (if not by Harry & Son then someone) its parents had been lying to it about its parentage all this time and confront us with it. Harry would be his usual cavalier self. 'Oh, it was for your sake,' he'd say to it (if it wasn't his blundering stupor that revealed it, then he'd be too blind to speak and think clearly), or 'Your mother thought it best for you, and it's been ten to fifteen to twenty years already so be cool and forget it, babe. And we brought you up well and without privations, haven't we, so what more do you want?'—but it'd devastate me. Incidentally, I'm no longer nostalgic for you and this is no lie (I don't lie!). The truth is I wish I'd never met you, or met you but said after a while 'Enjoy the party, Gid, or Gold, or Gould—sorry, I'm bad with names—and nice to meet you and toodle-oo,' because then none of this would have happened. And what good came of it? Did I pick up a sizzling piece of wisdom? Find my way out of a blind spot from my youth? Have my first adult orgasm, o-lay! So I pray—and I'm dead serious about that: with my back on my bed last night and eyes closed and mouth open and lips soliciting to the Lord—this letter will terminate our correspondence. I know I'll never respond to you if you write again, and if I happen to answer the phone if you call, then immediately on knowing it's you I'll hang up with eardrum-damaging finality. Be a pal, as you used to say to me to get your way and said your dad did too to you, and tear up the naked photo of me. I no longer look like that—what was in is out—and it could be of no use to you now—certainly not of the masturbatory kind either—and it's the last appeal I'll ever make to you and I do so most genuinely. Matter of fact, not the last: tear it up and send it back noteless but agglomeratively intact. Will you do that? Thank you, Gould. Good-bye." He kept the photo (at first, when he was still living with the other woman, around her house here and there but out of sight: in his desk or dresser drawer or favorite hardcover poetry anthology; after he moved out: faceup in his night table drawer so whenever he opened it he saw her, then facedown when he got tired of seeing it so much: her shy smile, or qualmish one, or reluctant or whatever-it-is kind of smile that's pulling back as it's being given—"I know I look absurd," it seemed to say, "or the bottom of my face that's left does, since I also know I'll be snipping the top half of my head off this photo, and if I was going to do it right I should have stuck a Coke bottle in my cunt, but as it is it's somehow wrong and can probably be used against me in the future or the baby—you could say 'Look at her, she's a whore who also poses for porno photos and I should have the child'—but I think I have to do it anyway, which makes no sense, okay?"—tiny belly bloat on her lanky frame, but it got permanently dirty and a part of it scratched across her arms over her breasts so he turned it faceup again; a short time later when he moved back to New York: in a see-through bag of most of his old photographs he kept in his shirt and sweater drawer and which included baby shots of him sitting up in a pram and on his mother's shoulders with her holding out his hands and looking as if she's doing a Jewish dance and as a summer camper and Boy Scout and several of him over a number of years sitting on a curb watching the Macy's Thanksgiving Day parade and pictures of old girlfriends or girls he wanted to be his girlfriends and half the photos in the bag taken on his European trip when he was nineteen and had his first camera, of girls he met and places he saw and road signs where he waited for a hitch and many of him in a sport jacket feeding pigeons in the Piazza San Marco and his folks at a table in the same piazza ten years later on their first European trip which had to be cut short because his father got very sick and also when they were young and on their parents' laps and uncles' and brothers' shoulders and together when they were courting and several don't-take-me-I-look-repulsive ones of his mother in maternity clothes; for a while in a letter envelope at the back of his socks, underwear and handkerchief drawer, keeping it hidden from some woman he might meet at a party or bar, let's say, and invite home and her coming upon it accidentally or because she liked to snoop or was looking for a pair of socks to wear because his apartment in winter was usually cold, which is what he meant by "accidentally," and maybe even questioning why, after explaining how she found the photo by accident, he had one of a slightly pregnant otherwise spindly meek-looking nude woman (some distinctive kind of kink?) and then lost it after a few years but doesn't know how: he removed all the dresser drawers several times that year thinking the envelope might have slipped behind or under them, once emptied out all the clothes and unfolded them and searched through the shirts and inside the pockets of the shorts and shook every garment out and things like that. Did masturbate to it a few times, usually—after the first three or four times—when nothing better was around like a just-bought or week-old issue of a men's magazine that was also known for its fiction and had a potentially interesting article or interview. He felt he needed a naked woman's body or several of them in different poses to do it to, focusing his attention when he did it to her photo (to the magazines' photos there were vaginas, clitorises later on, spread legs, raised rears, brushed bushes, nipples that had probably been rubbed with ice, he heard, just before being photographed or both breasts dunked in frigid water) to the little that was visible light pubic hair. Every year or so, then every two, three, three to four, but really at the most two to three he'd think something like his child would be one now . . . two . . . three . . . five . . . seven . . . ten . . . thirteen or fourteen. Would it have been a girl? Chances are, because of that test, which was new but not as reliable then and of what she felt at conception, yes. What would he have preferred? Both. Either, he means. Twins of opposite sexes he would have loved, for then he'd have it all in one. A healthy baby, that's all, isn't that what he's supposed to say? And it's true too; his father said first thing he did when he saw him after he was born was count his fingers and toes and check that his testicles had dropped. But after that: probably a girl. Easier, he's sure, meaning less conflict, they take fewer risky chances, like to read more and play indoors, theater, dance, voice, piano, imaginative games, other things that make it easier, and they seem to get sweeter and more compassionate and tender than boys as they get older, or stay that way more, or most, or maybe he doesn't know what he's talking about, and she'd have her mother, much more important to her than her father, while with a boy there's always that comparing, challenging, matching, outdoing. Would he have tried to see it, taken an interest in it? Boy or girl, he would have, as it got older, or tried, and often as it wanted or its parents let him. Would have even taken it a few weeks every summer, if permitted, car trip around part of the country, two weeks in a rented cabin in New Hampshire or Vermont, things like that if he had the money, maybe even camping—he'd learn how to do it—and he'd send presents every birthday and Christmas and books throughout the year: classics, poetry, things he'd find out it was interested in. About twelve years after he last saw the woman he tried contacting her when he was going to be in Madison but neither she nor Harry was listed with information. He sent a letter to their old address, having transferred it to each new address book, thinking maybe it could still be forwarded—they might have moved only within the last year or two and the expiration date on forwarding their mail hadn't been reached—but the post office returned it: addressee unknown. He phoned the university's law school and the secretary there said Harry had left teaching for private practice seven or eight years ago and she didn't know where. Could she find out? he said, and the next day she said all she could learn from personnel was that the law office he joined was in Milwaukee. He called Milwaukee information but neither was listed. Maybe they got divorced and Harry had left the state and she was still living in Madison or Milwaukee but under her maiden name or new married one. He didn't remember her maiden name and called the law school again for any information on the woman but the secretary said she didn't know anything and none of Harry's former colleagues still taught here and even if she had their phone numbers and names she couldn't give them out. He was seeing someone now, nothing very serious—dinner, movies and bed—and about once every three weeks called someone else or was called by this person for the same thing, so maybe the woman and he, if she was no longer with Harry and hadn't remarried, could get together for a couple of days in

Madison; they had been attracted to each other once, she in her way, he much more so in his, and not that many years had passed where they'd be so physically changed unless she'd gone through some major health problem or illness; some people even said he looked better than he ever had and he felt he was a more reasonable and interesting person than when she knew him and in much better physical shape: he ran and exercised vigorously every day. But he didn't know anyone who knew her. He couldn't remember the name of the friend she stayed with when he first met her in New York or exactly where she lived: some number Downing Street in the Village—he remembered he got off at the Christopher Street subway station and that it wasn't the same number as the British prime minister's residence; that, he thinks, would have stuck with him. He could go down there and maybe he'd recognize the building and then he'd look at the tenant roster or mailboxes and maybe recognize the friend's name, but he didn't think it worth the trip: she had probably moved by now too; in twelve years everyone he knew around his age had moved three or four times. A year later he was at a small wedding reception of a woman he'd dated for a short time that same year. They had split up amicably—she liked him and sleeping with him and thought he was intelligent and all that—he liked her too and loved her body—but she thought him unmarriageable and she wanted to get married and have children with someone who made a lot more money than he or at least whose prospects for it were better and who was readier for marriage—in other words, she said when she told him all this, and nothing that other women haven't said to him, she was cutting off their little romance to give herself the opportunity to meet other men before she got too involved with him—and though he didn't know why he'd been invited—they hadn't remained friends, seeing each other for coffee or talking on the phone or anything like that—he went out of curiosity and the chance of meeting a woman. A man came over to him and said "Don't I recognize you—were we once acquainted?" and he said "Not that I know of, I'm sorry, what's your name?" Their names weren't familiar to each other but the man was sure he knew him from someplace and that Gould even might have had an important impact on his life—"Something you said or did, I'm almost positive"—and Gould said "I don't see how that could be, unless something I said related to something else and you took it the way you wanted or needed to at the time— that can happen, though I'm not claiming to be a psychologist; and believe me, nothing I've ever done, or I'm aware of, I don't think could have altered anybody's life in the kind of way you said," and the man said "Let's see," and they went back where each had worked and lived and gone to school the last fifteen years and it turned out the man had studied with the host of the party Gould had met the woman at and that the man was at that party and had once been a good friend of Miriam's. "Miriam, that's right, I don't know why but I'm always forgetting the name," and the man said "Just think of the original Miriam's place in the Bible and you'll always have it," and he said "Excuse me, I don't mean to sound ignorant, but I don't recall a Miriam in it—in the Old, anyway, and I've never read the New except some quotes you see on Baptist signs along the road and maybe what was read to us at public school assemblies," and the man said "In the way you allude to them, she was in the Old T, sandwiched between Moses and Aaron, but I'll let you guess or do the research on the rest; granted, though, Gould, she wasn't the most significant sororial biblical figure. And I'm still wondering what it was that could have impressed me so much about you at that party, but it could be my memory of my own history's starting to flag too," and he said "Anyway, whatever happened to Miriam?—I know she once lived on Downing Street here," and the man said "Married a Canadian doctor whose family's reputed to own half a province or so, and moved to Montreal." "You know his last name?" and the man said "A French one with a *le* or *la* in it, but that's all I know." "Miriam's last name then—it's been a while," and the man said "Hildago, but she dropped it for her hubby's. If there are any further questions about her, all I can say is I've been out of touch with her for years—call it a falling out," and he said "Miriam had a friend from college with her at the party and I've lost touch with her," and gave the woman's name and described her and the man said "She I never knew, not even by name, and I must have seen her with Miriam on and off, but can't picture her from your description. It might help if you could give me her original name at school. But tell me about you. How have you been faring these past dozen years? Marriage, lots of squealing infants, or because of one reason or another are you a confirmed bachelor or just unsure about being one?" and seemed to be making a pass by what he said and way he said it and used his lips and eyes and Gould said "None of them," and excused himself. Four years later, when he was married and his first child was around a year and a half, he received a letter from the woman. She'd read a book review he'd done—it was good, she said, illuminating in parts and never stodgy but didn't go deeply enough into the reasons he disliked the book so much, which she thought he could have done with very little added effort as well as given a clearer summing up as to what the author was trying to say—and the contributor note indicated where he taught, which is why this letter's coming to him by way of his institution. "Preface completed as to how I got to you after so many years, as well as unasked- and perhaps uncalled-for capsulized review of your review, now let me explain why I'm writing. Naturally (as you can see I've adopted your old irritating habit of asides, which I think is the most honest way for me to write since it's how I think when I'm writing, though I realize the momentum and interest of what I write are often lost in these digressive interjections) I hope this letter finds you well. You're probably married by now—I hope you are or have been married at least once (my own feeling, based on the experiences of friends and partly on my own experience, is that it takes a bad brief rancorous first marriage to make a good harmonious second one, and that most first marriages are brief because they're rancorous, wrongheaded, misguided and destructive almost from the start and the relationships leading up to them aren't much better) and have children or a child, and if so I congratulate you (shades of my shade Harry, if you can remember back that far) which may be the most belated and surely the most recent congratulations you've received on the matter, unless you were just married or remarried or had your first child yesterday and this letter arrived the day after. All foolishness aside—all, if I can manage it, asides aside—and also because (there goes that resolution, made in earnest but which you should take as an exemplar of how much you can trust me regarding this, and after what I have to tell you, which I'm sure I'll eventually come to, regarding anything, perhaps) I don't believe any letter should extend beyond a bladderful of ink (as you can see, one habit of yours I haven't adopted, convenient and time-saving as it would be if I wasn't so inept with almost any kind of machine, is the typewritten letter)—but let me continue (this goes back, incidentally, to the previous page and that 'all foolishness aside' start) and a gold medal to you—it's Olympics time again and my entire brood's influenced if not, in how we use our hours, governed by it—so a gold medal in stick-to-itiveness if you've kept up with me in all this). About two months ago my youngest son Timothy was going through my personal library for a book—any book; he simply wanted to read something (and I've two sons, by the way, and no girls, and no child of mine has ever died or been taken away from me at birth or anytime after and tragedies like that, so this is all the children I've had and have or ever will; you'll understand what I mean momentarily—I'm sure it'll take a leap of faith for you with that 'momentarily'—if you haven't understood already) and found one that interested him because of its cover (you may not be able to tell a book by its cover but it can start you reading it—excuse me, I'm such an impoverished poor punster who's always tripping overself in the attempt, and four or five words into that pun I regretted having begun, and same with the overself, which is more a neowart or carnage than a pun) and he opened it (the book, if you forgot, and I'm not blaming you) and an old postcard from you to me dropped out. There, I've finally gotten to it. Do you know what I'm going to say next? I suppose that depends on how well you remember what you used to say too publicly at the time (though now I wouldn't care less) in your postcards, and what I just said wasn't what I was going to say next. Now I've given enough hints. If you haven't caught on yet then something, I'm afraid, and I say this lamentably, has happened to your once-snappy brain. You had drawn something on it—are you getting warmer? (And I meant the old children's game, nothing else, and shouldn't have even clarified it, since it looks as if I did mean it provocatively, when I didn't, I didn't.) And Timothy asked 'Who's the artist?' I told him you weren't an artist, or you might be now but you weren't when you drew it, and he said 'But he's done a nifty caricature of you as a pregnant lady standing on a doctor's scale with your head pressed up against the measuring stick attached to it. And he wrote underneath (this should all have been paraphrased or in indirect quotes, but permit me the license and also the pleasure in seeing how adept I am at replicating his voice): "Haven't heard from you in a while (that, of course, should be in the direct quotes it is). How's your confinement doing? Measuring up to scale?" So he knew you when you were pregnant with me, based on the card's dates (meaning yours and the P.O.'s). Pretty bold of him there, Mom, as if he knew you intimately. Was he,' he asked, "a lover or someone like that? (I inserted the 'he asked'

97

because I thought I might have lost you. Did I?) A good friend who you maybe only had some good friendly sex with and nothing else when Dad was still around? (That's right: Harry's no longer around; he's dead—'shades of my shade Harry,' several pages back?—but more about that later if the pen holds out.) I mean, Ma (here I'm trying to convey it as it was spoken, to bring the scene more to life for you so you'll be able to hear the boy, though he actually calls me Chris more than he does Ma or Mom), you say your marriage was open then, but how much so?' ('Nifty,' from a previous page, I now realize, isn't a word I've ever heard him use; it could have been 'neat' or 'nice,' but don't hold me to it.) So I told him the truth: you, me, your orgasmic duplicity, my lethargy, Timothy as blastocyst, Harry as goingalongwithist, and the truth's what I'm truthfully telling you now, truthfully. 'Not (and I also just realized Timothy would have used 'whom' for 'who' in that 'good friend you maybe only' many lines ago, since it's a discipline at school he's recently relearned again for good and has been practicing on us without letup or remorse) even as a friend,' I said of you. 'And for me, at least, not for the sex or rapport or because I was piningly lonely in New York, where your roots first started to generate, or the satisfaction and intrigue in deceiving your father either. He was just there—your father elsewhere—slippery, pushy and unstoppably priapic, and after my first few puny no's—I'm almost sure about that—I was my most typically submissive, unvocally suspicious and containable.' Principal reason I told him is because his father died in a motorcycle accident eight years ago, if one can call it that: Harry was stoned, driving with one hand, blowing kisses with the other, his lady possessor, an obsessive confessor who miraculously survived without only a spleen, reproductive system and one eye to brag about it all, giving him a handjob with Vaseline—she even said he was approaching out-of-body trans-send-your-socks-off-into-the-void ejaculation as they crashed—and having missed out having a father for so long during most of the important years for that I finally succumbed to thinking he should know he still had a biological one, feeling that if I ever died (at forty I suddenly became mortal) before he was on his own and John (my eldest, whom you met) was too encapsulated in his own life to tender to him, he could try contacting you. All this about the aborted abortion that I never gave so much as half a thought to having must come as a surprise and shock. I apologize for that, but at the time I thought it the only way to keep you from the birth and baby and then the child being raised. You were such a gushy sentimentalist about children and blood, which might be nice if one were married to you, that I knew you'd intrude deleteriously, in addition to all the other disadvantages he'd undergo which I wrote you of but now can't recall. Harry went along with my having the child so long as I continued to let him lay his many legal girlfriends (that was his profession almost: layman of lawyers) at any minute of the night and overdraft our savings and checking for his increasingly more exotic cars, two-wheelies and drugs. Then he died, I kept you a secret from Timothy, since I didn't see any point in his knowing, the secret spilled out of the bookshelf and Timothy, an aspiring trial lawyer he says but only for the money, easily grilled it out of me.

But now—for instance, regarding keeping you from the birth, your adamant ideas on circumcision: that a boy shouldn't have one; he can keep his prepuce clean just by washing it and the dismemberment robs him of a sexual edge; even if his brother and both his fathers had them and preputial men are more prone to penile cancer and sometimes suffer phimosis and are also supposed to increase the chances of cervical cancer in the women they lay. You were filled with that sort of unthought-out naturalistic mischief. But now, as I was saying, Timothy would like to have a relationship of some kind with you but asked me to initiate it with this letter: flamboyant, aggressive and (no pun calculated) cocksure in the courtroom as he's sure to be, he's preternaturally shy outside it, something I was in every setting and still am, except when I'm writing, and you said you were once too, which amazed me because you were so fundamentally forward and backslapping. So what do you say, Gould? He'll write back if you jot him a few lines. Just say who you are and what you do and you heard he wanted a letter from you, and if you have a wife and children or child then something about them. He loves animals so if you have a pet or two or your children do, tell him of it. Where you live and have lived and what kind of place it is: Ping-Pong table, swimming pool, little lawn where you might play ball or run around with your kids, what sports you might attend: all those things. In other words, what you're most interested in if it's clean, and if you mention me then simply refer to the place where we met: kids his age love hearing about parties and New York. Or write what you like— who am I to inscribe your lines? He'll be thrilled to get anything, though please don't feel you're committed to this forever. If you want to withdraw after the first letter or think your other obligations preclude any to him, even an exchange of letters, tell him so and he'll just have to understand. He's fifteen and quite mature and other than for his blond hair and if my memory serves me faithfully—too bad we never got to the stage in our relationship of exchanging photos, if only so he could have some idea what you looked like then and must still resemble a little now—he looks like you of sixteen years ago, minus fifteen or so (did I make my math too confusing to follow, as well as this labored sentence?). For certain he looks like no one else in his family, Harry's included, except for his hair, which is mine though now mine is a fading blond-gray (let's face it: I've aged and I swear I don't care; it's only a man or two who knew or screwed me fifteen-twenty years ago who do). Now he's standing beside me, and when I asked him to move because I hate anyone looking over my shoulder, then beside me, and is reading and now has read this page and after telling me I'm being too harsh on my facial lines, corporeal spread and dehydrated hair (those are my words; his were just 'face, body and hair'), wants to read all the previous pages. But I'm telling him and have just told him they're private and it's something he knows better than to ask. And he's telling me and has just told me and, because I didn't catch it all and it seems to be serious enough that I should, told me again to say he'll write you first if you will only give the thumbs-up in a letter or card to me or him that you're willing to receive (you don't even have to be eager, he said) and that you might even answer him (though just that you'll open his letter will be enough, he said; 'If you want, don't even read,' he just yelled). He's also saying—but let me get this straight (and fill, to be completely honest with you, and though I didn't want to go past one and after my second, thought I was being dishonest in not telling you, my third bladderful of ink—has it been that long; can you hold out?). Now: something about law and legal things I think he was saying—yes, that's what he was saying, he's now saying, and that you should never fear, the junior trial lawyer says, that your personal correspondence (his words) will be used in court against you. That he will never 'institute' a son's (he just told me to put quotation marks around that possessive) equivalent of a paternity suit, though for all he knows, he added, that's what it might be called. He only wants the two of you to know something about the other: it'll make him feel good and 'more whole.' Speaking personally—he wants me to strike out that last quote; says it makes him seem stupid for 'whole is whole, like unique's unique and pregnant's pregnant,' but it's my letter, Timmy, I just told him—he hates when I call him that; has said it sounds as if he's still a child. But, speaking pregnantly—*personally* (that was intentional)— 'Get out of here now, Tim,' I just told him—he's a great kid (but isn't getting out. 'Out, Tim, I said out!'), decent, sensitive, witty, gentle, polite, way-above-average intelligence and sensibil- ity, the boy of boys and all the other standard things people say about their children. (I hate that last passage: so bourgeois.) (And that last use of 'bourgeois': so bourgeois.) I just wish Harry had lived (of course I also wish it for other reasons) so Timothy would never have been shoved into this stew. (Such odd word usage, a stew itself, and if I'm preternaturally anything in this letter—why did I use such an unnatural word there, a question which acts out what I was about to say? The first time to show off, the second to poke holes in myself. And why did I think I had to answer my question, which is still portraying what I was about to say and that was if I'm preternaturally anything in this letter it's self-conscious. Meaning that I am, and not because you mean so much to me, if I can beg your pardon, because you don't. I'm self-conscious because I feel guilty withholding his existence from you till now and also that abortion trick I did, and withholding you from Timothy too. I've done the absolutely wrong thing, I think, which I hope this letter will begin to correct.) A boy needs his father (this goes back to my wish that Harry had lived), and whatever Harry wasn't to me (other than for the boys, begetting one and fathering them both, what a pointless marriage!) he (already said in the last paragraph) was always there for his sons. (So: sort of said. And John's in sleepaway college, by the way, and indifferent that his brother is only his half brother now.) Now Timothy thinks of you often, says he's dreamed of you, wants to go—what am I saying?—he's gone to the local library and run a computer check on your publications in the hope there'd be a jacket or newspaper photo of you and found that you haven't been productive the last fifteen years ago and that this seems to be only your second review in a publication that's important enough to be on a computer readout (Timothy told me the term). If that's so, I told him, then it could be that most of your work time goes into classroom teaching—which he immediately saw as a 'definite plus in biodad's favor'—or else our library hasn't the resources it claims it has. But Gould, like facing age— oh gosh, I was about to get philosophical. What I'm saying is face it, you have at least one son who, I believe, in addition to all the other reasons he's drawn to you (flesh and blood, a writer of at least two published reviews, etc.) secretly admires you for winning his mother over (fucking her in one night, though I told him two, and it was two, wasn't it? Since you can't count the first day we met; and I didn't, of course, say 'fuck' to him; I think I said, stumped for the moment as to how else to put it, 'when we were joined together as lovers') and knocking her up that first night too (I didn't tell him that; he just assumed). Because I think I lied—I did lie, didn't I?—and said that was the only time we were joined together, since the next day, I told him, I drove back to Madison with John. Who knows if that admiration for you isn't his way of getting back at his real dad—the nonbiological one—though for what, I don't know, other than—and this would be too ironical—his treatment of me, though pummel me with pumice stones for trying to get psychological on you too. Other than that (I'm in the closing mode, I swear) if you don't write either of us back I'll write you again. If you don't answer that letter (I'll give you a few weeks with both) I'll phone your university to make sure you're still teaching there or not on sabbatical or leave somewhere. If you are there or on leave but not writing back (first I'll phone your department's secretary to make sure you're picking up your office mail or having it sent to you and that you're not in a foreign country where it's rare for the mail to get through) or you write back you want nothing to do with any of this, I'll understand, even if I can't guarantee Timothy will; though that should be, after all I did (lying, disappearing, hitting you with this news, perhaps subconsciously inducing you to bed sixteen years ago with whatever whining and self-hurting and other unwily wiles I used to make you feel sorry enough for me to) of no concern or problem to you. You're in the clear as people say (I can't for the life of me, like that 'for the life of me,' get genuinely colloquial—maybe curtailing the adverbs and swanky verbs would help). Timothy, incidentally, is no longer in the room reading this and hasn't been since I ordered him out that second time (I'm afraid, since Harry's death, I'm able to get scolding, revolted and fierce). As you can see by the skipping light script in the last sentence, the pen's running dry again. I want to leave enough ink (to be honest, this is the end of my third—all right, to be absolutely honest: fourth—bladderful) and three (since it's a much handier if not facile number to make comparisons and analogies with and so forth) has always been enough, hasn't it? ('always' meaning 'usually' here), if not more dramatic: on a match, three strikes and you're out, three-time loser, Holy Trinity, is a crowd, etc., to address the envelope as well as forge a facsimile of a first-class postage stamp on the top right corner of it (naturally, not true and the end, you'll be glad to hear, of any of my fourth-class jokemaking attempts). So thank you (why'd I say that? I suppose in my hope you'll accept my apologies for all my wrongdoings to you) and very best, and if you do have a wife and child(ren) you're currently living with, my humblest regards to them. (Not 'humblest,' but you know what I mean.)" He showed the letter to his wife and said "Something, huh? I feel like I don't know what. Still shaking inside and like an ice pack's been dropped through my body to my feet. I mean, before I read it I had one kid and now I've two. What should I do about it?" and she said "Want me to make a joke about the ice pack or just give you a straight serious answer?" and he said "Both if you want," and she said "Well, I'd say you have an unusually—and I ought to be careful with my jokes here after what she had to say about them and also hold back on my aggressions—*digressions*—and fake slips and asides—that you must have unusually clear arteries, which should be something to be thankful to find out about. And then—joke flat, for you're not smiling," and he said "No no, it was all right, just maybe I couldn't find anything funny now . . . but what else, the serious?" and she said "To write back; I don't see how you can avoid it. What to say to her, though, right now I don't know. That's for you, as to how you feel. But one question you should ask yourself is why you're so sure the boy's yours." "I just know he is; the timing sixteen years ago; her pretenses during it—at the early stages, and now in this letter, meaning . . . meaning what? This has also confused me. That it just seems authentic, this letter. I mean, there does seem to be something askew with her in it, the way she puts things. Or maybe I'm wrong; it's just her way of putting things—she's nervous, self-conscious, was always turning away, not looking at me, bashful, if you can believe it; frightened, even, though she now says she can be aggressive—I'm sure that's what she meant—and fierce. Fooling herself there, I think. But, but, just by the way she says she kept it from me and is now revealing it. And because I doubt anyone could make up a letter like this, or if anyone could, she wasn't among them or was the very last to . . . all that, I'm saying, smacks the truth—*of* it. I'm repeating myself and also still not being clear," and she said "No, I understand, and how could you not be? What I'm thinking now though is why you're so sure she's even had a second son. It's possible she has gone a little over the who-knows-what and it isn't simply nerves and self-consciousness, since we don't know what's happened to her, like drugs she's taken or illnesses she's gone through and relationships she's had, in sixteen years. Or tragedies even—the loss of her first and only son, though that's carrying it too far. But she might only be imagining it or, as she said about the boy to his alleged deceased nonbiological father, is trying to get back at you for some reason. Though why would she be, since from what you've told me and this letter says she was the one who cut you off. But I'd look into the letter more deeply, read it for keys. Maybe she's getting back at you with this possible birth lie for originally getting her in bed and impregnating her when she didn't want to, at least the pregnancy," and he said "I don't know, but I have to admit she wasn't very keen on sleeping with me. More like, if I really had to or sort of insisted—her meekness again—she'd get on the bed, hike up her dress and spread her legs and I should just go ahead. But there's more validity in what you say about the pregnancy, since I did trick her. I should have pulled out of her as we'd agreed—I'm saying, the first time. The second and third, if there was a third, I assume she was protectively prepared, or else she didn't do anything because she already knew she was pregnant. But she wasn't a vindictive type or a conniver and nothing in the letter shows it. In fact, just the opposite comes out," and she said "Why, where's it say that?" looking at the letter, and he said "I thought I heard it come through, but I won't press it; I'm not as good a reader as you. But what she says here I'm convinced is the truth, though if it really came down to it I'd want a blood test to prove it," and she said "Do you know what they cost? There was something in the—no, a doctor acquaintance, Debby, and she was talking about it, or someone for some reason asked her, when I was with her, and the figures stuck. Maybe it was originally a newspaper article and this person wanted it explained or couldn't believe the costs. But Debby went into it: more than a thousand; that is, if you want ninety-nine-point-nine accuracy. It's a very complex foolproof process which no medical insurance covers, so you really have to want the tests. And you need their consent, mother and child's, and they have to take the tests the same day as you and their blood flown to the lab air-express if the lab's here, or yours to theirs same way, or maybe theirs is taken the day before yours so it can reach your lab the next day, but which has to be another hundred in costs: flying blood," and he said "Then that's another matter, which we'll maybe come to someday, but I'm saying I believe what she says is so and that I have to deal with it. And if it isn't so—now I mean that if she does have another child but it isn't mine; or what she says is a bit exaggerated . . . I don't know what I mean by that; I know it's something but I forget what—then I'll find out somehow in my letters to him.

But I will write her back saying the kid should write and I might even put something in the letter for him," and she said "For no furtive purposes, believe me, or that this is the wise wife telling the obtuse spouse what a mistake she thinks he might be making, but I'm still a bit suspicious. Out of the blue, sixteen years, this boy opens a book and his papa drops out?—excuse me, but it doesn't even seem a trace fishy to you? Maybe it's the truth—taller tales have been—but it could also be she wants you to start kicking in for him—private school, for instance, if he has a problem academically or his public school or school district does. College—he's getting to that age and may even be so precocious that this is his senior high school year and he's thinking of going to Stanford or Amherst or Yale. But big bucks and the living's high there. Or she comes upon one review, sees you're teaching in a good school, has read that some college profs make a hundred thousand or more and thinks you were sharp and smart so maybe you're among this elite and feels it'll be no hardship for you to help her with some serious bills because she's being evicted or had medical expenses she's up to her arrears in, and so on—the last wasn't bad, was it? and it wasn't anything I heard," and he said "As I told you, she wasn't like that and nothing she wrote suggests she's changed. She hated people who squeezed money or promises out of you. Hated advertisers, salesmen, promoters, professional handshakers, anyone pushy and aggressive and self-interested and unctuous, if I recall, is the word she used, but who wanted something from you like that. In a way, me at the time—that's what she said about me: pushy, sexually needy, other things, and

I was. Those days, nothing was going to stop me from trying to get the babe in bed and once in it or sitting on the edge of it with a piece of her clothing unbuttoned or off—even a shoe— from being even more forceful in frigging her. And once in her I sure as hell wasn't going to pull out—except maybe to quickly stick it back in some other way—and dimish my good time. Okay, that was me then, now I don't have to. I'm married, we can go for days without doing it if we want to, though we don't seem to—both of us; it's not just me. But sixteen years ago, or really since I was around eighteen, if she let me stick it in or didn't fight me off hard enough to stop me from getting in her, then screw it—apt phrase, right?—I left it to her to take care of the rest of it, meaning her own pleasure and the birth control and after-sex wipeaway, etcetera, though I might provide the handkerchief if my pants were near. My satisfaction, once it got under way, was paramount. You don't like what I just said, though I know I've said it before to you in various ways, but what can I say? Now I wouldn't act like that for sure if I were single, and I didn't, I think, when I first met you. I remember I'd decided to change my approach to fit my age and probably, without admitting it, my existent sex drive. But your face is saying something; what?" and she said "Nothing. You came on plenty strong with me then but it was all right. I knew what I was doing, which isn't a criticism of her. She was about ten years younger than I when you met her, you've said, though with a kid, and it was a different and I think much looser time then all around and maybe people, even intelligent ones, thought like that: 'Because I want another baby or am going to have another one some day, what's the difference if it's with him or someone else or even with my husband again, so long as the man seems to have good genes? It still comes out of me.' But I still think if I had been her age and without protection our first night and certainly if I was still cohabitating with my husband I would have clawed you off or grabbed your balls and squeezed them till they crunched if you had somehow got your stiff in without my permission or with my permission but I suddenly had second explicitly articulated thoughts about it and you refused to withdraw." "Anyway," he said, "looking at it all—and I know I didn't answer half your questions—in the end what's the harm? She only wants me to have a minimal relationship with him now—by mail. Maybe sometime later a phone call or a meeting, something I'd only do—the meeting—if I felt sure he was mine, and unless I get us all to take those blood tests, which I'm not about to, I don't see how I could. I don't know what I'll write to her but it'll all come out when I write it and I promise I'll be careful with my words." He started to write her that night, then thought he's only writing her to get through to the kid, so just write him, and started a new letter, saying who he is—"A friend of your mother's. We knew each other years ago, which she's of course told you, though I never met your father, who I understand passed away and which I was very sorry to hear"—what he does for a living, his family—"We've a daughter who's just started to walk and who seems quite bright, lots of clear words and a few communicated impressions: 'Look, bird! See, squirrel!' I'm not kidding. Early on kids talk like that, just verbs and nouns and commands, and not 'squirrel'; 'dog' "—and that "I heard from your mother you'd like me to write. I'd be happy to get a letter back telling things about yourself: what you like to do, school, job if you have one—I started working two to three hours a day and all day Saturday when I was thirteen, not recommended if one wants to get good grades, which I always wanted but never got except in music and art and if spelling had been its own subject, then I also would've got it in that"—his interests, friends, any pets? what he likes to read—"I'm assuming you do, no problem if not"—and so on. "Please give your mother my deepest regards." No reply from the boy. Month later he wrote the woman saying he wrote Timothy same day he got her letter and he hasn't received an answer. "In something like this the first thing I always say is I hope everything's all right (sometimes it can be illness and even worse, heaven forbid). That said and everyone's in good health and neither of you is going through comparable problems in other matters (fiscal, residential, social, etc.) then maybe he's even shyer than you thought, not that I'm saying you don't know your own son or that I have some special insight into his behavior because of this one action. (I'm afraid I'm being extraguarded here, not wanting to step in your terrain and feeling I've no right to draw conclusions about him, and I don't. I don't pretend to know him in any way other than from what you've said about him, but let's face it, as you like to say, or did a couple of times in your letter—and I didn't mean to make you self-conscious about that; it's really nothing. Damn, I forgot what I was going to say, so don't look for the closed parenthesis. But something about parents, because they're so close to their kids, often not being the best judges of them, which is an old notion but seems new to a new parent no matter how old he is and which I'm sure will be true of me too with my child (Fanny, *née* Francine, and it's been suggested, for obvious reasons except the big overlooked ones [force of habit and we like it] that we go back to the *née* one or call her, if we insist on an abbreviated or just less formal name and one we don't like, Franny). But have I gone too far in even saying what I just did about Timothy and you? Talk about self-consciousness (mine)! This whole thing, quite truthfully, has catapulted me into a tumultuous hazy maze (and also into blowhard overprosy writing just witnessed). So where was I? And I'm not saying you're one of the parents unable to judge her child sometimes because you two are so close (I don't even know how much you are but I get a feeling of it and fine, fine, why shouldn't you be?). But if Timothy's had a change of mind about contacting me or wanting to be contacted, that's okay, but please let me know. That's probably all I should have said. Most sincerely, and always my best to you and Tim." He showed his wife what he wrote, said "You think I should've called him Timothy, or maybe just change the 'Tim' to 'him'; I can do that with a correction tab," and she said "Why are you diving in headfirst like this?" and he said "What do you mean?" "Listen, the boy didn't answer you, so wait till he does," and he said "But what do you mean about diving in headfirst?" and she said "You're not being deliberative, prudent, patient, even the least bit skeptical; you're being impetuous, precipitous, reckless, even foolhardy," and he said "Adjectives, adjectives, all adjectives; fuck them and adverbs." "Okay," she said, "then this, since

I can see what I said made you pissed: what's the big rush? All right, not 'big,' but just 'rush, rush.' If he doesn't answer in another month or two, he'll still only be fifteen or at the most on the cusp of sixteen, but still young, with plenty of years left to begin to get to know you, and in the interim you can decide the next thing to do regarding him, which might be to do nothing. But you're acting like . . . this waiting for his letter the last month. You've been all hyped up and anxious about it as if it's a *fait accompli* or something that he's your son. In other words, a given, indisputable, no q's asked, and you're dying to hear from him. Perhaps, as you once intimated, to find some signs in his letters that he is who she says he is. Maybe by the way he writes or what he says or even his handwriting and signature, if he isn't already on a WP, and then oh boy, wait till the photos of him come in: 'Look, Sal, my chin, my nose, my lobes.' But that he's yours unequivocally. It's as if you're not already a father. And that you're forty-seven but unmarried, or married to a barren woman or you're the one at reproductive fault and you're desperate to go down in life as having fulfilled some universal or divine purpose and that's to leave a child behind with your seed in it, even if all this information about your fathership comes from someone you haven't seen in sixteen years, only was with two or three days—you two will never get that one straight—and has a history of being untrustworthy or considerably unreliable and for the most part simply not there. But there's Fanny and in a year or two we'll probably have another child or start to and if you want three I'll go for three. Rather, if we want a third we'll have it, and we've said we do, but we'll determine that for certain after we have two. But what can you do for this boy now that he's fifteen or for all we know soon to be or already sixteen?" and he said "No, it would be early summer when she and I met; that'd have him born in March or April, so he's only a few months into being fifteen." "Money for tuition and things like sleepaway summer camp and braces we can't afford," she said, "and I won't let you legally adopt him since that'll cut into what we want to give to the children we conceive. If you want to send him a few dollars—a few hundred—and it's from time to time, but money for his health or health insurance mostly, okay. I wouldn't even send this letter, though I won't do anything to stop you, and I certainly wouldn't write another one if you don't get one back from this one or the last. Take their not sending back as a sign, not that either of us believes in that," and he said "Truth is, but I told you this before," and she said "How would I know?" and he said "That I remember how much I wanted it to be true when she first said she was pregnant and then with that photo I told you she sent me and letters about her pregnancy, or maybe there was just one letter or two. And truth too is that I feel good now at the possibility of having a second kid in him. It won't stop me from wanting a second one with you and if we want, a third too, but that should do it. But if he's connected to me in the way she says then even at this late date in his life—fifteen's not late but you know what I mean—I have to take whatever responsibility's mine, all of which I'll find out what it is." "You don't. She kept it from you. You're off the hook as she said, or whatever so-called so hard to come by colloquialism she used—'out of the woods,' 'in the clear,' " and he said "Blood. If the kid's blood, then that's all there is to it, whatever's happened and no matter how much time's elapsed, though call me a misled sentimental sap." "You're full of shit," and she left the room. "Sally?" but she didn't answer. He mailed the letter and came back and said "I mailed it," and she said "So?" and wouldn't talk to him anymore that day or let him close to her that night. He woke up a few hours into sleep and wanted to put his arm around her and hold her breast and if he could hold both of them in one hand then both and fall back to sleep that way, which she knew was the easiest way he could get back to sleep, but she took his hand off and moved to her end of the bed. They didn't talk for two days. Sure: "Good-bye," "So long," "Excuse me," "Go ahead," but nothing much more than that. The woman didn't write back, the boy didn't, they never did. Two months later he called information in their city and was told the woman's phone number was unlisted. He wanted to ask her or the boy, which-ever answered, and if a boy did he was prepared for that: "Hi, this Timothy? I'm Gould; I wrote you almost three months ago," and if it was the older son he'd say "Let me speak to your mother"—but to either of the other two "What gives? You don't want to write, then as I said in my last letter to you" or "To your mother: that's fine, you had a change of mind" or "Your son changed his mind, but you should have done the right thing—either of you, or both, for he's old enough and you must have some control over what he does or doesn't do and could have squeezed a line or two out of him—and let me know where I stood. You bring me into it, you shift my life somewhat, you turn me around and around and upside down and send me into I don't know what consternations, in addition to what it does to my family or just my wife, then you shouldn't step away as if you never wrote" or "Your mother never contacted me to ask if I'd welcome a letter from you and you never asked her to, and which I said I would." Two years later he was going to be in their city and wrote her, saying "This is like something from ten years ago or twelve or fourteen, I honestly forget, but closer to the latter, I believe, when I wrote saying I was going to be in Madison and would like to look you up. Well, things come back on us, don't they, and I don't mean anything sly or snide in that, and I will be in your city in a couple of weeks and hope to see you if you're there and, if possible, your youngest son. I hope everything's well with you all. It is with us, and we've recently had a second child: Josephine." No reply from her. He called information there the next week, thinking maybe she's listed now, but there was no one with her or Timothy's names at that address or anywhere in the city. A week later, when he was there and after he'd done his business for the day, he went to their old address. He didn't expect them to be there, though they actually could be, something he just thought of, but didn't have a phone anymore—service could have been cut off because she hadn't paid the bill—but he also just wanted to see where they had lived. It was a large Victorian house turned into seven or eight apartments, the tenants' bells and mailboxes on the porch by the front door. Her name wasn't on any of them. Maybe she married again and took the last name of her new husband, but then she also would have had hers there, he'd think, and if she was remarried they probably would have moved out: the place seemed rundown. To find out about her he rang the first tenant's bell and when no one answered, the next bell and then the next and the man who came to the front door said the woman had moved out several months ago and he didn't know where. One day she was there with grocery bags in her arms and the next day she was loading a rented truck by herself with her furniture and stuff. "As for the boy, he was here a long time— she had two but the eldest has been away at college for a while and you almost never saw him, not even summers, and the youngest left home for Canada more than a half year ago I'd put it and seemed unsure about what for when I asked him. 'Work,' he said, and I said 'Work up there when they have a worse unemployment picture than we do down here?', 'Or maybe school then,' he said, 'or maybe nothing, just exploring, but not like up a mountain or in a hole,' is what he said. Young for going off on his own so far alone but he said he saved up for it the last year so it was okay. I never asked his mother what happened to him. Or if I did she never answered or else by accident I had my hearing aid in wrong or turned off. I suppose nothing bad did happen since she never showed any grief or anything and I used to see her almost every day—my window's right there and I was laid off and then retired so I had little to do but look out and snoop. But she had the same placid look, mood and voice for years. You couldn't get a laugh out of her, even when you said something really funny but unnaughty, not that she wasn't the nicest of ladies and also the most helpful in coming to people's aid here and troubles and things like that in the house." "And the boy, was he a nice kid—the youngest?" and the man said "Oh yeah, very nice, Tim, a real fine young gentleman. Civil, respectful, kept his music low. And listen to this: not the harsh angry clamor: 'Kill me this, beat me black and blue that, rape the world and its girls, drink and drug and party and buy my harsh angry music,' but good classical and jazz, to my ears. And no shouting matches with his mother, and when his brother was around, always a nice thing going between them. And things like after he rode his bike he parked it close to the building upright, saying good morning and hello, and helpful to the neighbors too with packages and opening doors, and errands when he was much younger, and you'd have to beg him to take a tip. That says a lot about her too, doesn't it? I wish my boys had had more of that in them. But I've told you so much and I don't even know why you want to know. They being investigated; the boy?" and he said "Far from it. I'm an old friend of the family's, Gould Bookbinder's my name," and shook the man's hand. "In town for the day and lost touch with them, so I came to the last address of theirs I had, hoping against the odds, when I couldn't reach them by phone, to meet up with them here, and seems I didn't miss them by much. You think anyone else in the building knows where she moved or the boy?" and he said "Nobody. I've spoken about it with them, the steadies. It's become something of a mystery to us we like to wonder about, since they were here awhile, though it's not like it's never happened before. Tenants here are always moving in and out at the spur of the moment or their roommates or lodgers are, and after they're gone I've never seen another one again, except by accident someplace, but that only happened once and I forget where." When he got home he found the letter he sent her two weeks ago returned by the post office: addressee left, no forwarding address. "So that's it, I guess," he said to his wife, "and I bet the next time I hear from her, even if I've nothing to back this up except that one long lull before I heard from her again, will be in ten to fifteen years. Somehow she'll find me—well, *here's* easy, but if we're in some other place or two removed from here—and say she's been thinking of me and my life. And also apologize for what she did to me ten to fifteen years ago and hope I'm well, family's well, everybody and everything's well and of course that this letter reaches me and even suggest I write her back but only if I care to—'There have been so many false starts from me that I can see why you might not want to,' she could say. And then something about Timothy, 'if you're still interested': married, divorced, remarried, children, he's become an undersea explorer, a real estate broker, an American folklorist, a professional coin collector, besides flying his own planes, but she won't give any hint where he lives or what airports he lands in. I'll almost be retired by then, or five to ten years from it. Have to wait till Josephine finishes college; that is, if we don't have a third child in the next couple of years, which'll make it two to three more years till retirement unless I'm somehow sacked—too befuddled to even find the classroom I would've been teaching in for thirty straight years; exposed myself when I thought the faculty club's fireplace was a urinal. Or they give me early retirement with the same tuition remission policy for my kids—I've never been able to figure that one out, how they save—but we'll talk about that some other time. But I know I won't ever be able to get in touch with her no matter how hard I try. If I called the landlord of the house she recently moved out of, what do you think he'd say? Let me tell you: No forwarding address, possibly not even one to send her rent deposit to, or if there was it'd be a General Delivery or P.O. box number in a big city. So I'll stop trying and it's unlikely we'll ever be in the same place in the next fifteen years where we bump into each other. Even if we were and we did bump, so many years would have gone by since we last saw each other that we wouldn't know who the other was except if my wallet dropped out of my pocket when we collided and a credit card or my driver's license or something like that fell out faceup before her eyes or she accidentally kicked it and picked it up to give it back to me and saw my name on it. 'I don't believe it,' she'd say, 'Gould? Or are you another Gould Bookbinder?' And for all I know she'd then say 'Sorry, though, something imperative and I've got to run, but I'll write you, I promise, and you can answer back if you were the right Gould.' And I wouldn't hear from her again, since that accident would serve as her every-fifteen-year contact with me, till I was in my eighties and on my death bed, though of course she wouldn't know who I was, and whatever kind of communication from her, like letters, that people use then would be placed on my chest, but I'd be too blind to read it and too deaf to hear it read." "So you tried," she said, "and it's over with and nothing more to be done about it now. How'd the rest of your trip go?"

He was almost forty, never married, childless, seeing a woman for almost two years, they'd broken up several times during that period for a few days, weeks, once for a month, had lived together for half a year till she said she wanted her own place for the first time in her life—she was with her folks till she got married at eighteen, separated from her husband a few years ago and moved in with an old high school friend—and got a small cheap apartment and he stayed in his, now he was seeing her one or two nights a week and spending most weekends with her and they were also planning a month's bicycle trip in Holland and France this summer and when he came to her place on a Friday night for a long holiday weekend she immediately looked distant or cool, said "Gould, hi, how are you?" and swiveled around after he said "Fine, you?" and went into the living room, hadn't kissed him when she opened the door, he thought that surprising, couldn't remember her not giving him at least a perfunctory kiss hello on the lips or cheek when he made some kind of head or body move toward one when they were alone unless they were still angry at each other over something from the previous day or two or that hadn't been resolved from a week back or only she was still angry at him or thought it hadn't been resolved, and things had been pretty good between them the last few weeks, holding hands or his arm around her most of the time when they were walking outside, her head against his shoulder in the movie theater and a few kisses initiated by one or the other of them snuck in during a particularly dark scene, long deep lively conversations or just chats with lots of play, not a single argument or minor spat, nothing either of them said or did to tick the other off, exchanging I-love-yous and things like that at dinner in a restaurant and at night before they fell asleep after they'd made love, when he phoned her two days ago she said she was looking forward to a three-day week-end with him, he thought they might even resume living to-gether after the summer trip if things continued to go this well though he'd tell her to sublet her tiny apartment just in case it didn't work out, it might even end up in marriage in a year or so, he thought, even if she told him a few months ago she was dead set against getting married again to anyone, so soon after her divorce, for three more years and if he didn't like that arrangement he better stop seeing her now, that she just wanted to continue being out on her own and entirely paying her own way for that long, and he said now when he caught up with her in the living room, she putting a record on the turntable, then turning the machine off and looking at him standing beside her, "Anything wrong?" and she said "Why, I look it, something I'm giving off?" and he said "Yeah, sure, it seems obvious to me and even more so after what you just said; what is it? . . . and your racing in here away from me, turning the record player on, turning it off," and she said "You're right, something is the matter, in a way. I've something important to tell you, didn't want to say it the second you got here and probably couldn't hide that it was bothering me . . . something you might not like but which you have to know," and he said "Come on, what, what? From you I'm up to hearing anything with equanimity unless it's that you're very sick with an incurable illness, God forbid, or you want to give me the can," and she said "The can?" and he said " 'Get rid of me'—it's not the right use of the expression or even an expression to you?" and she said "What I want to say is nothing like that, but you have to wait, I'm not done with the preparations before I go into what I'm going to tell you . . . if we don't want any music let's sit on the couch," and he said "I don't want any—it'd just interfere," and they sat on the couch and he said "Can I get even a smidgen of a kiss to alleviate this a bit?" and she said "Let's be serious," and he said "I'd really love one but okay, serious, right, let's . . . so what is it, you have a lover in the closet and you want me to leave for the next hour?" and she said "What are you talking about? What does it even mean that you're not aware it does?" and he said "Nothing, only kidding, it was dumb of me, really dumb, and he isn't in the closet, he's downstairs waiting for me to leave . . . no, sorry, dumb again, knock knock, what's there?" banging his skull with his knuckles, "I'm just nervous because of your so-serious face and everything else about you that seems so serious—I'm expecting the worst," and she said "Once again, it is serious, but please no more silly other-lover talk—men are the furthest thing from my mind," and he said "Good, I'm glad to hear that . . . okay, then this: after all your . . . your, wanting to hold off . . . no, I shouldn't say it, I've been dumb enough, not that what I was about to say was," and she said "What?" and he said "For two or three more years as you've said—marriage, that now you want to with me after all and are afraid I'll think, after everything you've said about it, that it's the most outrageous request I've heard and I'm going to stomp right out of here, when I actually wouldn't look at it as too bad an idea, and I'm now being serious," and she said "Oh yes, that's it; I wish it were as easy as that but this is much more complicated in what's involved between us and on my part solely in the yes or no," and he said "Don't ask me why but I've no clue as to what you're saying. Let's go back a bit: what preparations did you want to make for me before you got into the heart of what you have to say?" and she said "I'm not sure; hoping you'll be calm and truly consider my viewpoint and so forth—most of it by now I forget. Thinking of what you're going to say beforehand and how you're going to say it shouldn't be done, I think, when it comes to something like this. All I should have done at the door was say 'Hello, I've something very important to tell you, it's not about my health or someone else, come in,' or 'it is about my health in a way and to some people, but not me, it is about someone else,' and then 'come in,' and even given you a kiss because I'd really want to and you expect one when you come and then we'd sit where we are now and I'd say it," and he said "You're pregnant with our dear little baby, and I'm not joking there, I swear," and she said "That's right, though it can't show, it's too early. But I am, I just found out—yesterday; I even went to my gynecologist for a test—and I'm going to have an abortion, but how'd you know?" and he said "What do you mean?" and she said "Why, what do you mean? Wait, you don't think I'm having the kid, do you?—is that what you're saying?" and he said "Let's talk about it first," and she said "Do you or don't you?" and he said "Why not have it?" and she said " 'Why not?' We're not married, for one thing, but almost the least thing, but let me get this straight: you are talking of my having the baby and not having the abortion, right?" and he said "Of course, and why can't you?" and she said "That marriage business, to begin with, and also because, and this a more important

125

reason, I don't want a baby now and even if I did I wouldn't have it on my own," and he said "So situation solved. We'll get married and have it and if you don't want to zip into marriage because of it then you'll stay with me at my place unmarried or we'll get a new bigger place and that way you won't have to have the baby on your own. Because as I've told you—" and she said "You and a bigger place? You can barely afford your low-rent slum some months so how do you expect to pay for a more expensive apartment while also supporting me when I'm out of work having the child and also paying to have the baby and then taking care of it? There's doctors, hospitals, all sorts of expenses—carriage, crib, clothes, diaper service. And neither of us has medical insurance and if we wanted to get on a plan they wouldn't take me because I'm pregnant and if only you got on I couldn't join it because we wouldn't be married. Even if we were married they'd disqualify the pregnancy part for me," and he said "We wouldn't tell them you're pregnant," and she said "They'd count the months, and besides, it'd be wrong," and he said "How many months pregnant are you, one?" and she said "Whatever I am, I wouldn't participate in anything illegal and by the time you joined a plan there'd be lots of months gone," and he said "Listen, I'll work harder at getting a lucrative job— two jobs, what do I care? For I've told you, to get back to before—plenty of times I said this—I'd love marrying you and having kids. One kid now, more later; or just a second, and it could be much later. So one or the other or both: marriage or no marriage but living together somewhere and having the baby—it's all fine with me, great, what I want most," and she said "Really, you're going crazy with this talk, none of it has anything grounded in reality," and he said "It's not that way at all. It's real and I meant it and it's possible and—" and she said "See? Calm. I wanted you to be calm, reasonable, I knew this would happen, and you're not. That's why I should have been persistent in preparing you for this. Because as you told me, then as I told you: my marriage disgusted me so much about marriage that I won't be ready for another one for a few years and I'd probably never be ready for it with you. That I got pregnant with you is the mistake of my life. Excuse me—just letting myself get pregnant was, or almost as big a mistake as my marriage. No, more so, because now there's a life-and-death question involved. Anyway, to answer your thing about marriage, simply because we were all right for each other in bed and a few other things and felt very good about each other now and then doesn't mean we're right for each other forever—for marriage—for however long marriage is," and he said "Wait, don't jump into inextricable positions. Ones you can't—places, I mean, where you bind your— for things are different now, a kid's a kid, a pregnancy's not an ordinary . . . a— But let me get my thoughts collected, on line, I'm altogether confused. I won't say nothing like this has ever happened to me, but not at this age. Let me start again, that didn't come out sounding right, where—" and she said "Look, Gould—" and he said "Stop using my name, *please*," and she said "When did I?" and he said "That way, I mean, for I hate it when you use it like that, saying it as if—for I know what's coming next and I don't like what I see," and she said "What?" and he said "The worst, the goddamn worst," and she said "Now you're getting angry and I—" and he said "I'm not, my face isn't, I don't feel it, in the face or building up in the body, or my anger," and she said "Then worked up, because that's another thing I wanted to avoid," and he said "I'm not that either; I'm listening and maybe at times commenting or just answering," and she said "Then just listen, all right? Now: it's fun a great deal with you, this by way of introduction—" and he said "Oh boy, some woman said that to me years and years ago and the introduction meant the end," and she said "Will you please *just* listen?" and he nodded, and she said "It *is* fun and has been most times—well, not fun now, and it's been more than fun, of course—and I like you a lot, I think you're a very dear person," and he said "Watch it, Jack, here comes the kiss off," and she said "It isn't; now listen. And I once thought I was in love with you, before we—" and he said "Either you were in or you weren't and if you felt you were—thought it—you were," and she stared at him and he said "Vow: silence," put a finger over his lips and she said "love with you before we started living together . . . I'm sure it's what made us live together or encouraged us to," and he said "Excuse me, I know I shouldn't be talking, but I want to remind you that you said last week you loved me. It was at dinner, the Egyptian Tavern, over that mixed Middle Eastern appetizer platter if you want to get exact about it—I can even tell you what we wore, your hair was up not down, the main dishes we had," and she said "And what we drank, because we were a little tipsy at the time, bock beer at home—" and he said "Shared, one twelve-ounce bottle shared," and she said "Wine you brought to the restaurant. I think we drank a whole bottle, before even the main dishes came, and French too, which I always feel is more potent than the others," and he said "A cheap French wine, probably from Algeria, so not so potent; I even told you that at the table, making the Middle Eastern connection. And almost the whole bottle, though maybe half before the main dishes came, but we ate a lot over a long period because the service was slow. And we were feeling fine, just fine, couldn't be better, we held hands, kissed over the table—lips and hands, you even kissed mine," holding his hands out, "and a week or two before that in bed after making love we said it too—I love you, you love me—I don't know who said it first; you did, or I, but the point is we both felt it at the same time—it was obvious to me, obvious," and she said "Where's this conversation getting us, Gould?—oh, I'm sorry, I'm not supposed to use your name," and he said "I'm trying to replicate the circumstances of the events, disputing you amicably in proving that we said we loved each other then so *were* in love, for after you told me it at the table and in bed, I told you it too, or the reverse," and she said "All right, *then*, I felt and said it *then*, and we were *then*, but only after we were half smashed or had made love as you said and I was no doubt feeling good in bed, spirits high and body excited and satisfied and mind relieved of whatever shit this city and practically everyone in it gives. But I shouldn't have said it when I was in that particular state, not even to tit for tat your I-love-you if yours was first, since it's the equivalent of saying it when you're drunk," and he said "And that could've been the night you conceived," and she said "It's possible, if it was a few weeks back; but we're together two to three times a week and usually on those days, unless I'm hemorrhaging or down with a bad cold or flu, we make love. But it's unimportant now how the baby happened. Whether conceived in love or friendship or doggy passion or out of coercion on your part or generosity on mine when you couldn't go to sleep without it or because you were so nice that day I couldn't deny it or that some of your come dribbled off my stomach into me after your interrupted ejaculus, if it was a night when I was too tired to put my diaphragm in or couldn't find it and had asked you to withdraw, not to say that if I did use my diaphragm then it was the first time in about a thousand for that one that it didn't work. But it's still a conception we have to deal with and I'm dealing with it this way by getting rid of it. So whatever was said or done between us, I'm saying to you, ours is not the kind of love that sticks around and goes trippingly on and on and which I want to happen to me to get married again. And even if I were in love with you or anyone, and deeply, which I'm definitely not with you, the first point I made is the truest and most immutable and that's that I'm not at all ready to have a child now or get married. I have to be on my own more. I've said it and I'll say it again," and he said "You don't have to," and she said "No, I want to, because it's not getting through: I have to be on my own more—I must. All this comes too soon after my marriage ended, which I got too dumbly into to begin with, so do you understand now, this 'wrong time' business I've brought up again and again? Do you understand and that nothing will make me change my mind?" and he said "But I want the baby," and she said "Fine, but not this one and never with me. Break off with me completely and find a woman who does want one now and have it with her—I'm saying you should do that. In fact, I'm saying that this is probably the last time we should see each other; that right after this discussion—" and he said "So it is the kiss off," and she said "All right, so that's what it's ending up being, but it's not the word I'd use. It's more a facing of reality, confronting it full out, seeing things as they—" and he said "They're all the same and they add up to kiss off," and she said "Then fine, then that's what it is, this is the kiss off, but I'm also telling you we're not good for each other anymore. Maybe we were for lots of things—" and he said *"Maybe?"* and she said "All right, we were, but never for a long-term life-together-for-forever or what for a while could be that type of tie-in and connection," and he said "You just don't want to say 'love affair' or 'relationship,' " and she said "Certainly not 'love affair': I hate that term worse than 'relationship.' But also that the timing isn't and was never really right for us and we fought that and lost and now you should gather up all your things you have here and go. This will help you find that woman to have that child you want, while I'm—" and he said "But you're pregnant with our baby and I want that one, not just any woman's; yours," and she said "Believe me, Gould, if you want a baby so much that you'd have it with a woman who absolutely doesn't want it or want to live with you and who'd make your life particularly miserable after having it till you'd want to brain her, I mean that, then you'll find another more wonderful woman much better in the ways you want from me." "Speak

English," he said, and she said "Don't get mean and bitchy, I hate that too. A woman who's agreeable and very receptive to marriage and kids and who'll want yours and for them to look like you and you'll be happy with her because she'll love and admire you and give in and administer to all your needs and whims while with me you'll be unhappy and dissatisfied, always, I promise, and often depressed, with a brief respite from the unhappiness and rest of the mess only every now and then. I like and appreciate many things about you but as I said, I don't want our *relationship* to go on any longer than today or, if you want, from the time after you drop me off or pick me up at the abortion clinic, though where or why I came up with that drop-and-pick-me-up idea, I don't know—skip it," and he said "I have to have this baby. If we do then you'll see, you'll want to be with it and me and you'll love having the baby, you'll adore it and thank—" and she said "No, absolutely and unqualifiedly not," and he said "Then I'll have to force you to have it, that's all, if there's nothing else I can do," and she said "Oh yes, and how?" and he said "I'm not sure—by stopping you from not having it," and she said "And how do you think you can do that?" and he said "By locking you in your apartment or mine till you give birth, or that's one way," and she said "Look, no more playing around—just get out of here, will you? I don't like the tone or the import and you're becoming a moron. Collect your stupid stuff some other time when you're less moronic, or I'll send it over, but now I want you gone," and he said "It's no tone; I'm telling you, I could make you stay here, cutting you off from everything, or I'll drive you to some remote place someplace—Maine, Vermont—to keep you locked in. And then when it's too late to abort or miscarry, when your own health would be in jeopardy and there wouldn't be any doctor or butcher who'd do it, I'll let you out and you'll have to have the kid and if you want to give it to me, great, or if you think I'm too wacky to give it to or you won't to spite me and you want to put it up for adoption or hand it over to some relatives like your parents, then I'll say I'm the doctor—the *father*—and claim it and I'll make a good case for myself why I incarcerated you, and I'll get it. I'll get a lawyer to help me. I'll be willing to go broke and into debt getting a lawyer and other help. I'll do everything I can to get it. I'll get my family to back me, I'll get newspapers and stupid human-interest shows behind me. I'll contact anti-this-or-that organizations I've up till now had nothing to do with or never believed in . . . your own friends to say I was never nuts but just because I wanted this baby so much I became temporarily deranged or just overimpassioned," and she said "You know—calm down—but you know, I never knew but you really *are* out of your mind—how come I never saw this in you before?" and he said "I'm not. I'm just showing you, but being serious in this show, how much I want our baby to live and if it has to come to this, how far I'll go to keep it. I don't want to lose this chance. I've always wanted one—I told you that the first time we dated, at that bar on a Hundred Thirteenth, whatever its name—that I'd wanted to be a father for years, and now this might be, for whatever reason, my last sentence, I mean 'chance,' and the bar was the West End," and she said "But look, and I'm saying this calmly and I hope you'll respond in kind, look at what you're saying. You think they'll give in to a madman—even let you see the baby for two minutes—who locks up his pregnant ex-girlfriend to have that child? You mentioned 'sentence'; well, they'll give you a jail one, that'll be your baby. A five-year-old one, or ten, and where you can see it all the time, or if you're lucky just a few jolts with an electric rod to your frontal lobes should do it, if that's where it's done," and he grabbed her wrists and shouted "You're having the baby, no two ways about it!" and she said "I am not, and get your hands off me, goon," and he said "Then you're staying here with me for as long as I want you to," and she said "I said get your fucking hands off me, you goon; get the fuck off and out of here or I really will sick the police on you and press charges and see that you're dumped into jail and stay there," and he said no and held her wrists tighter and stared at her face, thinking maybe she'd agree to the baby if he just stared at her but knew that was stupid and she said "What the hell are you looking at? You think I'm a child and you can get your way that way? You look ridiculous, you look ugly, with your pointed eyes," and turned away and said "And now you're hurting me; get off, you're making it even worse for yourself, goon, much worse," and he said "I'm sorry, but say you'll have it, please," and she said "Yes, I will have it but I'm lying," and he said "Then I don't care how much I hurt you," and squeezed harder and she screamed and he put his hand over her mouth, twisted her around till he was behind her, kept his hand over her mouth and thought What have I got myself into? What am I going to do now? But she has to see she has to have it. You just can't kill something you say you'll one day eventually want when there's a chance you might never have another chance to have that something, and he said "Listen to me, you can't kill something you say you'll eventually want one—" when she bit his hand and ran for the door and he caught her, stuck his wrist in her mouth from behind and twisted her around in back till she muttered through his wrist "Sop, you're baking it . . . shoking," and started gagging and he let her arm go and took his wrist out but kept his hand loosely over her mouth and said "Don't bite; I don't want to hurt you; last thing I want to do; but I will, I might have to, you've got to have that baby," and she started crying and he said "What utter baloney, every trick in the book," continued crying, and he said "I won't go for that crap. Having the kid's more important than falling for your horseshit. The kid's what you should be crying for and particularly if you kill it, don't you see?" and waited but she didn't make any head motion or say anything but seemed to have stopped crying and he grabbed her hand, thought What should I do now? I should leave, give it up and get the hell away for all time from here, but maybe I can convince her, it's worth it trying, and said "Please, I'm not going to really lose my head, but change your mind?" and she said "You've lost it; you're going to pay you don't know how much for this, you goddamn goon," and he pulled her to the kitchen, she tugged back and he grabbed her arms and pulled her harder, took the dish towel off the refrigerator door handle and tied it around her mouth but there was only enough cloth left in back to make the first half of the knot, knew she could easily rip it off, if it didn't fall off first, and scream, so it was more a symbolic shutting-her-up and that he might do worse if she fought him, though he just told her he wouldn't, walked her to the bedroom pushing her arms from behind, she was crying again and he tried not to look and believed the tears but under his breath intentionally loud enough for her to hear, he said "Fake tears, don't tell me they're real, but go on, blubber all you want, see how it feels," though didn't know what he meant by the last remark: him, her, the baby? and when he got to the bed he shoved her cheekdown into it, knee up against her back but in a way where it wouldn't hurt and said "So this is what I'm planning. You listening?" and she shook her head and he said "You're having it, you're staying here, not leaving till I can sneak you to a place somewhere far away where you'll also stay. I'll disconnect the phone in the meantime. Or I'll answer it and say you're sick but you'll be okay, laryngitis, so you can't talk, or the flu, gastrointestinal, your stomach, and I'm feeding you soup, or sweet tea, taking care of you better than you've ever been, but no visitors, you're that bad off plus in no mood to see anyone. Then in a few days I'll say you miraculously recovered when you got a call from Europe for a job interview with a production company. I'll even tell your boss this if he calls, that the prospect suddenly appeared and it was too good to pass up, with the possibility to triple your current pay and complete medical coverage, so up his giggy for that's what you think of him and his part-time work and cheap company with hourly wages and no benefits or overtime pay, and who am I? Well, I'll say who I am: your man. I'll tell him, except for the last, all the things you've wanted to but have played too safe, though I can see why: money for the time being. And later that you adopted a cat weeks before and are still in Europe and I'm taking care of it, that's why I'm still here, not that anyone who knows us would think I need an excuse. Or I've sublet my own place for a few months and moved in here while you're away, that the renter offered me more money than I could refuse because of my apartment's location, not the building so much, and I was short of cash as I usually am, or something, but I'll work it out, what I'll say. Then I'll get a good friend who'll help me out—Benny would; he'd like the idea, not letting the woman get away with it and that the guy's got rights in this too. Not that so much, since he doesn't understand why any man would want a child, and one to raise on your own, if it came to that, even more incomprehensible, 'for how do you get done the things you want to get done,' he'd say, 'like your womanizing and getting drunk and sleeping till noon and going to the track anytime you want?' " He hoped for a laugh—that might start something good—but she kept her eyes shut: thinking, planning a way out or just saying, with her lids tight and face pointing away from him: This is the way I'm locking you out. "But Benny would help, get his brother's car and drive us up to this place the two of them rented for the year in upstate New York, near Albany, a shack, or 'electrified cabin,' as the owner called it, where they fished and swam from and hoped to do some cross-country skiing, but I'll convince him this is more important. It'll be nippy at first, but we'll get lots of blankets—you'll have your own bed or cot, don't worry, and I won't touch you. And kerosene heaters or the electric ones, since the kerosene ones really aren't safe, if it already doesn't have some kind of interior heating, and line the windows and tape plastic sheets over them inside and out and do everything possible to stay warm, and then I'll let you go once you're ready to deliver. Late April, early May—when do you figure?" and took the gag off. No answer or look, eyes never opened, but the way they were clamped tight he knew she wasn't sleeping. And of course no one was going to think anything funny, as she didn't to his Benny routine before, with a gag on. "Anyway, once the time comes, or I'm saying the month or two before—you be the judge—I'll take you to the hospital for a checkup and whatever preparations you need to have the baby, but I'm not leaving you till then. Benny can drive up with food and things once a week. He'd do that for me and I know he can get his brother to go along with it or at least to let him have the car and me the cabin. They're very close, one's friend is the other's automatically, and Benny's been a true pal, though I was always disappointed in him never seeing the good—the worth, what you are—in you that I did. It's strange, two people you like so much but they can't get together. He thought you too wiseass, he said, sarcastic, a ballbreaker—my balls, and I'm not saying this to make you feel . . . to disparage you in any way. But you knew what he had to say already and never cared anyway. You thought him a jerk and could never see why I hung out with him. But he was loyal, never two-faced—no betrayals—or reproachful, and we had fun. Though he did say 'Okay, go for it if you dig her'—his words, 'go for, dig,' he was once a jazz drummer so that's how he still speaks—when I first met you and introduced you two; and I do, love you, I mean, and he

also thought you pretty while I found you beautiful. And it—"
and she said with her face still down in the bed "Oh stop with
the love, your talk and what you're going to do with me in
Albany and this Benny business—he thought me pretty, you
found me beautiful; oh, big mushy pigwash, for it's all such
manure," and he said "It isn't, I'm telling you, and after it's over
that'll be the end of it," and she looked at him and said "End of
what? What are you talking about? Do you know? Do I know?
Endless minutes of it and it's all empty. You're talking like a
jerk, worse than Benny, as if you've lost your intelligence and
common sense, which you once had some of but he never did.
Besides—but forget it—but your decency, anything good in you
that was there before but which now resembles take-what-
you-can-get-grab-beg-steal-embezzle-from-life stick-it-up-their-
pisshole-asses giggy-giggy Benny. Just let me up—get your
stupid leg off me, you goon—and out of here. No, you get out,
this is my apartment, so I'm ordering you to and you have to
comply," and started squirming under him, tried sliding off the
bed and he said "Please, relax, I'm not letting you up right now
unless you calm yourself, and certainly not out, and I don't want
you getting hurt falling to the floor. I swear it won't be so
bad—having the kid and the months up to it with me. It might
get a bit boring sometimes but it could also turn out to be
interesting and even enriching. Anyway, different. All the books
you want to read, good air, time to think, a healthy intellectual
period and physical one too and I'll treat you beautifully
throughout what you'll call an ordeal. Read to you, cook for—"
and she said "Will you please!"—"do everything for you, that's

the absolute minimum I can do, and we'll listen to music if you want, whatever kind, the radio, good TV, but this is what I'm going to do. I'm not fluffing off this kid to the nearest scalpel or suction pump or spoon, so face up and confront it yourself as you told me to do with something else. What was that?" and she said "What do I care? You're sending me to sleep with your talk," and shut her eyes, face rested on the bed. "Maybe if I say and do nothing you'll give up trying to communicate with me and just leave peacefully and quietly but making sure the front door's locked when you go." He got off the bed, sat across from it, thought "What now, the next step?" said "Scream once and I'm putting the towel back around," but this time, the way her lids came together so loosely and forehead was uncreased, he thought she might be asleep. Later—half an hour, what he thought most about was how pretty she looked, soft features, beautiful hair and skin, wouldn't it be something now if she had gone along with it, he'd be flipping, maybe calling people, probably lying on the bed with his arms around her, and her head, as she used to like to nap, snug in his neck, maybe if he persisted gently and came up with some other strategy she'd come around but he didn't know what—she stirred, rubbed her eyes, he said "Have a good nap?" and she snapped her head to him as if just realizing he was there, sat up on the bed, he said "What're you doing?" and she looked contemptuously at him and stood up and he said "Where're you going?" she said "To pee, do you mind?" and he walked behind her to the bathroom. "Excuse me," he said, when she stood in front of the toilet, waiting for him to leave, "but I'll have to stay by the door while you go. I don't see what else I can do, under the circumstances," and she said "So ridiculous, so nuts, and the language: 'under the circumstances' indeed. Don't you feel stupid? Well, screw you, you stupid prick, that's what I have to tell you. You like to hear it? You don't know it yet? It takes that many times to sink in? You're even shallower than I thought. Then 'screw you, you stupid prick' again. I don't know how long you expect me to amuse you but don't count on it much longer," and sat down and peed and he looked away. After she wiped herself and pulled up her underpants she said "You're trying your darndest to humiliate me, your way of settling scores, and over something in the past—I don't believe this baby bull at all—but it's not working. This is what I've learned today about you: you've the mentality and emotion of the crude jailer, and you should have become a real one. Perhaps then you could have—" and he said "I don't, not at all. I—" and she said "That's my very last word to you on anything till you leave," and went back to the bedroom and he said "Oh, you'll—and I say this with no pride or self-gratutory . . . *congratulatory* . . . self-congratulatory feelings or self-congratulation—but you'll say more in coming months. You'll have to, for I'll just about be the only person you'll see," and she said "I'm breaking my silence oath, so don't tell me I did. If you don't let me go—meaning if you don't leave in the next five minutes—then I'll not only shout and scream but bite and fight and break windows and lamps and your head if I have to. And after I've drawn attention from the outside or the other tenants and the cops smash the door in or get you or the super to open it, I'll make sure you're put in prison for as long as possible—not only for keeping me here, and 'kidnapping' they'll call it—but I'll say you did ten times worse than that: beat me, threatened my life, anything where I don't have to furnish visible proof; the beating I can do with little pinch marks to myself. I'll lie my heart out, that's how I'll settle my score with you," and he said "I'm sorry you feel that way, but it doesn't scare me off," and she said "Who cares about scare? It's what I'll do to end this satire of male brainlessness, brawn and day-dreamy revenge," and he got a scarf from the dresser and stuck it in her mouth as a gag and knotted it in back, tied up her arms and legs with other scarves and tights, knew absolutely he shouldn't, that he should untie her and go but he still hoped, at the same time knowing he'd made the whole thing hopeless, that he'd think of something to change her mind about the baby or she'd change it on her own, quickly made two sandwiches and a salad and dressing, got a glass of water—no, water, she'll tie it to being a captive and say something like "How come also not just crust or dry bread?"—dumped the water and filled the glass with apple juice and ungagged and untied her and told her to come to the table to eat. She stayed on the bed, said "See the stain?" touching a dark spot on the bed cover; "that's urine—I had to go again—and I don't care. I don't want to go to the bathroom again while you're here and pull down my pants," and he said "Then do it that way, but you'll get a bladder infection and rash, and I'll eat in here," and brought in the food though he didn't want to eat, wasn't hungry, was only doing it for effect and she no doubt knew it—so why did he persist in doing it if he knew she knew it? because maybe she didn't—tossed the salad and put the sandwich plates and salad bowl and utensils on the bed and the glass on the night table—no, he was doing it because he didn't know what else to do, or was stalling, doing futile things to give her time to change her mind—and sat beside her and ate. "Surely you got to be hungry," putting salad on her plate and sliding it to her and she pushed it back. Phone rang and he said "God, the phone, you could've called when I was bringing in the food—let's let it ring," and she said "Anything you want," and looked away from it and then lunged for it on the fourth ring; he blocked her hand, knocking over the juice as he did, picked the phone up and held it till the ringing stopped. "Sorry for the mess," wiping it with his handkerchief and she closed her eyes and peed and he said "How do you expect to sleep in that smelly stuff?" and moved to the chair with his food. "Anyway, I know you're doing it intentionally, and it's not going to get me to release you," and she said "Intentionally, sure, like I now don't have to make number two. I was holding it in long as I could but I can't anymore. Will you let me do it in private or do I have to do it in my pants? Even when we were together I wouldn't let you see me and you also didn't want me to see or hear you," and he said "What do you mean 'not hear me'?" and she said "By turning the faucet on," and he said "That was a habit I got from my mother and I thought it polite, like lighting matches over the toilet after," and she said "I don't care; what about me now?" and he said "There's a little window in the john, so I wish I could but I can't. What I will do is not look," and he let her go inside the bathroom, turned around but kept his foot in the door in case she ran up to it and slammed it on him and tried to lock him out, and she turned the tub faucet on hard and flushed the toilet several times. "I'm a little tired from all this," he said, when she wanted to get past him; "we should probably clean up—*I* should—and go to sleep. You want to brush your teeth first?" and she said "I could care less what my mouth smells like with you. Worse the better I'd think," and he said "I was thinking of your teeth, but do what you want," and took the phone out of the socket, brought it with him when he took the dishes back to the kitchen, peed into the sink because he didn't want to make another stop in the bathroom, put the phone back in and said "I'm only doing that so everybody will think things here are normal," changed the sheets, said "If you don't mind, though even if you do, and again I'm not going to try anything with you, we'll sleep together, but this time I'll take the side of the bed by the phone," she changed behind the closet door into another pair of pants, he always slept nude with her but kept his boxer shorts on and they got into bed. "Maybe in the morning you'll wake up," she said, "—know what I mean?" and he said "And maybe you, I'd like that," and shut off the light. She had her back to him and after a few minutes he said "You want to talk about it some more?" and she said "No thanks," and he thought The "thanks," and it wasn't said harshly, was she softening or just saying it that way so she wouldn't hear anything harsh back from him or just anything back and she just wanted to go to sleep? And after about fifteen minutes, when because of her faint steady breathing he thought she was sleeping, he moved closer and tried holding her but she threw his arm off.

"Are you kidding? Never have I detested the guts of anyone more. You're scum to me, the worst perfect scum there is. I'll never be able to be anything but thoroughly repulsed by you, is that not clear?" and he said "I'm sure you'll get over it," and she said nothing and he said "Good night," and she said "Shut up." She slept awhile, or at least she didn't move around, he thought, and she made occasional grunts and sputters and snoring noises. When she got out of bed in the dark he said "No phone calls or running out," and she said "I have to pee—you don't see the direction I'm heading? Anyway, haven't you given this thing up?" and he said "No I haven't," and followed her and turned around and waited at the door. Phone rang in the morning and she reached over him for the receiver but he grabbed it and said hello and the woman who called said "Maria?" and he said "No, a friend, Gould; she had some very early appointment today and I'm still a little tired; I'll tell her you called, good-bye," and she said "Who was it?" and he said "A woman. I shouldn't have answered, maybe—so early, and tired, I could've blown the whole thing with my words—though giving my name out like that makes it less suspicious and now you know I'm serious," and she said "Oh yes?" and he said "About the whole matter. We're almost in day one of your double confinement—" and she said "Oh, wordplay, no less," "—and I'm still hoping you'll come around. Please, Maria?" and she said "I can't believe you're still harping on this. It's wrong, insane, inane and everything else, don't you know?" and he said "That line seemed rehearsed; you've been thinking of using it the last hour?" and she said "I'm not able to think of it spontaneously? What arrogance," and he said "You're right. I'm sorry, *that* was inane. All I should have said about it was 'So you've said, but here we are,' " and she said "It can't last . . . what, till this afternoon before you feel totally debased and revolted by yourself?" and he said "I'll try to hold off on that longer. We only have seven months, a feather in time or something, or maybe only six—I'll have to do some research on that; but at least here till tomorrow night or Monday, when I'll call Benny." "Suppose I said I would have the baby, why would you ever believe it now?" and he said "I wouldn't. This forced confinement is for the next six months or so no matter what you tell me," and she said "Boy, are you ever going to be bored with me. I won't even say what I'll be with you. You'll be lucky if I don't stab you in the chest in the next two days, and not out of anger so much as your presence driving me crazy," and he said "I'll look after myself, but one thing for sure is I'll never hurt you. I'll disarm you, overpower you gently . . . hold it, I have to pee," and he took out the phone, shut the bedroom door, kept the bathroom door open and went to the toilet, wiped, wanted to wash his hands and also brush his teeth but thought "Better get back, she could yell out the window," and went with the phone to the bedroom, put the phone back in and said "So where was I? About your stabbing me. I'd overpower you gently, if it came to that, but I promise—" and she said "What a good noble man," and looked away. "We have enough food for the next two days?" he said, and she shut her eyes, her expression: "Will this creep never shut up and leave?" He took her hand and went into the kitchen with her, looked inside the refrigerator and cabinets and said "There's plenty of food but just one beer and no wine. You'd like some tonight, wouldn't you, if just to blot me out?" and she kept her eyes shut with the same expression. "That didn't get to you? I didn't say what you felt? I'm not making this worse? No, I should sacrifice everything, right, everything, for you once said a self-sacrificing person is the best kind of person there is, or 'to be,' or whatever you said, for when everyone else is trying to get what they want, the self-sacrificer . . . well, he . . . oh, the hell with that sentence. But I should sacrifice the whole thing of it—the kid, what I want most in life, and after that the most, you, because you think it's the right thing for me to do, but you shouldn't give up anything, right? You're not looking at me. I'm not here for you now. And I sound angry-mad to you, don't I, but don't worry, I'm not. Because I'm going to get my way after all, except it'll be hard. And I'd have some wine and scotch sent over but I have no credit card or check account and I don't want to blow all the cash on me for that and I certainly won't use yours. I'll live," and he made coffee, toasted two English muffins and heated a little milk and set a plate of buttered muffins and a mug of coffee on the counter for her, with warm milk and half a teaspoon of unstirred sugar in it as she liked it in the morning, but she didn't touch them. "You going on a starvation diet? Very unlike you. One thing I loved about you, along with many other things of course, was that you always loved food and appreciated wine, when you were well," and she said "It's a way of aborting too, you know—fetus needs food," and he said "Then I think I'd force it down you gently if I saw it was becoming a problem for it," and she said "Okay, though don't take it as a surrender to your threat—half a muffin I'll eat, and food for energy to zip out of here when I see my break," and stood by the sink and ate the muffin while looking out the window. After she finished he said "Want the other half, or mine, which isn't buttered?" and she shook her head without looking away from the window. She looks so beautiful, he thought, so dreamy, in thought but nothing about what he's saying; maybe at what she's seeing, the sky almost, a bird gliding around up there. "All right, you win," he said, "no reason why now and not before or later, but there it is, maybe it was hearing myself with that forcing-the-food-down-you that did it, but I've gone on long enough with this, right? Right," because she was only looking out the window. "It is idiotic, debased, all the other things you said. It'll never—this baby—materialize, or it'd just be too hard for me to get it to, and I don't want to make you feel even worse than you've been. Seeing you at the window . . . I won't ask you to say what you were thinking then—before, right after I asked do you want my English muffin?—because you won't tell me and it's none of my business . . . but that too; so that does it. I do—speech, speech—want the baby more than anything and secondly for you to want it and thirdly, or really tied firstly, for you to want it with me, but if you got sick while I was keeping you here or in some cabin that does exist but never could have been, what would I do? It could happen, and the baby could have been lost that way, something I also hadn't thought of before, so, and with my usual confusion and tied-up tongue . . . just too many things working against it, that's all. So you're free to go—I hate put-

ting it that way. It does suddenly make me feel more like a jailer than someone trying to protect or save his kid, and you don't have to go, for I'm going," and collected his things in two shopping bags—"I'm taking two of your big paper shopping bags, the kind with handles, do you mind?" and she just continued looking out the window—books, extra pair of running shoes, clothes, shaving gear, his exercise towel—and went into the living room. She was in a chair reading today's *Times*, which had been delivered to the front door—he'd forgot about that— and said "You won't—last shot?—change your mind?" She didn't look up. "Only joking; not joking, but of course you won't. So, tell the cops I'll be home in about half an hour, that's how long it should take me if I make good subway connections, and for them not to come with their weapons drawn, as I'm prepared to go peacefully and . . . anyway, long life and much luck," and put the keys to her apartment on the little table by the door and left. She didn't call the police or she did and they didn't come and he never saw nor heard from her again. A few years later he was walking up the aisle of a city bus and saw a friend of hers in a seat and said "Oh, hi," and she said "My goodness, Gould, hello," and he stood beside her and said "You are . . . your name? Excuse me, it's been some time," and she said "Sharon LaVerge," and he said "Right, I remember you and Maria and once we all went to a movie—*Passions of Anna,* I think; one of the more intense Bergmans around at the time . . . how's she doing?" and she said "Anna?" and he said "You know, or maybe you've lost contact," and she said "She's fine, married, to an extremely nice fellow, living in Worcester, Mass., but she gets in every now and then. They have a house, with a patio with a tree growing right through it, and are trying to have a child . . . wait a second, I shouldn't be telling you this; I probably shouldn't even be talking to you," and he said "Why?" and she said "You're saying you don't know?" and he said "Some incident she might have told you?" and she said "What else, that isn't enough?" and he said "You realize—I'm sure she does—I was mostly kidding at the time. It only went on for less than a day—overnight, granted, perhaps making it seem worse in the retelling of it than it was, and right after sunrise I was out and never saw her again," and she said "She didn't think it funny. She called it horrible and that she feared for her life during part of it and for more than a week after she was still fearful you'd come back and that she thought of calling the police," and a man and woman in front of her turned around and looked at them and then quickly turned forward again, and he said lower "And I told her 'Go on, call them.' I mean, admittedly I was upset if not in a certain way out of control for a while, but never so out of it where I was going to flip over the edge, because of what I didn't want to lose—*you know*. But I knew she wouldn't call them because she knew I knew . . . I mean I knew she knew she had nothing on me. It was a spat, a very troubling argument, a major point I was trying to make about what there was at stake, and I was serious about the objective of it—what I wanted but not what I'd do to get it—because she did tell you the reason I acted up like that, right?" and she said "Yes, naturally, would I be sitting here nodding all this time if she hadn't?" and he said "Well, I wanted it so badly, so of course I wouldn't have hurt her for anything; to do that would be to hurt what I wanted more than anything in the world then, and I kept telling her that and she knew it. She also had to know that in telling you different she was only trying to turn it into a larger event in her life than it was. Or maybe, in addition to everything else she was also distraught she was going to have it . . . an operation," and motioned with his head to the couple in front of her, "so that did it, or could have, for what woman, even if having the, you know, was the last thing she wanted at the time—a baby—wouldn't also have tremendous regrets over the—" and slit his finger through the air, "am I right?" and she pointed to where he'd slit and said "That finger across; I didn't get it," and he said "The end, the procedure, the termination," and she said "Ah, I see. But no matter what, you'd never convince Maria you weren't serious then in your threats. But that was between you two and is long in the past and I'm sorry I brought it up in the short time we have to talk—my stop's coming soon," and he said "Oh, too bad. So how have things been with you?" and she said "Fine, fine, but you know what life's like: the good often looks better than it is and the bad often looks worse, but on the whole everything evens out and is nice. Married too . . . happy; a good unharried life, exactly the way I like it. We've decided not to have children— made that decision; people always ask so I'm telling you this right out. It's simply not anything we want," and he said "How would you know so long beforehand?" and she said "We wouldn't be good parents; we're both too involved in what we do and see this as a lifetime practice, and we thought this individually long before we met. But don't start on me too," and he said "Sure, I wasn't saying, and I'm glad everything seems to be going so well for you. What kind of work you do?" and she said "Same as then, computers, which I like, my husband too . . . and you, how are you getting along?" and he said "Work, health, spirits, all fine, and I've been seeing a woman the last year and a half and we'll probably get married end of the year or early next—we don't foresee anything that'll stop us—and right after that have children . . . I've got to before people think I'm their grandpa," and she said "Why worry about that?" and he said "I really don't. And, well you wouldn't know but I don't live here, I live in Baltimore and only come up weekends to see her, till she eventually moves down with me," and she said "So she's still working here; that makes sense," and pushed the stop tape and he said "Yours, huh?—I forgot where you lived, or you probably moved. Anyway, if you see Maria—I hope she won't mind this—but please give her my regards and congratulations on her marriage and, between you and me, I hope she has a child if she wants one that much," and she said "They both do but they've taken all the tests and it seems each of them has something wrong for it, so it doesn't look good," and he said "I hope the a.b. had nothing—" and she said "No, that's been ruled out, it must be something since then, though I did say it was both of them," and she got off and when he got to his woman friend's apartment he told her about whom he met on the bus and where he knew her from and for the first time about how he tried to force Maria to have the baby.

The last was when his wife was still walking with a cane, or a cane mostly but often with a walker and sometimes she needed a wheelchair to get around. They had two children and nearly three years after the second was born—that was the spacing they used between the first two and she became pregnant in a week—he said "What would you say to our trying to start having a third and what I promise will be our last child?" and she said she knows how much he wants another one—that he always wanted three—but she doesn't see how she could have one in her condition, which he knows that unless the present drug works or some other new drug suddenly turns up, is only going to get worse. "I could get pregnant—I don't believe that's stopped in me; having my periods regularly certainly hasn't. And if I was very careful—staying in bed through a lot of the pregnancy and taking extra good care of myself—not falling, staying off stairs—I could probably deliver it without a hitch. But what would I do with the child once it was born? I'd nurse it, if the doctors said I could after all the toxic medicines I've taken, but after that . . . though they'd take me off those medicines if I became pregnant. Would probably have taken me off them months before we started to try to have the baby, to avoid complications in the pregnancy, and because of that, who knows?—my condition could deteriorate even faster than it's been doing. But after that it'd be too difficult taking care of the baby the way I'd want to and you already have your hands full with the girls and your job and the house," and he said "I wouldn't mind doing more. I'd love to—really, my kids are everything to me. You're everything too and I'd devote all my free time to the three of them and you. I'd make more free time for myself to do it—I know how to: just cut out just about everything else but them and you, which wouldn't be a big loss, though also making sure the toilets and kitchen floor and such are cleaned every so often. And I bet getting pregnant and then lactating, or they go together—I forget, what do you do, start with the milk at conception or three or so months into the pregnancy or even just when you give birth or right after? But the doctors have said that could happen with your illness, that pregnancy often arrests and even corrects some of it, and we've seen what being pregnant does to women already healthy—you with Fanny and even a little bit with Josephine," and she said "I don't remember that," and he said "It's true, take my word, it made you healthier and more energetic and I swear, even more erotic, and everyone kept saying you looked much better, more beautiful and so on," and she said "The better-looks part happens with most pregnant women, maybe to compensate for the swollen body but which I'm sure comes from the glow of knowing you're carrying and has little to do with physical health other than you're supposed to be less disposed to colds," and he said "The point is that it'd work and you'd be healthier and I'd see to it that it did," and she said "It also wouldn't be fair to the girls. I'm barely half a mother to them now and with an infant around I'd be a quarter of a half the first year or longer," and he said "So? Say a year, say two, but they can make that sacrifice also to have another sister or a brother," and she said "You forget that to most children an infant sibling is an intruder, the worst sort of nuisance-scourge—stealing your parents and making you double up in your room with your sister or even worse

154

in your sister's room because for a while this ugly stinky baby's got to have her own space and all the other folks mewling and drooling over it," and he said "Not our kids; they'd love it, I know them, and they'd be helpful, learning how to change the diapers and burp it and so on—you'll see," and she said "Besides, much as I'd love to give you another child, two's more than enough for us at our age and perhaps the planet's and when you consider college and who knows what else for them—shoes, piano lessons, a word processor each—" and he said "Nah, never them with computers," and she said "Hey, turn around and face the future—anyway, practically all we can afford." Some days when they wanted to make love she said "I'll put my diaphragm in," and a couple of times he said something like "If you think you're so close to having your period where you're not even sure you need protection, don't bother: you're usually more precautionary than you have to be," and once when he walked into their bathroom and found her drying herself after a shower he said "So, what do you say? No diaphragm or anything—just stand where you're standing and grab the grab bars and I'll come into you from behind. I'm that ready to go and the kids will be home soon with their school bus tooting so we have to do it fast," and she said "I still have it in from last night. You really want to get me pregnant, but I've told you: I can't chance it; an abortion could cripple me faster than the normal speed of the disease." About a year later putting in the diaphragm became so difficult for her that she instructed him how to do it and then she'd check to see if it was in right. "You don't trust me, eh?" he said once and she said "Matter of fact, I don't. Not only because you haven't had years of practice at it and that you admit to being clumsy with your hands, but when we start doing this you're always too much in a hurry and you want another child so much that you might leave it somewhat askew so a little of you leaks in." Sometimes he couldn't get the diaphragm in right no matter how many times he tried and he'd pull his hand away and she'd say "You got it?" and he'd say "It feels okay," and she'd feel it and say it wasn't and that he should just give up and get inside her and then finish his sex on her stomach or someplace, "but please pull out in plenty of time and keep your cock away from my cunt when you come," and he said "Ah, now that's a familiar line from my youth or sometime after, or maybe I only heard it once when I probably rejected using a scumbag, as we called it then, and the only other way was on the girl's stomach or where she'd jerk me off till I did it in the air," and she said "With my hands stiff and uncoordinated the way they are I doubt I could even do that to you now," and he said "I wouldn't choose it over the stomach anyhow, but then, you know, when I could do it two to three times a night, who cared if I wasted one?" One night he didn't pull out in plenty of time but let a little of it dribble inside her—he could control it like that—and after when he thought enough had dribbled in for her to conceive but not so much where she'd feel or later notice the semen, he pulled out and made all the noises of orgasm on top of her, though he didn't feel anything when he came, and she got pregnant, he was sure she did by the swell of her belly a month or so later, so it was because of that one time when he dribbled or maybe some other

time around then when he'd unintentionally inserted the diaphragm in wrong and when she checked it had felt all right to
her, though with her hands shaking and there being less and less
feeling in them, did she even know for sure what she felt with
them anymore? But the belly. One night, about a month after
he'd dribbled into her—on that particular night a month ago
he'd wanted to get her pregnant; other times when they made
love the thought didn't occur to him or if it did it was that he
didn't want her getting pregnant because of the harm she said it
could do her or because what the medicine she was taking
would do to the fetus and once they found out then what they'd
have to do to the fetus or that they already had two kids, more
than enough, and if they had another even nine months from
now he'd be close to his mid-fifties when it was born and when
it was ten he'd be in his mid-sixties and when it was thirty and
getting married, let's say, or having its first child he'd be an old
man, possibly doddering or senile and very sick . . . but he
lost it. Go back. Her belly. He was watching her, she was
undressing, he liked to watch her undress, especially when she
had her back to him—well, he liked to watch her stepping out
of or kicking off her underpants from the front too, or trying to
kick them off, getting them caught on her toes and then having
to sit down to take them off—but best when she had her back
to him, sitting on the bed or standing up, but was a little turned
so when she took off her shirt or unhooked her bra and pulled
it from around her arms a little of her breast showed. . . .
Anyway, it was about a month after he dribbled into her, and
while she was undressing he noticed her belly—she was stand-

ing sideways—had a quarter-moon-like swelling to it like the first two times she was pregnant a month or so. She showed early, though she always denied she did, and with one of their kids—Josephine—he said "But look at your belly, it's a bit bigger and has that particular pregnant swell, I should begin calling it if it turns out I'm right again, like the last time with Fanny and when I pointed it out then you said, though we'd been trying to conceive and probably did the first time we tried, 'It's not that, it must be something else. Maybe I need to lose a few pounds or, God help us'—I remember that expression especially, for any use of the word God like that is unusual for you—'it's just gas. If it is,' you said, 'we'll find out soon enough,' and then you laughed, hand over your mouth, that kind of laugh, something you also rarely do, since you didn't mean it as a joke. You meant . . ." But off the point again. This night when she was undressing and he was watching, preparing to make love to her—that's what was on his mind and he thought hers too by the way she smiled at him but not saying anything when she was unbuttoning her shirt and saw him watching and also the slow way she was undressing and because she knew he usually got aroused when he watched her undress unless they'd made love in the last few hours—he saw a little swelling . . . but he said that. Recognized it from the previous two times, but that too. But didn't mention it, feeling that if she was pregnant and didn't know . . . but he's gone over that too: later she found out the better, etcetera. Also, the longer she was pregnant maybe more attached she'd get to the baby, so less chance she'd want to abort. And this was one of those times he thought she'd stay the same or get healthier rather than sicker and where the medicines she was taking wouldn't affect the baby much and that if they had to abort because of what they later found out in the various tests she'd take, then at least they'd tried to have another baby, though he didn't know why he constantly switched his opinion on all this: maybe because he had no basis for either, where one way of thinking about it was as good as the other, meaning the chance of something good or bad happening to her or the baby was about as good as nothing happening. A few nights later she said her period's late this month, probably due to the new drug she's taking and he said "But you started it a couple of months ago," and she said "It's possible it's only now beginning to have an effect on my period as it's already had on other things: hair falling out, little more tiredness during the day, discoloring of my stools, the occasional feeling I need to vomit," and he let it go at that. Her stomach did seem a little rounder than it had a few nights before but he was probably only imagining it. He still hoped she was pregnant but now kind of doubted she was and that it was the new medicine changing things for her as she said. Several mornings later she pointed to her stomach when she was getting up and he was doing exercises in their room and said "I'm not getting fat, so don't worry, as I know how anxious you can get about that. Fat women—oh my dear; even unpleasantly plump ones—quite the turnoff, right? While I'd think that in some ways, all that meat, more to put your arms around and maybe another layer to get into and so much juicier to the squeeze, might turn a fellow on. But it's the constipation now, which I was also told to expect from this new drug," and he said "Have you started your period?" and then thought Damn, shouldn't have mentioned it, for all the obvious reasons, but she said "No, though I thought I felt it coming on two days ago. It's maybe a day or two away, but not even spots yet. Look, when you're at the drugstore next time or Giant— their generic brand is as good, I hear . . . in fact, soon as you can, if you don't mind, could you buy me something to relieve it?" and she said it came in a tall container and gave the name. "But generic or otherwise, the powder with no sugar in it," and he asked how to spell psyllium and when she spelled it he said "I better get this one on a piece of paper." He looked at her exposed belly whenever he could the next week and felt it when they were making love or lying in the dark and going to sleep and it seemed to be getting a little larger and harder, and because the Tampax box wasn't opened on the floor by the toilet bowl and she wasn't spreading a towel under her when they made love it meant she hadn't started her period. "I bet she knows," he thought, "and maybe even wants the baby but hasn't decided on that yet, so is holding off telling me." Then she was going to the doctor's to learn how to catheterize herself, something she had to begin doing to empty her bladder a couple of times a day to prevent the accidents she's been having. He drove her there, went downstairs for coffee and a sandwich after he left her in the examining room, and when he came back she was sitting in the waiting room. "Something terrible's happened," and he said "What, the catheterizing?" and she said "We didn't even get to finish it, so I'll have to come back for that another day. But the nurse teaching me was poking and sticking this self-catheter tube there when suddenly blood came—" and he said "Blood, Jesus, you're all right now though, aren't you? I mean, what do we have to do, the hospital?" and she said "No, we can go home, I'm fine, it's over. I thought it was my period starting, which I was thankful for, of course, and went to the bathroom—" and he said "It was a kid—you lost a baby," and she said "I'm sure that was it. A very tiny fetus, infinitely tiny, almost nothing, a nothing blob, it was so tiny . . . I never had anything come out of me like that where I saw it . . . but how'd you know?" and he said "What about the bleeding? How bad was it? You call the nurse?" and she said "It went on a little while, but they helped me, even gave me a new pair of under-pants—paper, but it feels funny, I don't like it, I want to get home and into a real pair—and a bag for the old ones," and she held it up, ". . . but how'd you know it was that? It could have been anything," and he said "I just assumed by your expression when I came in; so worried, pained, almost afraid to tell me— that more than anything gave it away. Not 'afraid' so much, but you know. But you sure that was it, what came out?" and she said "I didn't know it right at the time. I was so dumb. I'd had an abortion before—long ago, but the third or fourth month, and I was put out, so I never saw it and never wanted to. Here I thought it was a little menstrual blood at first. But also, because of the stomach cramps and my constipation, it was me all filled up with gas and crap and maybe the crap was finally coming out of me down there, but of course I wasn't thinking. All this before I looked, because I heard it plopping into the water, so for sure thought it was crap," and he said "That stupid fucking nurse. So what did she do, poke you up your hole without looking or even the wrong hole intentionally because she wanted you to lose the baby?" and she said "Of course not. She didn't know; I didn't; nobody did. She was putting it in the right place, showing me; maybe she wasn't the greatest expert at it, because it hurt when she did it, but in the urethra, when the blood came," and he said "And she didn't see what hole it was coming out of?" and she said "It was just a trickle, and it was all so fast her getting me into the bathroom that she didn't have time to look," and he said "It was a goddamn botched-up job, a stupid screwup . . . which nurse was it? Did you tell the doctor? Did you even see him after?" and she said "Shh, please, and it wasn't her fault. And the doctor saw me and said, from everything I told him, that it must have been a very early fetus and there was no major hemorrhaging and everything came out and I was in no danger. It was just that this thing, this fetus, didn't have it in it to live—that's my opinion; the doctor couldn't say for sure what made it abort—" and he said "He doesn't want to take responsibility . . . the insurance and so on," and she said "That's not it. But he agreed it could have been related to my illness and the way I am, so weak at times, and all the drugs I've been taking, and that he never specifically warned me with this new one because I'd told him I had no intention of getting pregnant again and that if I had changed my mind about it he knew I would have informed him," and he said "Warned you about what?" and she said "You're really upset about this," and he said "I am, what do you think; look what they did to you. But warned you about what?" and she said "Of getting—what I said; that women shouldn't be . . . that it shouldn't, this new drug, be taken by women contemplating getting pregnant or by men with my disease who are married to women who are planning to get pregnant, though the drug company has no extensive studies on that yet, the drug's so new; but in the little data they do have, there wasn't a single miscarry. They were just being extra careful by making that warning," and he said "Extra careful? If they were extra careful, or the doctor and nurse were—" and she said "He did the right thing based on the information about the drug and what I'd told him. But that—all those things working against me—coupled with the fact that the fetus wasn't healthy itself, which can happen in women much younger than I and stronger and in perfect shape and not taking any drugs or anything—" and he said "What did it look like?" and she said "Can't we continue this in the car, or even later? I've had it with it for now," and he said "Just, while you can still remember it, tell me what it looked like, please," and she said "I told you: nothing; a glob, dark, red, bloody. I flushed it down fast, almost before I knew what I was doing, it was so sickening-looking. But I almost think . . . but this has to be impossible. I'm sure they don't even start growing those things yet. But from some quick look, as it was turning around in the bowl, that I saw limbs—something, two of them sticking out on either side," and he said "Oh sheez, that's awful. Fuck it, I knew you were pregnant; I saw it in your belly. The way it was shaped, which I knew from the two other times," and she said "Why didn't you say anything?" and he said "I had my doubts, didn't want to alarm you, raise my hopes—you know—and I thought you knew yourself and all those signs much better than I. But I'm really sorry now. I could have stopped you from going in for that catheter. I would have asked you to have the baby if it had stayed," and she said "How could I have? I can't even pee right or stand up straight anymore," and he said "We could have done it; it would have worked out; women have had them under worse conditions: paralyzed; in iron lungs. Three's what I always wanted; three's the best. Maybe we can still have another. You can go off this drug; for a while you don't have to take anything. I'd take care of you from day one to the end. We'd get someone to help, you'd stay in bed—" and she said "No, this one was an accident; we just have to be more careful from now on."

Evangeline

She put an ad in the newspaper of the university he'd been a grad student at: "Garden and lt. handyman work for room and bd; 2 months minimum, 3 preferred." He calls, says that if she does take him he can only give her two weeks. That he was driving to New York with a friend in the friend's car and his apartment lease will be up in three days and he'll need a place to stay. She won't even have to provide him bed linen; he has a sleeping bag and pillow and pillowcase, though he would like a real bed or mattress to sleep on and to have his own room to write in a few hours a day before or after he does the work she wants done.

She says to be honest the ad's been running for several weeks and no one's answered it so far and she'd like to get the work started, so could he come by for an interview and to see if he'd like staying here? She has a young son; he has nothing against children, does he? and he says "No, why ever would I?"

He bikes over that afternoon, rings the bell, nobody answers. Walks around the house calling her name. "Mrs. Tylic? I'm here, Mrs. Tylic—Gould Bookbinder, at the time you said." "In here," she says when he passes a screen door at the back of the house. The laundry room. A beautiful blond boy, around two years old, is sitting on top of the washing machine, stretching inside for clothes and dropping them into the laundry basket on the floor. She pretty, girlish-like; in shorts, T-shirt, long hair in pigtails, thin, almost no breasts, though a bra on, small, five-two at the most, bright blue eyes, black hair, pale skin, holding clothespins, one in her mouth which she takes out, shy smile, very white teeth and perfectly formed it seems, slender muscular legs, high behind, young, twenty-two, twenty-four. They talk while she sticks certain clothes in the dryer and hangs on a line above his head other clothes: man's sweatshirt, seems an extra large; two bras, several small underpants, but a woman's, not a kid's, and all with bloodstains in the crotch; leotard, the boy's socks, which he'd think would go in the dryer. She says another reason she'd like a man here is for her son, since he's missing even a semi-steady male image with his father almost never around. He points to the boy, shakes his head a little and she says "Bronson knows; his biological pa, B-senior, pops in every third month for lunch to bitch as to how much of his inherited dough he's given us and to spin Brons-J around in his newest nifty sports car. Now it's a psychedelic-painted Lotus; that goofer's loaded." She doesn't work, for the time being takes marketing courses at a community college and is also trying to sculpt and pot, lives off the little money her ex-husband is forced by law to give their son and what she manages to pad on the kid's medical and daycare expenses, which her ex also pays; the house was bought with the money she got from the divorce settlement. "So I don't have much; the meals will be skimpy. Lots of pasta and canned tomato paste and jug wine, unless you feel like springing for the real McCoy and also one night treating us to a restaurant meal. I need lots of work done that I can't afford anyone to do. I don't expect major plumbing repairs but I do want simple electric jobs beyond just changing light bulbs, and the fence fixed, some bamboo dug up from a friend's property and replanted here, and if there's time, help in wallpapering the two bathrooms, besides all the ugly old rose bushes removed. Their roots go deep, I want you to understand before you sign on."

She takes his references, calls that night to say they all checked out and could he start in two days? and he says "As I said, my residence is only a single small room in a large house full of other small rooms filled with rowdy grad students and at night their loud mates, so I can even move in tomorrow. I've almost nothing to pack and I can use the sleep too before the long mostly sleepless drive back to New York."

Years later, maybe twenty, she writes "Why are you still writing me? I don't think our correspondence is healthy. It's been enjoyable hearing from you. You always wrote interesting and occasionally witty letters, not that I was ever interested in anything that happened in your rat nest of a city or thought that wit was such a great thing to have. I prefer sincerity and plain-spokenness and not to think of cockroaches and rowhouses. But you're married now and your wife probably resents your writing me and I don't want to be the cause for any strain in your marriage. I know I'd resent a husband who was getting letters from a former lover he says he was once in love with and almost married to." He wrote back saying "Sally accepts what I say, that we're only friends now. And how often do we exchange letters, three times a year? I get the feeling the main reason you want to end the correspondence is because there's nothing in it for you; in addition, you don't like the act of writing: it takes too much of your energy and time. The phone would be far simpler and less physically taxing if all you want to know about is what's happening and not what I'm thinking. So okay, I'll stop, and a long good life to you and of course always my love to B-J." She sends him a postcard: "That was extremely UNFAIR!!! Don't be the louse and bastard you once were; I thought you had climbed out of that. And sure: 'good life' to me but 'love' to Brons. You couldn't be more obvious. You're a fuck!" He sends her a picture postcard of the New York skyline, and says "I'm sorry, I'm sorry, I apologize; I swear my remark on the physical cost of letter writing was only a little dig I was giving and I meant no deep harm. As for the good life instead of my love, I thought saying anything approximating affection to you would be inappropriate after what you said about it. I hope this clears it up. Best ever, Gould." She doesn't write back, so her postcard was the last he ever heard from her.

Thinking about it soon after, he was glad to be through with the correspondence. He always answers when anyone writes him, so he felt stuck in it. But she was cutting him up too much in her letters and for no reason he could see and he'd wanted to say something about it but hoped she'd stop on her own. "You were usually such a sourpuss and at times acted like a fruity prude. Everyone we knew here felt that but they also thought there were decent and worthy things to you too. . . . You bitched too much when we were together, but about everything (especially the music and movies I liked and what I read and how I was raising B-J) and I've been wondering if you complain as much now to your wife. . . . Nothing was ever good enough for you and I doubt that anything will ever be. You thought California culture the dimmest but you never convinced me that your depressing falling-apart East was superior or even its equal. And as for Europe: oh, you loved that place despite its fastidiousness, *ooh-la-la*-ness, long serious faces and cruddy toilets and all their bloody wars and what they did to your poor Jews. . . . Our weather was always too beautiful for you, our shores too uninhabited and pristine. The people around here too open, good-natured and lighthearted and just all-around easy to be with and relaxed. You craved New York nastiness, impoliteness, uptightness, backstabbingness and hardships of every sort and snow so cold your skinny balls froze till they cracked. Things shouldn't be so 'naturally good.' " He doesn't remember saying that, nor does he see himself as ever saying it, since he never believed it, so if she wasn't quoting him why'd she put it in quotes? "I'm delighted you've finally found a woman to marry—not 'delighted'; that was one of your fake poofy words. I'm just *glad* you're getting married and I hope it works and changes you for the better (like helps you mature) as every marriage should. But honestly, I thank all the stars there are that I didn't become your bride and that you're no longer hassling me. . . . Brons doesn't consider you his second father anymore. He became disappointed and then disgusted with you when you refused to fly out here for a week in what had become your ritual annual visit. You said you couldn't afford to any longer because the plane fares had gone up, but do you know what it did to that kid? Now he's too busy making money to be interested in anything you do: your work, who you marry and what's on your mind. If there's one person you can bet will be a multi-m man by the time he's thirty, it's our junior B. . . . Why deny things for yourself so much? You were the same skinflint with us too. True, you only had menial jobs then and were basically supporting us—your 'family' as you liked to say (*that* I appreciated)—but you still could have treated yourself to something when you had a little money, or not been so penurious (cheap, man, CHEAP!). What I'm saying is that you inherited your cheapness from your father and because it is genetic it's probably impossible to eradicate."

Years before, maybe two or three after they split up and he moved back to New York, he wrote "I'm no longer in love with you, you're for sure no longer or never were in love with me. And you're with someone, I'm with someone, and you constantly gripe about me in your letters and occasionally say how much you hate my guts. So would it be okay if this is my last letter to you and I don't get one in return? Give my love to B-J . . . I'll of course keep in touch with him and try to see him when I can." "Give Brons your nothing," she wrote back. "Keep in touch with your nothing, you great bullshit artist. Besides, although I've rarely bad-mouthed you to him, he said 'If he's against you, Mommy, then he's against me, and I never want to talk to him again.' I told him that his relationship with you is his business and apart from me, but he doesn't see it that way. So I'm sorry but he doesn't want to be bothered anymore with my passing on your feeble greetings and bogus love. For a little unurban kid, he's hip to your schemes." He got a letter from her two years later (he'd written Brons a few letters during this time but got no answer) saying an old letter of his popped up from behind a file cabinet she was giving to Goodwill because she's redoing her house outside and in ("I've come into some family money and this savvy stockbroker fellow I know pretty well invested it for me and I made a killing") and she read it and thought of the days they were close and how good he was for Brons at such a vulnerable age and for so many years and she harbors no ill will to him anymore and just wanted to know how he was, and the correspondence resumed and Brons wrote and called that he wanted to see him, so he flew out, stayed in her guest room for a night and in her bedroom the rest of the week. Or a few years after that he remembered one of the many things he'd left behind in her house—a drawing several centuries old he had when he met her and hung on her wall but had never given her and now wanted—and included in the letter more than enough money to send it special delivery and apologized for the inconvenience this would cause her and swore he'd never ask for anything else of his again and she wrote back "Why not fly out to pick it up personally plus the rest of your little art treasures—none of them fit in with anything I own anymore—and see Brons along the way? He's dying to see you but is too shy to ask and can't face the hurt if you refuse. As for me, I'm comfortably with someone now (if I can be juvenile for a second: the coolest, cutest dude I've ever flipped over, and he's nine years younger than me), so I'll make and receive no demands. In other words, if you think I'm encouraging you to come because I'm lusting after you, you'd be nuts. This is all for Brons." So he'd fly out and the new guy had gone backpacking in the Sierras for two weeks and he'd sleep with her after the first night. "Why not?" she'd say each time he came out. "We were always great together in bed and I'd only get horny in a few days knowing you're in the next room beating your meat." Or she'd call after a year and say "I was thinking of the three of us in Portugal and Spain, hitchhiking along back roads—people there had never seen such a gorgeous towheaded boy before, it seemed, the way they kept mussing his hair. And I wondered what you've been up to, working at, reading and yes, even though she disliked me—I liked her, by the way, or admired her—how your mom was holding up too. . . ." Anyway, always resumptions in their correspondence, overtures to fly out from both of them, he'd scrape up the dough to go, for a few years, annual visits in June and the same arrangements at her house every time. Till she wrote that last letter, his to hers, their postcards, then it all stopped.

So he was immediately drawn to her in the laundry room. The day?—sunny and dry. And her hair up or down?—now he's not sure. Up, he thinks. Down, he thinks. Either way, she looked great. Through their entire relationship she had bangs, so she had bangs that day, but wore the rest of her hair many different ways. And she seemed vulnerable in the room, also protective of her son, more so with both those at the same time than he thinks he ever saw since, for a while clutching Bronson's shoulders from behind, using him as a shield or device of some kind—well, literally to hold on to and hide behind—because she felt so discomposed or shy, and saying "shield" and her placing Bronson between them or keeping him there would make her less protective of him than he just said, and she also seemed interested, even attracted to Gould. Of course, the vulnerability and shyness, which he noticed when she first met other men she was attracted to, but it was probably mostly an act. And was it shorts she had on or long pants? Jeans, tight . . . not jeans but these thin summerweight cotton pants, he just remembers, red, and tight to her skin, and he now thinks a yellow tank top. But long solid legs on the small short body, but perfect legs, it seemed, and if the pants were long—they *were* long—then he could see the outlines of her skin through the cloth. "So-and-so" (she mentioned a well-known West Coast writer a little younger than Gould) "once said my legs were the most amazing and dazzling—lots of z's—on earth. 'Naturally,' he said, 'I haven't eyed out every woman's legs, but there are just so many kinds and I doubt any pair could be better than yours.' Am I sounding too conceited and slight?" and he said "It's okay, what else did the big brain say?" and she said "That I ought to model them. Or have a fashion photog take black and white shots of me only from the top of the thighs down and to blow up the best one to poster size, stencil the word 'legs' below the photo and to make a half-million copies of it and have someone market them to poster stores. That men would want to marry me just for my legs or pay five dollars for a thirty-second peep at them in some sideshow or porno place where just my legs were visible. Then he got really gross about my legs, where he'd like them in regard to him—he was pig rich from his novel by then and had big strong arms and a wrestler's neck and chest and beautiful bushy blond hair but an ugly face on the largest head I've seen on someone who wasn't a sad idiot and decrepit breath . . . could that be the right word?" and he said "If you mean 'stinky,' no, but I get the point." "And would I mind if he told his best pal about me—the Playboy of the Potato World, he called him: a fat cat from Idaho, you see, or son of one, and all from tubers—since he thinks I'll fall for him madly and he wants to know someone who's seen my legs with nothing above or on them in bed. 'Tell whoever you want,' I said jokingly, and his pal—Brons Sr., though without the S just yet—shows up at my place a day later, says who he is and that he's selling eros but not from door to door, just to mine, and swore he never used that line before," and he said "Why, did he think it a good one?" "And I tell you we flashed on each other right there and were on the floor in five minutes with not even the front door closed—that must be a record—with him lapping my legs up and down and around till they were greasy from his spit, and in a month we were married and with kid. Really, I don't know what the big fuss is with men over legs. What are they, at their very best, but shapely sticks to walk on and cross. You guys get gunned up by everything. Even some with my poor chest: they must think of it as a pubescent girl's and that turns up the heat. Or they see me as a boy or something in between, the creeps, where they then get both. But I'm being too egocentric again, aren't I?" and he said "No, I swear, I love your stories."

He liked to lie close to her in bed while she slept, or pretended to, and stare at her face if there was any moon or room light on it. Beautiful from all sides and the front and from in back too: the head shape and little perfect ears poking through the hair. Hair what he already said: long, black, bangs, different styles, etcetera. Eyes, small nose, chiseled lips, he's so bad at descripts, tiny waist, didn't mention that before but it was probably assumed and he'd wanted to say "minuscule," slim hands, small delicate feet or delicate hands and small slim feet, flat muscled tummy, and so on . . . the works. "This writer also said I had the best-looking ass for a woman my size he'd ever seen, so a qualified compliment but one he still thought I should appreciate. That there'd be men there too who'd want to marry me just for it. But through him I hooked up with Brons-S and from that I got J, so something good came from the legs-and-ass man." He loved her ass too. Turning her over in bed—no, that doesn't sound right. If she was on her back, then sort of encouraging her to get on her stomach and she'd say "Why, what do you have in mind?" and he'd say "Nothing, really . . . you know," and massage her shoulders and neck and rub her back and legs and butt and then, or after some preliminaries with his fingers with at first a number of quick furtive forays, lift her butt up and try to get in her from behind. Hold the porno. "I'm a little small down there," she said several times, "and I'm sorry if I can't accommodate but it hurts too much that way," and then "What are you doing?—you know it hurts," and finally "Jesus, you rat" or "Schmuck" and once even "Hyena," "Will you stop that! You know I can't do it and unless something with age happens to my cunt, I never will. Try it next time and I'll tell you to get lost for good." Only one position she liked. He on her right, both on their backs side-by-side, her right thigh raised, he in her that way. Tries picturing it and it seems right, though remembers it always took a bit of twisting and doing, he never went in easy and straight. Became frustrating, unexciting sometimes, even uncomfortable, and humdrum too—more than three years of it and, when they weren't fighting or sulking, they did it about four days out of five. He wanted the variety of positions two people living together for a long time would do and she kept saying she didn't have the anatomy for anything but the double-back one and that sometimes even then it was only a little more pleasurable than painful for her, though about once every couple of months she let him come in her a different way. One time, when he knew better, after about a half hour of pleasant foreplay, he got on top of her when she was still on her back and she said "Get off, you tub." Another time, on an unusually hot humid night for that part of California, they didn't even own a fan, and she was naked on her back and seemingly asleep from the heat as it was around nine and they'd been reading in bed just to be on cool sheets, he said her name and she didn't answer and he repeated it and her eyes stayed closed and he slowly bent her legs up at the knees till her heels almost touched her thighs and her vagina opened, smeared his penis with saliva and positioned himself above her without touching any other part of her body and tried gliding it in and she opened her eyes, winced from pain but calmly said "I'm not going to fight you. You're halfway in and it already hurts like hell. But fighting you will end up hurting worse than allowing you to proceed, but I'm warning you I might be capable of doing a lot more to you when you're done than just ordering you out of the house and cutting up all your precious things," and he withdrew.

She once lunged at him with a steak knife after he'd made what he knew when he was saying it and even a few seconds before was a cruel remark about her. He flinched, the knife whisked past the place his face would have been if he hadn't moved back, and then he jumped behind the table—it was in the dining room, they'd been clearing off the dishes after dinner—and said "What're you, crazy? You just almost killed me," and she said "I didn't, I knew exactly when to pull back. I've got plenty of reserves; you're the one who hasn't, in anything. You're fantasizing again, thinking I'd waste my time trying to stab you and then the next twenty years of my life wasting away in prison because I did. Please, get your freaking things together and leave the house now," and he said "Don't tell me you didn't try to stab me. You did, so of course I'm going—how could I trust you again?" and she said "Listen, you're raving, but do what you want," and her face said she was trying to forget the incident and he wondered what to do. She put the knife and a couple of other utensils back on the table and looked at a photo on the wall of the three of them in a rowboat, Bronson and he rowing, she looking as if she was barking comical orders to them through cupped hands, and then left the room. He cleared the rest of the dishes, washed them in the sink, continued wondering what to do, leave? stay? What would he say to Brons? "Your mother and I just don't get along. We do some, but not enough. It's a pity too, because I love you, but I'll see you and we'll do things if I stay in the area, you and I, but that's the way it is, I'm sorry to say, though it's nothing you've done that's sending me away." She came into the kitchen and he expected her to say "What are you still doing here?" but she started drying the dishes. "How do we pile up so many dishes and pots and stuff for just three people and a simple dinner?" and she said "We're extravagant," and he said "Oh yeah, that's us." Then he called Bronson if he wanted to carpetsweep the dining room as he did last night—"You did a great job. And it needs sweeping badly, kiddo; lots of everyone's crumbs," and Brons said from his room "If it's okay, can I not? I'm busy playing," and he looked at her and she smiled and said "He's playing; what a life," and he said "So, what about that thing before?—our argument. Does it mean we're over it? Fine by me if we are, but you don't want it discussed?" and she pressed her cheek to his chest and put her arms around his waist and her hands went under his shirt till they were on his lower back and he kissed the top of her head and said "Your hands are wet, but you can keep them there," and she said "I'd never try to hurt you like that, never. If it looked like it then that can only be because when I was pretending to wield the knife, but with no intention of coming close, I must have stumbled frontwards a bit, though I don't remember that. But I'm sorry and it's finished, the incident, all right?" and he said "I'm sorry too if I misjudged the distance of the knife from my face, if that's what I did," and she said "It had to be, or like I said, it was all to sort of scare you a little, more like a harmless jolt, but I got too close by accident or mistake."

He left her house for good a few times—three or four—but always came back and stayed. Phone call to her about something—Brons, important mail he's expecting and if it came, though he was probably hoping she'd ask him over—and she said "What are you doing now, want to come by? Brons is at a friend's for the night," or he took Brons for the day, dropped him off and she said, which he was hoping she would, "Want to stay for dinner, even spend the night? Brons will love it if he sees you in the morning and I'll be honest—one of us has to—I haven't had sex for weeks and from what you've indicated about all the women you're not seeing, you've been dry for a while and could use it too," and he said "That'd be okay if that's all it'd be, a deal?" and stuck out his hand and she looked at it and said "Oh sure, we're gonna shake." It was Brons. Fine, for that night he wanted to get laid as he was as horny as she said—hadn't been with anyone since the last time he slept over a month or so ago—but he loved that boy and wanted to live with them again almost solely because he didn't want to just see him once a week or every other for a few hours that day. Once she called his deep feelings for Brons as bordering on the sick and he said "Why? I think of him, though I have no illusions about this, as like my son. One would think you'd be pleased he has someone who feels that way about him besides you," and she said "Sometimes I am but other times I think it's carrying it too far. He has a father. And even if they rarely see each other now, I feel in five years or less Brons-S will grow up to the point where he'll discover what he's missing and he'll want to see him as much as J wants to see him now. And so they'll see each other a lot and if you're still around, you'll be in the way, and maybe even J will go live with his dad. That's how it often turns out, not that I'd love the idea. But you and I? Come off it, we'll never stay together and we'll be lucky, the way we hack out at each other sporadically, if we last another two months. Then when you really leave—and it might be the next time or the time after that. But when every one of your books is with you and you have a rented apartment instead of a cheap room and nothing of yours remains in this house, the boy will be clobbered the hardest by you so far. Maybe double what it was with his father, as he's older now and remembers more than he forgets and this bad shit tends to get etched into kids his age permanently, but anyway, that for the second time he's been blown off by the big man in his life. How this will affect his future relationships, male and female—you never liked my psychological specula-tions but here it is—don't even ask."

Used to imagine her with normal-size breasts or just ordinary small breasts but not completely flat. Sometimes he'd suck one up by the nipple, close his other eye so as not to see the second breast and look at the distended part and think is it really possible that if she had breasts like this one he'd feel much better toward her, might even want to try sticking it out with her for life? He wanted a few times to get her pregnant just to see her breasts enlarge, also to have a kid. She'd said she loved— wait a minute. What he means by that "also" remark is that even though he knew they'd never marry, or chances were slight, and that he'd probably end up living apart from her and their child—or maybe they would marry now that they'd had that kid and it could even be that their relationship would get infinitely better because of it—he was thirty, a little past, and felt he should be a father by now. Not the attitude he'd take today, almost thirty years later, if he still didn't have a child, though who knows. And she'd said she loved being pregnant with little Brons because not only was her marriage then as close to being euphoric as it ever was ("Nobody believes this, but between periods of contractions we made love right up to the moment we drove to the hospital to have the baby") but because for a few months, till she went dry a few weeks after the delivery, she had breasts, she said, that could fill a small-cup bra and even gave her cleavage when she wore an evening dress once and a man could hold on to, and so on. Brons-S took lots of photos of her breasts then with and without clothes and might still have some, and if Gould wants he should write him for a few; she's sure he would appreciate the craziness of the request and part with them gladly or make dupes if he still has the negatives and send those. But most times he'd tell himself "What's the difference? Big breasts, no breasts, middling breasts, if there's anything there it's just fat and flesh, and she has a cunt, small too, she says, but most times sexually okay and adept in the limited way she's set for it, and the sweetest little horizontal hairline right above it but no other hair around (she swore she didn't shave the area and it never felt that she did), and one that never smells of anything—urine, sweat, soap, deodorant, perfume (no chance of contraceptive jelly since she was on the pill)—or that's how she prepares it before she comes to bed: maybe just water and a washrag, and a beautiful ass and great legs and all the other things, and she does have normal nipples and aureoles and he does what he can with these, more than he thinks he would to a woman with more heft to her breasts. "I should wear a shirt to bed, I'm so ashamed of my top," she said in different ways a number of times, her hands covering her chest, and he said "No, your nipples are gorgeous, the red circles around them exciting, I love when they're erect, sucking on them and the rest," and she said "You're just compensating," and he said "So what, but my feeling is you get what you get, both of us, me with that, you with my hairy shoulders and back, so make the most of it, though I don't know what you could do with my furriness."

Night before he's to come to her house he rides his bike into a pole on a bicycle path. The pole's there to keep cars off the path. It once had reflectors but someone had smashed them, or what? When he went back with her a few days later to photograph the pole for insurance purposes, the reflector frames were still nailed to the pole but the reflectors were gone. So he doesn't see the pole in the middle of the path—he's biking by flashlight, sky's dark and moon's not up and path runs through a grove of eucalyptus trees—the smells, he remembers, well, not then, but other times and perhaps especially at night—and bike's front wheel hits it, he flies over it and breaks his shoulder and cracks his head. Drags the mangled bike about a half-mile to his house and then, when he realizes how hurt he is, calls a friend to take him to a hospital's emergency room and next day calls her and says he broke his shoulder and has a concussion and he's sorry but it's obvious he won't be able to do any two-handed heavy manual labor or garden work for a while—he doesn't even see how he can help his friend drive to New York in two weeks—so he guesses their arrangement's off, and she says "Deal's a deal. You can still get on your knees and pull up weeds, can't you? And instruct me with repair work around the house, if you know how, and look after my son while I'm out, and so forth. I can't be paying for your food now, though—your labor won't cover it. We can go fifty-fifty, or forty for you, sixty for me, since I have the little boy, but all depending on your appetite. If it's enormous—you're not the biggest guy but you might have a high metabolism—it's back to fifty and maybe even you're the sixty. Actually, maybe you should be, since I bet I weigh a little more than half what you do and I'm not much of an eater. As for your room, it's here and costs me naught to keep up. But maybe you can also go in on the laundry detergent, just to be absolutely fair, and help me hang the more delicate wash on the umbrella clothesline outside, something I was also going to have you dig a deeper hole for and reinstall."

She went to Portugal with another man and her son, by this

time he'd left her for the last time and was living in New York. She called from Oporto and said "Why don't you join us? We always said we wanted to stomp around the Iberian Peninsula, so now we can all do it together. Brett said he wouldn't mind sharing me with you so long as he gets to stay with me two consecutive nights out of four. We can do it that way, always getting two bedrooms. And the one who doesn't sleep with me shares his room, and if there's only one bed in it, then his bed, with Brons," and he said "But he still wets it sometimes," and she said "Don't worry, he's just a kid with a wee bladder, and I brought a pad."

He'd left from her house, driven a U-Drive-It car to Indiana, flown from Indianapolis to New York. Called her every day along the way. "I'm in Nevada now, in the middle of a desert, I swear half the cars driving past are going at least a hundred-twenty miles per, but from this phonebooth I can see the mountains I'll be camping in tonight. . . . I miss you, isn't that stupid?" and she said "Enjoy yourself, explore the wild, curl up with a coyote or bear." "I'm on the outskirts of North Platte, Nebraska, and from this rest stop I just saw the most stunning sunset in my life and an hour ago a tornado. To catch what promises to be a glorious sunrise and to save some cash, I think I'll sleep in the car here. . . . I still miss you, maybe not even out of loneliness on the road, and more than I did yesterday. It's ridiculous, because when we said good-bye we both never wanted to see the other again," and she said she missed him too and would love for him to fly back soon as he unloads the car in Indiana. "We wouldn't work anything out but we'd have a helluva hot and heavy few days. Brons began peeing in his pants day you left. He says he can't sleep knowing you'll never come back," and he said "Tell him I'll see him at least once a year, though probably twice that. I'll send for him when he gets a bit older but meanwhile I'll fly out there just to be with him and starting a few months from now and one to two weeks at a time," and she said "You tell him because if I do then when you go back on your pledge he'll blame me." "Hi, Gould. I miss you, I love you, I want to hold you in my arms forever and ever. When are you driving back? Where are you now? Will you be away long?" "Oh, my little boy," he said and started sobbing and Brons handed the phone to her: "I think he's crying. I didn't do anything bad, did I?"

Flew to Lisbon (cashed in the savings bonds his mother had bought him twenty years before), slept with her that night and it went well for a while. He had her for two nights, Brett for two, they bussed and trained around Portugal and Spain together. Then Brett hooked up with an old girlfriend for a week and he and Evangeline and Brons hitched from Salamanca to Zaragoza, where Brett met up with them. Then it was time for those three to leave; he still had a week. They had a chartered flight back; his was regular round-trip fare. Why's he think all this info's essential? And he's never been good with facts, stats and grammar and things like that; he knows where people were in a room and what they did and generally what they said. He got angry a few hours before they were to go to the airport, said some things, she said some; he remembers the scene vividly: she was sitting in the sink peeing, he was packing Brons's things, Brons was napping on their bed (they'd made love on the floor while he was asleep), Brett was in the adjoining bedroom. They argued (she jumped off the sink, wiped herself and put on her pants); he jostled her (more a tap), she hit him (fist against neck), he grabbed her chin and squeezed it and said "You fucker (bitch, bastard, stupid cunt), why do you think I should take that without heaving you across the room?" She spit in his face and said "Oh so brave; let me see you just try it." He squeezed her chin harder till she screamed. (He knew what he was doing was all wrong, that he should apologize, say he doesn't know what the hell came over him, that he doesn't even know what started the goddamn argument, anyway, forgive him, and then leave the room and walk around the city for an hour, buy them going-away presents, etcetera.) By this time Brons had his arms around his legs and was trying to drag him away from his mother. Brett burst into the room. "Ladies, gentlemen, please," and pried Gould's hand off her chin. "You maniac," she said to Gould, "we're going just at the right moment," and he said "You're right, on everything, just as I'm wrong on them. But why am I bothering with any of you? This has all been a dopey sham. A woman shouldn't be shared—that's my problem or what set it off. We've been so freaking hip about it. Oh, you get to stick it in her, oh, I get to do it next, two for you, three in column four, oh aren't we all so *nouveau classe.*" "What?" she said. "Every time you hit the sack with her," to Brett, "it drove me nuts. Now I went over the peak. I couldn't stand your goddamn sounds through the wall. You had to make them, knowing I was in the next room sleeping right up against your wall? You had to shout, you had to say ouch, ouch? She's a slut, we're both pimps, the three of us are flaming exhibitionists, and you're a dumb asshole for agreeing to the arrangement in the first place. Once she left with you she should have stuck with you. It hasn't been good for Brons besides," and she said "And what you're saying now is? As for who's the loony hypocrite, we won't even vote." "Shut up, you bastard (fucker, bitch, slut, stupid cunt, A-1 manipulator). Shut up, shut up!" She spit at him again, punched his chest. "Ladies, gentlemen, please." He grabbed her chin. Brett said "Jesus, did you have to?" and jumped on him, threw him against the wall. Brons was bawling. "This is so sad," Gould said, "I'm such a wreck, everything couldn't be worse. How'd I get to this? I'm sorry, sorry, forgive me," and got on his knees and rested his head against Brons's shins. "Get off me. You're crazy," and he said "I know, I'm so ashamed, to you most of all, but to all the rest. Ah, enough," standing up. "I'm hopeless. I hate everything. Deals, contracts, egos, appetites, it's all getting to me. Nobody else here may be a sham but I certainly am." He punched the wall and when Brett said "Stop, you're gonna cost us a fortune," he threw a radio across the room, ashtray to the floor, picked up a chair to smash it against something but put it down and sat on it. Manager was called. He said "It's all because I don't want to be so solely alone again." Didn't know why he said it. Never really minded traveling alone. Had been looking forward to it after they left: Granada, Seville; they hadn't been there and he'd wanted to go. Toledo, the Prado, to sit in what he'd heard was a small square room there filled with tall El Grecos. He yelled "The freedom of the open road is hell. Ah, that's so asinine," and clenched his eyes closed and grabbed his head. "He was never like this," she said to someone. "Never melodramatic; in fact, bewailed that state. A schmuck sometimes but never so sophomoric. Maybe cracking up was the best thing for him; he was always too judgmental and tight." "That's unfair," Brett said and she said "You're probably right. Please get our bags downstairs. You help him, Brons. No good-byes, let's just go. He'll pay for everything he breaks," to the manager. "Otherwise, we're all paid up." She quickly threw the rest of her and Brons's things into a duffel bag, made for the door, said "Wait, I can't leave him like this," and he thought She's going to say she wants him to come to California soon as he can. That it wasn't all his fault and she takes most of the blame. That she still loves him and he doesn't have to think this is the end of them. Even if she won't mean most of it, it'll give him hope through the next week. "Please get a hold of yourself, Gould. I feel somewhat responsible for you but not that much where I'd miss my flight. I don't have that kind of cash to blow. And if you didn't like the arrangement, you always could have said. Take care. I don't quite know why it happened today, but like you I think it stinks," and left. "Bye, Gould's" from Brons and Brett at the door. The manager, with a young nervous elevator operator on both sides of him, said "Pardon us, sir, but we don't wish you to remain. The radio was old so we won't ask and we'll also excuse the glass. Now, can you go?" He's reached an age, he wanted to say to him, where he should have his own children. You, a Spaniard, know about that. One's own children and a good wife can stop a man from unacceptable behavior like this.

A job like yours too: full-time, relatively well-paying, respectable. He's become a leech on people for lots of things: money, emotion, having a kid. Something snapped that won't again. His life's become ugly and he must start changing that today. Okay, settled, he knows what's the problem but he's not sure how to carry out the solution, but one thing at a time, yes? and ran past the manager and his men—should have said he was sorry to him; he'll do it later, but everything can't come that fast—out of the hotel, walked around for hours, had lots of coffee and saw some sights, they were gone now, plane had taken off, were probably still discussing him, but don't let that stop you, went back to the hotel to pick up his things, someone had packed them for him, asked for the manager, he'd left work for the day so Gould wrote a note: "My apologies, señor, my deepest and most respectful. Thank you for being so courteous, understanding and just plain nice about the whole matter. I'm completely ashamed and shan't repeat that behavior again." Changed his departure flight from Madrid to Marseilles. Bussed to Aix-en-Provence; met a woman there on vacation for two weeks and started sleeping with her. He was getting healthy; when the woman said that as much as she adores him this is only a summer fling and she'll return to her husband in a week and never see him again unless she comes to America on business or they meet by chance, he said he understands, that was the arrangement from the start, he'll regret when they separate but it's been a wonderful few days so far and it isn't over yet. "What a marvelous disposition," she said in French; "so clear and clean and where there's no rancor or stain. Normally, a man would demand I stay till he has to go, that I lie to my husband why I'm delaying my return and then desert me in a few days, having won an uncontested contest with my husband and triumphed over my compunctions and better instincts or make a tearful tirade and spectacle when the time came for me to leave." "I used to," he said, "but learned." They went to museums and concerts and chapels designed by artists and restored homes of famous painters and composers, discussed art, philosophy, religion, books, music and the more serious European movies; Evangeline never wanted to talk about things like that; thought all conversation about art was "for faggots" and that America made the best movies and subtitles ruined your eyesight and good music started with Dixieland and jazz and books were for falling in love with and not trumpeting your highfalutin views and philosophy was unreadable when it wasn't laughable to read and religion you should just shut up about even if you're a believer and looking at art in books was better than on walls because you didn't have to tramp around huge stuffy buildings and try to peer over people's shoulders to see it. "That's because of your height," he said; "so get in front, no one would mind." He's never been so nuts, he told himself repeatedly, so let that be a lesson to him: it was terrifying and painful. Sure, when he was eighteen he was a depressed kid on and off for a year and contemplated suicide, or entertained that idea but was never serious about it and it was probably more romantic and hormonal than anything else, because it suddenly disappeared, and when women broke up with him when he was in his twenties he used to make some terrible scenes, punching doors, throwing things across rooms, once even threatened to slap the woman he'd been briefly engaged to when she called it off, but doesn't think he ever felt so icy and hollow inside and partitioned from the world as he did that day: there were voices in his head for hours that said "You're crazy, that's all there is to it, good-bye, cuckoo bird, you're now never gonna get out of your cage, mission accomplished: over the line for all time because an enormous wall's been built on it that you can never climb over, you'll have to be attended to forever or stay on powerful calming drugs but always in locked institutions where your keepers occasionally beat and bugger you and with no chance to be playful and creative and sexual with women again, all that's been erased or will be, so what can one say: it's too late and you shoulda seen it coming." The preventive solution? Forget what he came up with that day, that was only to get him through it. You just got to be aware of what you do and say and work your darndest at what you like pursuing and don't make unfair demands or expect success or the good things to last and bad ones never to happen and better to be hurt than hurt someone and gratitude is good too and politeness and genuine kindness and living alone has its pluses and drawbacks but things change, try not to have too many illusions and preconditions and musts, just be someone—well, he was going to say be someone others can come to and count on rather than warded off by his often being frazzled or on the border line of falling apart, though for the time being best he just take care of himself. It'll all take time; you can't be razed or destroyed in a day except by some devastating drug. Also the job, his own place, living normally or just quietly and simply but not obsequiously and never greedily, and independently and eventually the wife and kids will come. Why's marriage so important? Oh, for most of the old reasons and he knows so little and so much is too complex to make all the decisions himself and he's also tired of going out looking and even hunting, and kids he's always loved.

During the trip she said "This isn't easy to say but if you and Brett are getting weary of the two-in-a-row routine and want to do it to me together and at the same time even do things to each other, I won't object." He said "Never. It's got to be one-on-one with me or if there's a third, then a woman only." "I think that's what I prefer too," Brett said and she said "You're both scaredy-parrots," and Gould said "No, I just don't want to touch another man that way," and she said he was lying and probably Brett too and he said "I don't get it. What good's it do you having me screw around with a guy, maybe stick it in his rear and get shit on my prick and then put it in you—but especially the guy you're going back to California with and say you've loads of affection for?" and she said "You ever hear of soap? And it'd turn me on, for one thing, just as it would you seeing two young chickies going at it. And for another, it'd be good for you both, free you . . . heck, I've fooled around a couple of times with girls, when we were all zonked but I knew what was happening and could get into it, and I still really most like doing it exclusively with men and the same would happen with you. Just think if you ever wound up in prison; you'd be a little happier there than if you had never done it or at least not so afraid. I think though I'll always be a woman where one man will never be enough. You'll probably say that's because of my size and build and I'm trying to compensate for something, but you don't know how far off you'd be. Usually when either of you is finished, even if I've had my display, I still want to continue and wish I had the same, and if I can't, then another guy's joint in me. My number-one fantasy—one of you has heard it—is an orgy with just me and six to eight guys. But each a gentleman, nobody rough, and strong and sexy and a couple of them funny and making quips and two of them beautiful and even one guy very hairy and all of them no older than you two are and they also have to be at least nice-looking and big-muscular to wiry or lean. And each one gets to fritz me my way, but while one is, the rest are kissing and fondling and sucking me every which way and maybe one of them's doing it to himself and two others to each other, but I wouldn't know how to arrange such an event. And I suppose I shouldn't think I should, since it'd kill my poor little pussy for good. But I wonder, with enough jelly and breaks, and if I told them only to go in a little, not too deeply, had them swear not to, if I could pull it off. How about just one of them entering me that way and the rest at one time kissing and sucking me all over and that sort of stuff, things I'd never dreamed of. It'll all never happen, of course, and I'd get too oddball a sex rep and after a while there could be guys lined up five-deep outside my front door whom I'd never want to mess with. Though maybe it actually could happen with two or three good guys or even four, but that would be the max."

First night he's to stay there his shoulder's in a sling. They have dinner, some wine, she puts her son to bed, he says "He's a cute kid, I like him, very sharp, you can tell," and she says "He's the love of my life. I'd die if anything disastrous happened to him and would become violently insane if he was seriously mistreated, know what I mean?" and he says "Hey, don't look at me, absolutely the wrong pervert," and she says "Just saying, which I'd do to my father if he ever slept over or baby-sat, and as far as I'm able to remember he never did a filthy or untoward thing to me, but I was a girl," and he says "Personally, I'd think you'd be overstepping your anxieties there or honesty or outspokenness or something, if your father had never shown any inclination or sign, etcetera, or done anything along those lines to any sex or age. But do what your want, that's your business," and she says "No, I like that, you're right out there and put it well in a fumbling way," and they sit on the floor playing a board game she suggested while listening to records of her favorite music, free jazz, which he's never heard and now doesn't much like but she keeps closing her eyes and smiling and bobbing her head to, and she looks at him—she's killing him in the game, mostly because he's still learning how to play, or maybe she'd always win that well anyway: it was the only time they played—and it's the look of someone wanting to be kissed and she's pretty but small, very small, her body, he wonders, if it ever got that far, if she'd even be able to take a guy his size, he never made love with someone so short and slight and thin and he thinks Give it a go, why not for two weeks? though maybe he's wrong about the look and says "What?" and she says "Did I say something?" and he says "Your look . . . okay," and thinks Just forget it, don't want to press and based on a misperception get berated for it, and she leans forward with that look and he thinks It must be, and moves to it and it's just a peck but once she pulls her face away she brings it back to within an inch of his and puts her arms around him and he says "Oy, watch the shoulder, it's separated bad, they think it could even be a break," and she says "I don't want to make asinine double-trouble remarks and say 'I'll be gentle.' I'll just play it safe and keep my hands off," and he says "Sorry," puts his left arm around her and rubs her back but recoils his hand when he feels the bony knobs, but maybe it's the way she's bent forward that they're sticking out like that and rests his hand there and she grabs his penis through the pants and says something and he didn't hear what and wishes he did but won't ask her to repeat it, that'd be stupid, and puts his left hand on her shorts and then inside them and so on and she says "We can rip at it anytime, you know; you don't have to worry. But won't this make your shoulder worse?" and he says "We'll stay off it."—shoulder hurting like hell now but he doesn't want to say, she might think it's too dangerous for him and stop—and she says "What position would be the best for it?" and he says "Let's wait till we get to the bed before we decide, unless you want to do it here," and she says "On the floor? Or the couch? No support underneath for the former and the latter with no room? What could be less appealing," and he says "All this talk," and she says "You're right," and when they get to the bedroom he takes his shirt and socks off and lies on the bed with her and says "We don't have to do it immediately, but probably—wait, the door's okay?" and she says "He sleeps for the first few hours like a stone, then has to pee or has peed in his bed and I have to get him up either way," and he says "Then probably if you got on top of me, though only when you're ready and if it's okay," and she says "No good for me; the way I'm built. Would side-by-side be all right?" and he says "Fine," and she says "It shouldn't hurt you—we'll make sure your right shoulder's not involved—and if it does, we won't continue it. Later, if we like each other and want to do it again—not tonight, so much, but another time—we can do it once the way you like; but for now my way till I get the hang of you, is that all right?" and he says "Again, what's good for you, though you'll have to show me what you mean, I haven't a precise picture of it . . . may I?" and slips off her shorts and underpants and starts taking off her shirt and she says "I have petite breasts—I hope you don't mind too much; some men do; or my being concerned about it. You might not even think I have breasts when I get my bra off. I don't want to scare you, there's nothing freakish there or any scars, and I promise I'm not a boy," and he says "What are breasts anyway? I mean, I like them—" and she says "All right, okay, thank you," and he says "I was about to say I like them but I don't think they're essential to my liking a woman," and she says "Good, for the truth is mine are practically nonexistent. They're there, of course, two dots and circles, but they just don't bulge. Everything else is in place and relatively normal, although I love sex inordinately, do you?" and he says "Inordinately? I don't know. But I like it, sure, what else am I to say at this moment?" and she says "I love it, love it, with the right person and setting, though it's always good. And you look like—you even felt like, little I was allowed to feel, as if you have a nice body for it," and he says "What are you saying? That I've something against you touching me?" and she says "No, even if we didn't play around too long. But by nice body I mean that you're not too soft or fat or small or crooked," and he says "Crooked? And small I'm not, which you saw when I was standing up. I'm average, maybe a little above," and she says "I meant in the joint department," and he says " 'Joint.' You said that word before and I guess it means—" and she says "Yeah."

Screams, thrashes, pulls his hair, feet bang against the bed, does all that, digs her nails into his back till he says "Hey, lay off, your fingers, it's excessive, and it's not just my shoulder." A little later he says "Listen, I'm tired, my shoulder really aches—I have to get some aspirins or, if you have, something stronger. Besides, I don't have to prove anything to myself or you that I can do it three times in an hour. I can't; too bushed and maybe I put almost everything into the first and what's left into the second and a third's virtually impossible for me so soon. Anyway, twice is fine, even for the first time, and should be more than enough," and she says "There's always the chance you'll change your mind after you snooze awhile; men have," and he says "It isn't a question of my mind. And snooze a lot. Really, I'm out till daylight unless we're much further north than I was in my room last night and daylight comes an hour earlier here," and she says "You're getting too abstruse for me which I don't like because it sounds so phony. But I do tend to ask for too much in almost everything and I'm sorry," and kisses him and holds him as she dozes off. He listens to her as she sleeps; she breathes so quietly through that small nose. He'd like to take her arms from around him so he can put his sling back on and get the aspirins and go to sleep, but doesn't want to disturb her yet. Is this what he wants? Her body; so scrawny. And nice and smart as she is most times so far, he bets she can be a bitch and anti-intellectual, snapping at him in the bitch mood, if he comes and she doesn't, and demanding he go on till she does. Well, just for two weeks, and for that time, even if it turns out he doesn't like it here much, he's sort of stuck.

A year later they all went to New York. Acting was what she'd decided to do. She'd study it, he'd work as a per-diem sub in junior high schools, Brons would go to a cheap preschool, they'd live simply and frugally. She sublet her house for two hundred a month more than it cost to keep up, so barring any sudden expenses for it, that would be her contribution to their living in New York. It had come to her in a dream. She was acting on stage, a period piece she said—she was in a long dress and twirling a parasol—the performance ended a minute into the dream and there were lots of whistles and applause, people in the audience tossed flowers at her and shouted her name and yelled *Brava, Bravisima*—"I know this is mostly what's done at the end of every act of an opera, no matter how corny the opera is and dumbly performed and poorly sung, but this was my dream"—and when she awoke she said "I've never wanted to be anything in my life—not even a nurse or schoolteacher when I was very young—no professional till now. I want to be a stage actress; not movies or TV, just stage. I love great plays—

Shakespeare, Lillian Hellman, the one that *Carousel* was based on—and have a clear strong voice for speaking and singing, a decent-enough face—a couple of photographer acquaintances have even called it an exceptionally photogenic one—and lots of ambition and spunk. I want to give myself two to three years to make good, but only one in New York studying it. If I flop, back to the same old shit till the next inspiration; I won't continue something that's obviously coming to nothing and paying off with zero funds. But this is how things get done: you get a wild idea, make a quick decision and do it; all that holding-your-head deliberative stuff and plugging away for decades to get a toehold in your field is for losers. Will you come with us?" and he said yes because he wanted to return to New York, spend time with his parents and friends there, and the West Coast, or areas he's lived in or seen, was too relaxed and unexciting for him. He wanted to walk along jammed city streets—he got some of his best ideas when he did—and to be stimulated the way only a place like New York or Paris can—let's face it, he was a city kid—and for the first time to live in one with a woman, and he loved her son and wanted to show his friends what a good surrogate father he was, and living there would make her grateful for what he'd call his urban expertise in that city and also more dependent on him. Now whether she could be an actress? He didn't think she had the looks, voice, projection, personality and literary intellect for the roles she wanted to play and he never thought she was that good at mimicry or in even recounting incidents that happened to her or someone else or telling jokes. But you never know.

Several months later she said she wanted to move back to California. "New Yorkers are miserable and cruel. Your folks dislike me. Your friends all think they're superior and so smart and because I'm from the West I'm a hick and dummy. The air stinks. I want to smell clean air, see a blue sky with nice white clouds and later some stars. I don't want to go to the park just to see rotting trees and dirty grass or brown or ripped-up patches of ground. I want my old house back, my own backyard. I hate the walls of apartments and our so-called neighbors are the biggest creeps that ever lived. This one overdrinks, this one plays her loud music all night, this one looks as if he'd steal my kid, this one has caged birds that squawk all day, this one has an apartment that stinks as if it hasn't been cleaned of its cat shit for seven years. The view through our dingy windows is putrid. People on the street try to run you over even on their bikes. Nobody here has any respect for old people—few of the old people even do—or warmth for kids. I'm tired of car alarms at two in the morning, garbage trucks at three, hotheads bashing out their windows at four in the morning, someone being robbed on the street at five and the cops not showing up till six or seven. Bronson's made no friends. The kids in his school are too competitive, aggressive, argumentative, Jewish," and he said "First of all, if you didn't know it, I'm Jewish, goddamn you," and she said "They're not Jews like you. These kids are like their parents, I'm sure: pushy, angry, obsessed with money and just very Jewish, even the Christian ones," and he said "Will you stop using the word *Jewish* like that? You're not seeing and you've no sense of history, recent or otherwise," and she said "Listen to

202

me, I'm not made for this craphole—you are; you go and buy milk that's twenty cents a gallon higher than in California and which turns sour in two days, not me. Get cheated and insulted by store workers all day if you like. But Brons and I were made for the more peaceful and reasonable and civil West Coast where there aren't depressingly deteriorated faces mooching money and digging through trash containers at every subway entrance and bus stop," and he said "This city isn't entirely what you sum it up as by any stretch. And have you figured how much it cost us to settle here? There's the month's security on the apartment which we won't get back and if the landlord doesn't find a replacement tenant we'll be legally responsible for the rent till the lease expires in a year. I happen to, in spite of all its, okay, annoyances and difficulties, like this city and to dislike most of California for the very tranquility and civility you talk about. Okay, not the civility. But your area's too suburban, dull and uniform for me. There's no real change of seasons except maybe a few falling leaves and some sweater weather for two months, and the rest of that, mostly about art and culture—that California's twice as far from Europe as New York is—which are sort of my argument clichés to match yours," and she said "People clean up after their dogs in my town, that's why you don't like it. You like dog shit on my kid when he rolls around in the park, or on your shoes and when you come into the apartment, to stink up the floor with it. You like lunatics tossing bricks down at you from building roofs," and he said "When was that?" and she said "In the newspaper, not five blocks from here. You like bus drivers intentionally riding over mud puddles to splash you or parking twenty feet away from the curb so you have to jump over those puddles, and subways screeching till you can't hear." "Most of that's unusual," and she said "The mud-splattering isn't typical, I'll admit, though it happens too frequently, and same with buses stopping that far away to pick passengers up. But the subway screeching and express trains roaring through our local station happens every time, always, and will turn this into a neighborhood of deaf-mutes." "If it's too loud, you put your hands over your ears, that's all, but it never bothered me." "That's because you're already deaf by it." "That's a dumb old joke." They argued more, voices got stronger, she slapped him, he grabbed her chin. This was before Spain. In Spain when he did it she said "What is it with you and my chin?" Here she knocked his hand away and said "Forget it, I'm done with you, your rough stuff, your quirks, now your insanities; I'm moving back home," and he said "Just because you found you weren't much of an actress— oh yeah. You really gave it a lot of time," and she said "If you want to know, I found I hated acting. It's a completely fake profession. It's for phonies who are even more vain than I am . . . much more. I look in the mirror a great deal, but these people live in it and can't talk of anything but themselves or the famous or influential people they know or hope to know or know people who know," and he said "That's a cliché on a very familiar type; if you're going to present an argument about such a subject, go jugular," and she said "It isn't a cliché; you don't go to my school. If it sounds surface it's because they are surface. You met a few of them for an hour and they're so simple and sweet and interested, but playing that role. They don't know who you are yet; you could be a producer. But that's what they know how to do and are always practicing for in all their social contacts outside the theater: roles. Actors have no interest in being real people in real situations, and not even in real acting quality. They're unrelievedly jealous, in fact, of true talent and wouldn't give a snitch of credit to anyone who showed it, unless the person was dying or dead, the few times they're actually able to recognize that talent. They only want parts. I thought that at least—the very least—that having a small lean body would mean nothing on the stage. Look at the two Hepburns and a couple of others before they went movie-land for good. But they're the exceptions, for some reason, because every theater man I met, and men control it, let me tell you, is obsessed with wraparound breasts, legs and behinds, if he isn't sticking his hands on men's flies. I know I'll never even get a walk-on role in twenty years because of mine, nicely formed as my behind and legs are, or maybe a walk-on if I screw one like mad for several nights. It was a stupid move on our part—*mine*—and from a dream, goddamnit, and you let me go ahead with it, but all right. But at least I know when I've made a mistake, you don't," and he said "What mistake did I make, moving here? I like this city, I've told you. If there was any mistake, not that I'm blaming you, it was first moving in with you, but my dick has always ruled me," and she said "You're sick and sordid, do you know that? Sometimes I only think you moved in with us—" and he said "Oh, we're on that again? Why, because I feel for the boy more than I ever felt for you and

205

even love him more now than I used to, which is natural, for that's what time does to it if the kid stays as great as he always was," and she said "Then as I also said, you maybe love him too well. But don't get any ideas you'll be number one with Brons for too long. His real father isn't so much waiting in the wings now but he's there, smoking a cigarette or joint and looking at the beautiful actresses and their undulant hips and behinds, but he'll soon come on and do his part," and he said "Oh boy, are you ever into the metaphor or analogy or whatever the freaking figure of speech for it is. But you missed 'miracle play,' 'domestic tragedy,' 'comedy of errors,' 'theater of cruelty' and 'of the absurd,' and 'farce,' 'burlesque,' 'slapstick' and 'swan song' and so on."

"He misses you, pines for you, has returned to wetting his bed every now and then," she said on the phone week after she and Brons left. "When are you coming back? We both need and miss you. My bed wants you. The whole house is groaning for your return. Just skip out on the future rent and let them follow you to California if they'd ever do that," and he said "Can't do, it wouldn't be right. If I come, then I first pay them what I owe," and she said "Dummy, nobody in New York would and the landlord knows and expects that." She wants him, he thought, so she can have someone pay the bills. Maybe in three months, just so he can save some money from substitute teaching every day and also to give him time to get someone to take over his lease.

His mother said "My advice is not to go. She doesn't seem the right girl for you. She's not soft, her background's too different, I've a feeling she'll end up bossing you around and treating you like a schmo. You were always such a proud and independent guy but something's happened to you." His father said "She's a pig, no personality, ugly as sin and with brains to match. She treats you like a doormat. Her son's not yours but you play around birdbrain-like that he is, and this is going to ruin your future life and keep other women a hundred miles from you. Get rid of her fast. Don't waste your money calling her anymore, don't write, for sure don't go back. Get a real woman who looks like one and not like a boy and who has a body that can have babies after you marry her. This one's an operator and schemer, cagey as they come and only thinks of herself and her gorgeous garish clothes and layers of makeup, as if she's a rich princess who all the eligible men adore, when she's more like a witch. How can she walk on such pin legs and breathe when she has no nose? You two look stupid together— Mutt and Jeff, she's so short—and she also has no respect for your parents when she knows you love us and we've been good as gold to you. She comes in here, always wanted to be waited on, never once said thanks, and when she left, 'good-bye' was a dirty word to her, and no note since for the two weeks we put her up and the mattress her son ruined." His mother said "Not true, the no-thanks part. She was usually polite, had very nice manners, cleaned up after herself and her son, and the boy is a darling. If she could raise him to be so good, even if I bet some of that the last year had to do with Gould's contribution, then there's a lot to be said for her. She simply isn't right for him though. There doesn't seem to be that necessary thing between them, the lights and respect, nothing. Maybe because they were financially strapped here, but they were usually backbiting, fighting—in front of us—almost never agreeing on any one thing." "She's flighty," his father said. "Had a husband devoted to her—" "He wasn't so devoted," Gould said. "Then had a husband, period, and leaves him in a week or so after the boy's born and takes up with who knows what and eventually you. Now she wants to be an actress, or that's finally over. What did she want to be before?" "The part about taking up with other guys right away is wrong, all wrong." "When you were in California you wrote us she was going to be an interior designer, before that a furniture designer and before that an architect," and Gould said "Those things were momentary aspirations; more ideas to think over and discuss the possibilities of than anything concrete, and I did her a disservice by mentioning them. I suppose I wanted to—you know—build her up to you." "Just because you felt you had to do that shows how little you thought of her," his father said, and he said "That's not how I see it. Anyway, theater, an actress, becoming one, that was the first serious thing she really wanted to do and you have to give her credit for uprooting her life to pursue it. That it didn't work out . . ." and his father said "It didn't because she couldn't act to herself alone in front of a mirror if you gave her two hours to. And she was never pleasant, always that sour mug of hers, or something where you had to tickle her silly to get out the simplest smile. So what was there to her? Tell me, I'm asking. Did men stop dead in their tracks on the street for her?" "Yes, as a matter of fact, sometimes." "Bull. And if there's one thing a girl ought to have, if she doesn't have good looks and personality and a great job or lots of promise and there's no big family money around, which anyhow you don't care about—money, hoo! what does it mean to you—is brains. And for you especially she should have this and maybe most important: an intellect, to be a member of the intelligentsia you aspire to, and that she also lacked, take it from me," and his mother said "I found her to be quite smart, well read and full of interesting insights into life. It's the chemistry between them that I think was missing," and his father said "Chemistry and brains, then, but a lot else wasn't there. If her only attributes were that she was an all-star in bed and a good mother, big deal—you can't live off the first forever and the second shouldn't affect you much if the kid isn't yours. I think you're only going back for the boy, and a greater mistake couldn't be made. You aren't his father, you'll never be his father, and no matter how much the boy loves you now and you feel close to him, in ten years—in fifteen, you name it, if his real father doesn't grab him first—he'll be out of the house and in college and then you'll be stuck alone with her." "We could have other children," and his mother said "I'd advise against hanging your hat on that. She told me a number of times that having Bronson was the worst experience she ever had—throwing up violently for three months and then the long delivery, which nearly drove her mad with pain till they put her out—that she'd never want to have another child." "I overheard that too," his father said, "since of course she'd never say it to me. She never said boo to me. She knew I was on to her the moment she stepped into our house. And that despite all her primping and painting—toenails, fingers, face, eyes and hair, the whole can of worms—what I also thought of her looks." "Some people think she's beautiful," Gould said, "everyone at least thinks she's pretty. But what are we talking about, for the one thing we haven't mentioned so far and is more important than anything is that she's a very good person inside," and his father said "In my eyes she isn't, and the ones who think so or see that ought to get their eyes and heads examined. She's got a homely face and a shifty mind and a heart that's like a stone. There's a combo for you, one only an idiot would go for," and his mother said "That's not so—not even near the truth. Though there were some things I questioned about her, she has many fine qualities," and on it went, till his father said "Enough; nothing's going to sink through his hard head. And besides everything else, as if I have to say this, I'm not well, your mother can't do all the taking care of me at her age, and I'll probably get a lot worse before I get a little better, if I don't drop dead in a year, so it should be easy for you to see we need you here or just around the city for sudden calls," and he said "I wish I could; honestly, there's nothing I'd want to do more; but I can't be in two very far-apart places at the same time and I'm going out there. If you really need me—a sudden emergency, or just some help for a couple of weeks—which I'd hope not because I'd hate for you to get worse—I'll fly right home."

Years later he was standing at a bar with a friend who said "You know, you might not want to hear this. But since you brought her name up before . . . or maybe you do, now, or wouldn't mind, when it's so long after the fact, but I never knew what you saw in that California broad—Angel, or Evangel, or Angelina. She wasn't—" and he said "Evangeline. She never liked it shortened or would tolerate any nickname," and his friend said "Evangeline, then. But just *that*, that she wouldn't, with such a mouthful of an uncommon name. But she wasn't smart or sharp or good-looking. Her body was like a board. She didn't like one person you knew, me most especially, I think because I was your closest friend. She in fact looked on everyone we knew as if she wanted to spit great wads on top of their heads. She hated the city, was afraid of everything, and treated you like shit. She wouldn't even cook part of the dinner when Beverly and I came over—you had to do it all because we were your friends, not hers. What possibly could have possessed you? Usually your taste in women was pretty good," and he said "You sound like my dad there, may his soul, etcetera, and the rest of him . . ." and his friend said "Then your dad was right. He knew a looker; look at your mom. He also knew—I could tell, even sick as he was the last times I saw him and with not much use for talking because of his paralysis problem—what was up and who was phooey and what in life was hype or gauze or fake." "There was something between her and me that can't be explained. But I'll try, right? That's what I usually do. If you don't think she was good-looking or smart or anything like that. . . . Wait, did you say anything about her not being smart?" and his friend said "She wasn't, was she?—not too much." "Anyway, nothing I can do about that. Eyes, taste, your own handicaps or prejudices or just that you never engaged her in a deep conversation, or that she didn't fill your bill in the bones and flesh categories . . . But we had lots of fun together. I mean, where I really went hysterical with laughing, both of us together, and not from pot. And she had a very good mind. Would read a difficult novel, poetry or as much as she hated the subjects, an article on philosophy or some literary criticism I handed her—unlearned, you see, never got through high school—but would understand it more incisively than I most times and more than lots of scholars could. Why? Intuitive knowledge, instinctive, common sense, saw through things and could read between the lines and so on—incisiveness, as I said, all easy and natural. So we discussed things like that—long discussions, no fancy words or references or quotes from literary big shots or other books—and movies and plays we went deeply into too. And we both adored her son. Another plus. You don't have a kid or want one so you're shaking your head it's nothing, it's nothing, but you don't know what you're missing," and his friend said "The art bullshit sessions don't interest me either," and he said "I know, it's not what you like or appreciate— movies, you do, even talking about them at length. She also made a nice home for us. Very nice things; she had great taste, picked up treasures in Goodwill and St. Vincent de Paul; I felt very comfortable there. You're a slob so this doesn't mean anything to you, stinky jockey briefs in the kitchen sink, greasy pots piled high in the toilet bowl," and his friend said "Thanks a lot; you really know me." "I like things neat and attractive and a house in order and uncluttered, with serious paintings or prints on the wall, nice light fixtures, and that's what she did, with a little help from me. In ways our tastes in many things were almost identical; that doesn't hurt a relationship. And she was good in bed. Now your eyes light up. 'Good, bed, fuck, ug,' " and his friend said "Looking at her, I wouldn't've thought it; but knowing how much you like sex, it sort of makes sense." "She always put out for me when I wanted—not something every woman did—or most of the time. Handed me her body almost, or turned around with her backside to me, as if saying 'Here, I'm sleepy, not even up to performing, do what you want with it'—but with restrictions of course. Though I think I have her mixed up with someone else. Sorry. She, actually, couldn't be persuaded to do anything she didn't want to. And sure, she was a tremendous ballbreaker too and we wouldn't do it for weeks at a time sometimes because we loathed each other and wanted to live any way but together and even did the separate rooms bit," and his friend said "So why didn't you leave? If something like that happened to me with some girl, I'd say 'Man overboard,' and jump," and he said "Good question. I never understood why, several times, I didn't leave absolutely and indisputably and unreturnably for good. It was during my needy way-down-on-myself period maybe. Maybe I got too comfortable in her house and with her kid and in being to other people a much-admired pretend father. The pleasures of pre-dictably recurrent sex once the enmity ends. That I was a poor lonely putz but at least had a nice house and some family life. Also, I was going nowhere so at least for the time being was somewhere, and so on—you need more reasons? When it was good it was almost okay, blah blah. She needed me lots of times too and when I was out of her life no one missed me more, till the last time when she was giddy at my being gone and stayed that way. 'Aren't we better off now?' she'd say on the phone—I forget who called, probably me with some lame excuse for calling. 'Isn't life really better for you now that we're split?' If I said 'Well, I guess so, but still . . .' she'd say 'No, it is for me and if it isn't for you yet it will be. Wait, my new beau wants to talk to you.' But sometimes, before that, I thought we broke up just so we could get back together again in a month and for a few days, or a day or two, have the wildest most uninhibited and saddest—cries, tears, whoopees—time a couple could. In other words—well, in other words what? I can't think; Elephant beer we had to order. But I found her beautiful—I shouldn't forget that as a reason for staying. I'd look at her nose, eyes, the lips, everything. *Tout le* face. The most gorgeous I'd ever seen in a woman I was close to," and his friend said "That's nuts," and reeled off names. "And they had tits, these women, gigantic to big to medium to only a little bit small, but something there you could squeeze or push your face into," and he said "*Tits.* Why's it matter so much? You need them to feed off of? But I'll never win on that with you. Some guys are like that and some—a few—could care less. None could care nothing, I suppose, but you have to understand there are many other things in a woman, physical and emotional and so on, to supersede if not go way way beyond them. Just as if one guy has an enormous dick and the others don't, big deal, there are so many other things in those men that should be important to a woman, or one would hope they'd be there. Believe me, after the first few days with Evangeline, they didn't—" and his friend said "Bullshit."

His mother's younger brother came out to California on business and took them to dinner. They got a baby-sitter. "If the sitter costs a lot," his uncle said, "since I know how expensive services can be in California and how financially short you two are, I'd like to take care of it," and Gould said no. She laughed a lot at the table, especially at some of the remarks his uncle made and jokes he told. Held his uncle's hand as he walked them to their car, gave him a big kiss and hug good-bye, waved to him as they drove off. She seemed sincere in all this. During the drive home: "I had the most wonderful time tonight, best in ages, and I know why. It was that man. He's so unlike your mother—anyone in your family. Extremely funny, smart, successful, gentle, self-effacing, mannerly. Dashing, even—clothes he wore, things he said, way he spoke, how he handled himself with the overbearing headwaiter and waiters, as if educated at the best prep schools and then at Princeton or Yale and later a year at Oxford or someplace. A very generous and big-hearted person. It was a great evening, thank you," and he said "The food was good too," and she said "Food, food; yes, it was good, excellent, but those things don't make an evening. If the food had been lousy and the service terrible it still would have been a great evening because of him," and he said "I didn't know you went for older men," and she said "Don't be stupid." "I've never met anyone quite like her," his uncle said on the phone a few days later when Gould called him in New York to thank him for the dinner. "She bowled me over. She's a knockout from the word go, a dear young woman too, and intelligent? Oh my gosh. I should have a few like her working on my staff.

What does she see in you, I wonder?—only kidding, my boy. You're one lucky stiff. Don't lose her for anything or ever ruin it by becoming a scoundrel or pretending to be a fool," and he said "Say, when I'm through with her, or vice versa, or by some magic it's mutual, I'll give you her number, though I don't know what Aunt Dee would say," and his uncle said "Excuse me, Gould, and I don't want you to take this as harsh criticism, but as far as foolish behavior's concerned, what you said is exactly what I meant."

Bronson was asleep when Gould passed her room on his way to his and said goodnight to her. She said "May I detain you for a moment?" and he said "Sure, what?" and stood by her door. "Despite all our previous differences, I have to say it's nice having you back, if only for a few days. For all the turmoil and shit we threw at each other, we had plenty of fun too, am I right?" and he said "I'm not complaining." She was in her nightgown, sitting up in bed, holding a book with one hand, other was under the covers on her crotch, it seemed, and seemed to be rubbing or scratching it. "I've seen lots of guys since we split up—you know me—but so far no crushing *inamoratos* or permanent live-ins," and he said "Oh yeah? I'm surprised," and she said "Nobody who interested me that much—I'm so pick-and-choosy as you well know. But there are plenty of single men in the area, not to mention a million college studs who perhaps have become a mite too young for me, and things will eventually work out," and he said "I'm sure." "Do you like my new bed? I bought it a few months ago. Cost me a bundle but I figured if I don't have a live-in to be comfortable with when I sleep, might as well have a great bed, am I right?" and he said "It's what I'd do if I had the dough. The bed in the apartment we sublet is mostly lumps. We sort of sleep around them," and she said "Yours here isn't that comfortable either—I've never slept in it but I have slept on it—but you'll get a good night's sleep if you're tuckered out from your flight," and he said "I hope so. I don't know which time switch is supposed to be harder on your system, east-west or west-east, but I'm all in." "You know, I might as well come to the point why I stopped you, other than to reacquaint ourselves cordially with a pleasant chat. I'm dying to get fritzed by some guy. So if you'd like to, not for old time's sake but only because you'd want to, I'd be willing. Some nights I'm just randier than others and this is one. It could be because you're here and old memories float up—you think that's it? And we were always compatible in the sack, when we weren't pissing each other off famously," and he said "Really, I'm living with someone now and I'd just feel funny about it. And will you please stop whatever you're doing with your hand under the covers? It's distracting, in a way," and she said "I'm scratching myself, my leg, so what's bugging you? I've a bad itch. You want me to put some cortisone cream on it, I will. As for your decision, good, you're entitled, and your girlfriend will be proud of you when you report back on your abstinence, especially when I practically offered myself to you on a saucer, and I'm not going to get testy about it. I'd probably feel the same if I were seeing someone steadily and was a guest of yours in New York, even though wild horses and a million bucks wouldn't drag me to that city, and you were living alone and put the make on me.

But what I'd wish now is that you weren't here so I could place a call to some guy to come over; there are a couple who would," and he said "Do it then, I don't mind," and she said "It's not a question of your minding," and he said "I mean I've no hold over you. I'll keep my door closed; if I have to pee, I won't even go to the bathroom, I'll do it in a jar in my room. And you can explain to the fellow who I am or was and that I won't be disturbing the two of you and if he wants we can all even have a coffee and bagel together in the morning, since I brought a dozen of them with me, and that'll be the routine. Go ahead, call," and she said "Tomorrow, soon after I get Brons to school, I don't want you around here. I want you out, completely, so I can create a little space for whatever choices I might want to make for myself later on," and he said "Listen, you're making it very tough for me, and Brons. He asked me to come. You agreed to it. I'm supposed to be here a week. If I can do it I'll change my reservation to five days, even four. But you knew I couldn't afford a hotel and it cost me some to fly out here," and she said "You're being paid for not working this week, aren't you? so that wouldn't have happened without us," and he said "I took a week's vacation, which means I'll only get one week this summer instead of two. And I put in more than ten unpaid extra hours last week at work just so I could get away. And the flight—the money for it—that's where this week's salary went, for I don't make much, I've told you; it's a crappy job. But if you insist on acting the bitch, then I don't know what. I'll stay with someone a few days, I don't know who, but that'll mean I won't see Brons as much as he expects me to," and she said "You keep writing and calling him as if he's your real son. 'Oh damn,' the kid would say, 'a second week's gone by and he didn't contact me.' Three weeks and it'd be like you disowned him and he'd go into a funk. So then he naturally asked you to cut the whole pineapple and be his dad here for a week. Stop tantalizing him, encouraging him and he won't ask you to come out anymore; that is, after he goes through a month's depression getting over you," and he said "Okay, that's next week, but what do we do about this one? But I'm tired, want to sleep—the east-west, west-east. I don't want to argue; no bad feelings or for Brons to hear us. What do you say we talk about it some more tomorrow?" and she said "You've become so reasonable. When you were last here it would have been all shouts, insults, lots of go-fuck-yourselfs to me, plus under your breath 'you scrawny cunt,' but no discussion. It must be your new girlfriend's influence. Go to bed; and go fuck yourself, you son of a bitch," and picked up her book and resumed reading and he didn't say anything and went to his room. A half hour later he was awakened by something scratching on his door. Scratching stopped and he lay his head back on the pillow and a few seconds later it started again. Went on like that: started, stopped, started, stopped, till he was sitting up in bed. Do they have a cat? Didn't see one today and neither of them spoke of one but he thinks Brons mentioned a cat in one of his letters or on the phone. This might even be the room it most likes to sleep in; a kitty litter box could be somewhere around, under the bed, though there's no smell of one, and wouldn't one of them have told him that the cat might come in for it? It could even be Brons scratching, pretending he's a cat, but so excited he's here, wants to sleep in the same room with him and even has his sleeping bag with him. He said from the bed "Yes? Anyone there?" "Excuse me," she said, "I hope I didn't wake you, but I was wrong before and want to apologize, may I come in?" and he said "Sure, it's your house," and she opened the door and said "Say no if you don't want me in here; it's all right, guests get special privileges, which is just one of the things I want to apologize for," and he opened the covers, since he knew it'd really get bad between them if he didn't screw her and then maybe indicated it was what he'd wanted since he got here, and said "You probably can't see it, but I've turned back the covers for you on the left side of the bed—my left—so if you want to join me, come on, it's late," and she got in bed, hugged him and said "I'm not so bad and you're kinda keen," and pulled off her nightgown and they started to make love. A minute later she took her lips off his and said "Don't you have anything to say?" and he said "About what?" and she said "That you really don't want me here and are only cooperating because you think I'll be a shrew to you the next few days and you have no other place to stay," and he said "You got this from my kissing? Not at all. We're doing it, I'm enjoying it, so let's continue till we've finished it. And though you usually felt that talking during it, or muttering or howling some sexy or bawdy words—'sexy, bawdy, lips, toes, fingers, ears'—heightened it, I never did," and she said "Okay, we'll be silent for now." "Still side-by-side on our backs?" when they got to that point and she asked "The bed's too narrow for it?" and he said "That too; but the truth is it's never been my preferred position for the ultimate thing. So I'm asking if you still insist on it?" and she said "That part of my body hasn't changed since you left. And you used to get off on it, so what are you looking for, rockets, red glares? Maybe it is the bed. Why don't you sleep in mine with me while you're here," and he said "How would Brons take it? He thinks I only came out for him," and she said "He can still think that. But he's hip to all the shit older people do and lay on each other and their demanding needs and is also able to separate what you mean to him and what you and I do together as an adult team. He hasn't the hangups you eastern idiots do at his age and I've done everything I can to help him avoid them. Believe me, if he happened to barge into my room tomorrow and saw us screwing away he'd say something like "I knew you two would end up doing that," but know that if it makes me happy then it's gotta be okay and can only benefit him with my bettered temperament. You forget what he was like."

He's sleeping with her the morning after they first made love when Brons wedges himself between them, finally pushes him apart from his mother—he's been holding her from behind with one arm, other's back in the shoulder sling—and curls up to her with his arm over her shoulder and falls asleep. She has her nightgown on—must have got up sometime after they first fell asleep to do it—and Brons is in diapers and rubber pants and T-shirt. Gould doesn't like the feel or smell of him in bed—the kid must have peed in his diapers—and gets up, dresses, shoulder's killing him and he takes aspirins, wants to make coffee but doesn't see any grounds or a pot (turns out she

221

only drinks herbal tea; for guests: instant coffee or Sanka, both of which he can't stand), wants some toast (only bread here is packaged sliced white; rolls he brought for dinner they finished last night), has a cracker and glass of water (juice in the fridge is apple and much too sweet and he hasn't drunk milk for twenty years) and sits in the kitchen reading a book (would have liked starting the day with a paper; she'd said she has one delivered and he went outside to look for it; turns out it's the local afternoon daily she gets) and waiting for them to get up. He doesn't know how she lives like this: sliced white, instant coffee or tasteless tea, kid in her bed (turns out Brons has been coming into her bed almost every morning for months and despite Gould complaining about it, continues for another half year) stinking of piss. Two Siamese, looking like twins, both cross-eyed and with dark coloring and skinny sinister faces, meow at him, probably for food. He finds a box of cat Kibble, replenishes their food bowl and gives them fresh water and they hiss at him and don't eat or drink and one swipes at his ankles with its claws out. He wants to toss what water's left in the glass at them but she might later ask how'd they get wet and if he told her—oh, he could make up an excuse but he thinks she'd see through it—bad things could start between them and he wants to stay the two weeks. House is nice, sex good and she's lively and bright in her way and funny sometimes and good-looking.

He was going out there again two years later and called a few days before he left. "I'll be in the area, staying for two days at a hotel in San Francisco, and thought, if you and Brons were going to be around, I'd rent a car and drive down, would it be okay?" and Brons got on the extension while she was saying "I don't know, let me look at my schedule," and said "You haven't been here for years, Gould, and you promised. If you don't want to see me, say so, and you won't have to come all the way here," and he said "I wanted to see you—a lot—but didn't have the money to. This time my job's sending me, but if you're really that angry with me and don't want—" and Brons said "I didn't say that; I do. It'd be interesting," and she said "Sure, come; Brons wants to check you out and see if you lost any more hair. Funny, because we were talking about you last night," and Brons said "Two weeks ago, Mommy," and she said "A few days ago then, but mostly about hereditary and your hair," and Brons said "She said I'm never getting bald like you because of her and my dad." Drove down; she had a frame shop now and barely got by. Took them out to dinner. After it Brons said "Stay the night? We can play together and tomorrow you can have breakfast with me before I go to school . . . or maybe I don't have to," and she said "You have to. Gould staying overnight is all right though, and I'll make no demands," and Brons said "What, having sex with him?" and she said "That's not even a question. I meant I won't ask him to do any repair work for me, which I need dearly." Later, after reading to Brons in his room and then sitting in the dark talking to him till he was asleep, he knocked on her door and said "Goodnight, Evangeline, sleep well," and she said "Open the door and see what I've done to my room; you haven't even looked." "It's okay," and she said "Please, I've remodeled it entirely at a terrific expense that wiped me out financially for a year. I'm such an ignoramus about such things, but you know me and aesthetics and where I have to get the absolutely right thing," and he opened the door, she was in bed nude from the waist up, rest of her under the covers so maybe she was nude there too, four-poster with drooping canopy that looked as if it was going to fall in, flowery wallpaper, the flower parts furry and raised, gas lamp fixtures and globes on the wall, textiles and fabrics gracefully draped over much of the furniture, electrified kerosene lamps and Oriental rugs, thick blood-colored curtains that dragged on the floor. "What do you think?—Oh, my chest; I thought you'd never notice." He quickly looked around the room for one he must have missed. "As you can see I'm no longer self-conscious about my tits. People have taken me for a boy so long that one day I just said 'screw it' and I've even sat around like one on the beach and nobody seemed to know the difference. So that's where I am. Feeling much better about my bod. Next time a ladies' room is jammed and I'm wearing pants and I have to go bad, I'm going to comb my hair back and pee in the men's john. Not even a bra anymore. It was presumptuous of me all these years to wear one, and I've begun to appreciate the freedom of nothing swinging there and it's a big help when I run. Which I do a lot these days—I didn't tell you. I'm even getting to the marathon stage and Brons occasionally alleviates the boredom of it by bicycling beside me, although there I always wear a top. But you haven't said yet what you think of my room. You look numb-struck." All this talk and her breasts—her goal? even if it wasn't—got him excited and he said "Nice, I like. Not a single guy's room perhaps, but handsome, in good taste, well designed. Almost like a stage set, and the comparison meant in the best sense, you understand—for a Chekhov play maybe if one of them had a scene in a bedroom. And maybe that's what you should go into—study and later work at—stage designing, but I'll leave that up to you," and she said "No, the stage, my biggest bust. Oops, I didn't mean that, I swear," and slid under the covers to her neck and suddenly he caught on and laughed. "By the way, and I can see your erection through the pants, or did a minute ago, so it's not like what I'm about to suggest is coming out of nowhere or you should feel obligated to be taken aback by it—" and he said "Really, Evangeline, it was fun last time but ultimately didn't work out. Brons later wrote me—" and she said "That little conniver was only putting the screws on you, hoping it would make you feel guilty enough to fly right back. But fine, no pressure, though I want you to know there are no preliminary preps for it anymore or chance I could ever get pregnant. I had my tubes tied, another move to free myself completely. Such a relief to be able to fuck without inserting anything right before and that stinky cream or taking potentially risky pills or slowly getting bled to death by those intrauterines or having a man snap on one of those deadening balloons and then clog up my toilet with it when he later drops it in," and he said "The bags don't do that, do they? I mean, once they're off, they're so small and pliable they'd just go down," and she said "It happened once or else the plumber was teasing me, and he even said he'd show me it in a pail. Anyway, I suppose you have to leave tomorrow, so tonight's gotta be the night," and he said "It's not that I don't feel like it. But there's also this woman in

New York who I'll probably end up marrying—that's how far it's gone," and she said "Oh come on, what's one time? If it's only her, you don't say anything, and if you have to tattle on yourself, she'll understand we were once like man and wife so it's sort of natural we'd do it. If it's also Brons, we'll be quiet and discreet, barely a peep from me and from you just a muffled groan. And soon as we're done, you scoot to your room. Or even if you're done and I'm not even halfway there, though I hope that won't happen—you scoot. So what do you say? It's just something I really feel like doing now and I'll try never to ask it of you again," and sat up and held out her arms for him, covers fell to her waist, and he shut the door, undressed, said "Maybe I should pee first," and she said "In a jar or something in the room, but no going down the hall again and waking Brons," and he said "I always feel it's better with an empty bladder and that I can stay up longer, but okay," and got in bed. She was naked, immediately grabbed his penis and said "Now you're cuffed and going nowhere for a while, you got that?" and they laughed and kissed and in a few minutes he was ready to come and frantically grabbed her to get inside her and just did when he was done and she said "If I was brand-new at this I'd have to ask 'Is this all there is to it? What was all the hoopla over losing it for?' You wouldn't rest a little and then start again, just so I could get even close to halfway there?" and he said "I better not, we were pushing it as it was," and she said "Then give me something to wipe myself with; it feels like your girlie hasn't let you do it to her for weeks," and he got up, gave her his handkerchief, she used it and turned over and said "Before you leave, shut the light." Just then Brons knocked. "What are you two doing in there? That's not fair. You said you only wanted to see me, Gould," and he said "That was the main reason, why do you think different?" putting on his pants, kicking his sneakers and socks under the bed. "I was fixing something for your mother—the curtain, it was falling off," and went to the window while he slipped on his shirt. "Come in if you don't believe me," and Brons came in and Gould tugged on the curtain, one eye cocked to the top of it and said to her "I think it's okay now. This thing come down on you, oh boy, it's so heavy it could have smothered you, or at least him. How'd you ever get a rod strong enough to hold it?" "You bullthrower," Brons said. "All you wanted was to do sex with her, that's why you stay with us," and ran to his room and slammed his door. "What should I do?" he asked her and she said "Like everything: deal with it, make an excuse. You're an adult, so think of something winning and convincing. Lie your head off if you have to, or tell him the truth, that we're adults and this is something we sometimes feel the need to do, even when we're not on the greatest terms with each other: screw," and shut the light. He went to Brons's room, knocked, no answer, went in, room was dark, said "Brons? Brons?" and sat on the floor, felt around the bed for a hand and took it and put it to his cheek and Brons pulled it away and Gould took it again and just held it. "You know I love you more than I do any kid there is. If you lived in New York I'd want you to stay with me. Your mom wouldn't like it, she'd want you with her, of course, but it's what I'd want most of all. I'd send you to school. I'd be there every day when you got home. I'd arrange my work schedule around you. I'd have to get a better job, meaning a steady one rather than the freelance junk I do now, but I'd do it for you. But we got these three thousand miles between us, and I don't know what . . ." and Brons said "Then what are you saying?" and he said "I'm glad you weren't asleep," and Brons said "I asked you a question," and he said "That it makes things so tough," and Brons said "Besides, I have a father. He sees me when he can and he mostly lives in California or is always driving through here and Evangeline says he'll be with me much more in two years. I don't need you and I never want to see you again," and Gould said "Don't say that," and Brons said nothing and Gould said "Have it your own way then but it's certainly not what I want," and thought of going to his room but felt that'd hurt Brons so he stayed on the floor holding his hand, wanting to say something that'd make things better between them or just leave Brons feeling good but not coming up with anything, till he was sure Brons was asleep. When he was in his own room he thought Funny I didn't think this, it would have made me feel better while I was there, but all the time I was on the floor he didn't pull his hand out of mine. Though maybe he was too tired to. Next morning he got up early to go to the toilet, flushed it when he was done, Brons shouted "What's that?" and Evangeline yelled from her room "You moron, Gould. Didn't it occur to you the flushing would wake him? Now he'll never get back to sleep and he got to bed late last night because of you," and he said "I flushed it because there was crap in the bowl," and she said "So what! We can live with crap, even yours. It won't stink up the place right away. First one in later would have flushed it down. It's you effete faggoty Easterners who can't live unless you flush everything down at once, even just a drop of pee. But there's a water shortage now," and he said "There's always a water shortage here," and she said "But this is a real drought going on and we're supposed to be conserving water, something you wasteful New Yorkers wouldn't know of because you have all the water in the world. The water goes to the wrong people," and Brons said "Mom, I'll try to get back to sleep; I'm still tired," and he said "Brons, excuse me, but I'm going to be leaving shortly," and Brons said "So? Leave," and she said "Just don't make noise slamming the front door either, and make sure it's locked. We never had to do that till you people started settling out here in droves," and he said "My people?" and ran to her door and said "My people! What *about* them? If they can afford it they can't live where they want?" and she said "I said 'you people,' not yours. I didn't mean Jews this time. I meant people from out of state the last five years, and mostly not from the West Coast. Good-bye, Gould, and don't forget your sneakers," and turned over on her side, away from him. He got his sneakers and socks, shut her door because he didn't want her hearing him talking to Brons, dressed and went into Brons's room and said "Your mom would kill me for this, my waking you up again if you're asleep, but one last kiss good-bye?" and got no answer and Brons's eyes stayed shut and he repeated the last part about the kiss good-bye and got no answer and he left.

She took a dance class one night a week and once he peeked into the teacher's dance studio to watch. It was dark, not even a moon, Brons was sleeping in the car, slight smell of fall: decomposing leaves, smoke from a nearby fireplace, crisp air. She was in a leotard and tights, hair pinned up, thin face radiant, lively eyes, forehead wet and sweat dripping down her neck, barefoot. She danced so well, terrific leaps, bounds, twirls, strides, whatever the steps and things dancers do are called, it seemed she had the perfect body for it, even the neck was right, hair, long thin fingers and arms, legs looking more solid in the tights, square shoulders with a little knob on top apiece, her hard rear, small waist, the chest. She should have been a dancer, he thought. In the car, for he'd come to pick her up, he said "You should've been a dancer," and she said "Were you playing voyeur before? Themis hates when people look in," and he said "No, just that you look and move like one, so graceful, athletic. And the way you're still even breathing hard, which shows what you must have put into it, and you seem to love it so much," and she said "You really think so, you're not just saying? Because I've been thinking the same thing, but no 'I should've.' Even if I'm past twenty-five I thought there's still time. Not to be a lead dancer or anything like that. I'd be happy simply to be in the corps or maybe a little past it—a small ensemble role, you know the kind: all six together doing the same steps—of a good company. If I got into the San Francisco Conservatory would you move with me there if it became too difficult to commute?" and he said "Sure, I like that city and always wanted to live in it," but that was the last he heard of it from her and he never spoke of it again. But something about her looks and outfit, sweaty serious expression, yellow leotard and black tights, bare feet, hair up, hands on her hips and one leg sort of pointing out as she listened to the teacher, hand on one hip as she stretched on the barre in front of the long wall mirror, everyone applauding her, it seemed, after she did one piece of dancing where she raced across the room several times and made lots of big leaps, head bent down afterward modestly acknowledging the applause, that made him feel he was never so much in love with her as at that one time. Looking through the window, no light on him and hidden on both sides by bushes, he thought if he were a stranger looking in now he'd love to get to know that woman. She's beautiful, serious, unpretentious, seemingly intelligent, talented and with one of the supplest most agile little bodies he's ever seen. She said in the car "You're a real dearie for saying things I occasionally need to hear, but meaning them, not just to please," and pulled him into a dreamy kiss. "The kid," he said, thumbing to the back and she said "Another real dearie, still fast asleep." They drove home holding hands most of the way, he steering with his left and only when the car was lurching back and forth or about to stall, taking his other hand from hers to shift gears with the floor stick.

He was once very high, thought he was going crazy, was seeing and hearing eerie things he couldn't make out, then he was a bug with his head clamped between another bug's legs, next he was in a dark cell, his arms and legs chained to the wall, rats crawling through the ceiling grate and chewing his shoes off and then biting his toes, she talked to him, said what he thinks he's experiencing really doesn't exist, he was home, in the living room, on Euclid Avenue, right next to the Presbyterian church, the choir's practicing right now but you don't seem to hear, Brons is sleeping in his own room and please don't wake him with your groans and yells, walked him around the house for an hour, fed him coffee and aspirins and a couple of tranquilizers and then called a friend who drove over with a combination of stronger pills that would bring him down and make him sleep, she got him into bed and held him, saying things like "It's okay, nothing to worry about, only a bad trip that's ending, last time for that, right?—we're off that junk for good because it can happen to anybody no matter how stable and placid you've been till then. I'm here for you always, my baby, and tomorrow you'll be up and at 'em and bouncing around as usual. Now shut your eyes, it's all going away from the medicine you took or will soon. Rest, rest," and rubbed his forehead and stroked his eyelids and put her head on his chest and they slept like that till late morning, Brons awaking much earlier and looking in, he said, and seeing them asleep and knowing it was Sunday from the church bells tolling, got his own breakfast and then played outside with his Tonka steam shovel and trucks.

He couldn't stand her smoking and she was constantly giving it up. He once dumped her last packs into the trash can outside when she asked him to and she ran out a few hours later to retrieve them and smoke from one. She smoked before she went to bed, sometimes in bed while he was reading, first thing when she woke up, in restaurants over their food, in the car with the windows up, on their walks and the one camping trip they all took, spoiling the fresh air, on the beach when she'd ask him to help her light one because of the wind. He told her that his mother, when he was a boy, always seemed surrounded by cigarette smoke. "Two packs a day, sometimes three, and these extra long ones—Pall Malls; the smell in the house was execrable; even my father, who smoked a lousy cigar at night, complained of it and her breath, though his smoke I didn't seem to mind that much and for some reason quickly dissipated. To kiss her I felt I had to wave a wall of smoke away just to see her face. She kidded me about it but I hated the stench and I don't know how many times I got burned by her or one of her cigarettes left around. It kept me—I'm sure of this—from getting closer to her even emotionally and I didn't even want to use a towel she'd used, because of the cigarette smell on it, or get too near the clothes she had on." She laughed and said "So it at least stopped you from having a too-comfortable relationship with her and becoming a mama's boy or from even marrying your mother—a good thing, I'd think," and he said "The truth is— and of course what you say about my mother and me is absurd—that I could never marry a woman who smokes," and she said "Why in hell would you ever think I'd marry you, if you were referring to me?" "So I should cross that possibility off my list, is that it? But if it doesn't remain one then I don't see how I can hang around here that much longer. I eventually want to get married to someone, have my own kid, maybe a second," and she said "Yes, for certain, cross it off with me. I've had my child. To me one's more than enough, to have and to handle. I want to do things, not just bring up babies. You want to have one, two, as many as you want—many bedrooms filled with them; I don't want many bedrooms; two's fine and a third for guests—do it with someone else or several women. You could still live here while you're off inseminating, I wouldn't mind, unless you took one of these reproducers too seriously and I wasn't getting my time's worth from you and began to look like a fool. And when the baby's reached a certain age, long past being toilet trained in both departments and a good clean eater. What I'm saying is no big messes on the floor and in its pants and broken bowls. When it gets into kindergarten or first grade, really, so is out of the house a minimum of six hours a weekday, it can come live with us, if its mother doesn't mind, and permanently if she wants to give it up to its dad. I think I'd like a second child that way, and by that time, but only with your assistance and financial support, and because Brons should pretty well be on his own by then, there wouldn't be that much work to do for it, so it'd be something I could manage while doing all my other things," and he said "But your smoking, and I'm being serious here—you don't think you could do something about it? At least cut it way down and try to keep it out of my food and hair and the room we sleep in?" and she said "Giving it up entirely or cutting back on it is something I'd only do for myself. And after all my starts at it and quick stops, it's obvious I'm not ready yet. I suppose I can keep it out of the bedroom and blow it away from your plate, but that's probably as far as I can control it for now."

Soon after she awakes she says "Goodness, I just remembered, I have a lunch date with an old girlfriend. Do you want to join us or do you think I can leave Brons with you here?" and he says "What do you prefer? It seems like you want to go alone, which is understandable," and she says "No difference. You certainly won't embarrass me and I feel confident, short a time as I know you, that you won't jump the first gorgeous friend I introduce you to, and even if you did—well, that'd save me a whole lot of aggravation later on," and he says "Actually, my shoulder hurts, from last night, I think, so I'd like to stay put today," and she says "Then I can leave Brons with you? You won't doze off and let him run into the street?" and she tells him what Brons might like for lunch, "though he can be a fussy eater and there's no guarantee he'll open his mouth," that he still takes naps once or twice a week, "so if you're lucky, this may be the day," gives him books to read to Brons if he gets too wild or bored, "or really anytime, he loves them," and goes and he asks Brons what he wants to do while his mother's gone, "play alone awhile, maybe?" and Brons says "Play," and he says "But alone, by yourself, here, in your room, what? Because if you do then I have things to do myself," and Brons says "Play," and he says "Okay, I know, but where, I'm saying, and with whom? Yourself, alone, with me, here or some other place, outside or in? You have to understand, Brons, I'm not familiar . . . I don't know how to take care of kids . . . I haven't done it before, though you'll be safe with me, that you also have to understand, but I really don't even know how to talk to them . . . kids, I mean, little boys and girls like you. So once again, what do you want to do? Because if you just want to stay in your room alone, or here, and play by yourself awhile—" and Brons goes into his room and Gould says "Okay, fine, but I'll be here, and if you need any help in the bathroom, call me," and gets his typewriter out and Brons comes back with a box of blocks and empties it at Gould's feet and they start building things, later draw with crayons, dress several stuffed animals, go outside and he pushes Brons around in the bed of his big dump truck, puts him into his high chair and the food in front of him on the chair tray and Brons stares at it and he says "Want me to feed you? Your mom said you might and she even instructed me how. Showed me how to do it. With a spoon, only a spoon, you're too young yet for a serrated knife and pronged fork. Well, all forks have prongs—that's the pointy part—and I'm only kidding . . . just the spoon, and a special one, I see, with Daisy Duck on the handle. Where'd you get it? Because you look like a Donald fan, but that's sexist . . . you know what that means. Nice applesauce, so open, open wide. Do I sound like a dentist about to extract a tooth rather than a surrogate mother wanting to shove food in?" and Brons laughs and Gould says "For my own information, because maybe it's something I can use with you later on, but what was it particularly that made you laugh?" and Brons just looks at him deadpan and he says "Why did you laugh?—you know, ha-ha, ha-ha," and makes a face as if he's laughing and Brons laughs and he says "But why, before?" and Brons says something that sounds like "I dunno," and sticks his spoon into the bowl and bringing it to his mouth half the applesauce on it goes to the floor and Gould takes the spoon and feeds him the applesauce and a mashed-up hard-boiled egg mixed with mayonnaise and later he says "So, that was easy; my motto should be 'Yuck it up, feed the pup,' right? . . . no?" and Brons starts raising the chair tray and Gould helps him out and down and they walk to the market a few blocks away, get pastries and bread and lettuce for tonight and a juice for Brons now and after Brons drinks it Gould says "Listen, first thing before we head home, and maybe I shouldn't have given you that juice till we got there, but do you have to make caca or pee pee or whatever you call them? Because I remember seeing a boys' room in the market," and Brons points to his pants and says "Wet," and he says "Oh great . . . okay, but we'll deal with that later . . . I guess you'll just take your underpants off and put on another pair of whatever you wear. Why didn't your mother warn me about this, or why didn't I ask her?" and Brons says something again that sounds like "I dunno," and then something accompanied by motions that seems to mean he can't walk home, too tired, and Gould says "I'm afraid you have to. I've a bad shoulder—this part—and it hurts like the dickens, very bad, very bad. I think I broke it. Break, like you break a stick—smack!" and demonstrates with his fists, "and I can't carry you, okay?" and Brons looks as if he's about to cry and he says "You really can't walk home?" and Brons says no and he gets on one knee and moves him onto his good shoulder sidesaddle and carefully stands so as to put all the pressure on that shoulder and carries him this way, every half block or so getting on the same knee and letting Brons off and saying "Can you walk now? All rested?" and Brons saying no and looking as if he's about to cry, so Gould continuing to carry him. At home Brons says "Ead," and he says "Eat?" and Brons shakes his head and says "Ead, ead," and he says "What?" and Brons takes his hand and leads him to the pile of books Evangeline left and

Gould says "Oh, so which one do you want me to? . . . wait, your pants, you said you were wet," and Brons says "No I am," and he says "Excuse me, but do you mind?" and sticks his hand down the back of Brons's shorts—cloth diapers—doesn't want to put his hand inside but the outside of them feel dry and he says "You think you should go to the potty now?" and Brons shakes his head and he says "You know, to pee pee, or even caca; just so you don't do it in your pants," and Brons says "Ead," and they sit on the couch and he reads to him and explains each illustration and during it Brons gets on his lap and then holds Gould's hand and he thinks it's such a small hand, those finger-nails, it's like a little dog's paw and puts it against his and says "See how much bigger mine is? I'm not boasting, but some day—" and Brons says "Ead, ead," and he finishes the book and starts another and Brons almost falls off his lap reaching for the first book and puts it in front of Gould and says "Again." Evangeline comes home while he's still reading and he says "This kid's such a sweetheart, I can't tell you, he couldn't have been better," and she says "I'm glad you two got along," and he says "More than that and I'm not saying it to impress you. Ask him. Just one thing though; he didn't urinate once since you left. Not in his," and points behind Brons to his shorts, "or in the WC, though I didn't walk him there. I hate to be a worrywart but I was wondering if it could be some kind of urological problem," and she says "It's okay, I like it that you're worrying. But he's probably done it by now, or if you felt in his pants you just didn't dig deep enough. I'll change him," and when she comes back he says "Truly, I never knew a kid that age could be so charming," and she says "A lot can, some are even more advanced than that, but I'm glad it's him," and he's not sure what she means but doesn't ask her to explain: she might think him dense.

She liked taking baths with him—"Gould, I'm in the tub, want to join me?" or "Want to take a bath together?" and he said "I already showered today," and she said "So take it just to relax"—sitting on him with her back to his chest and his penis floating or sticking up between her legs. "So this is what I'd look like with one," she said the first time. "But I'd like mine clean, I never see you really wash your cock—go on, show me how you do it," and he said "Come on, what am I, Brons? I'm the cleanest guy around, often to the point of manic-compulsiveness," and she said "Your hands, yes, but I'm serious about this: I want to know how clean something is that goes so deep inside me," and he washed it with his hands and then splashed the soap off and she said "That's washing it? You didn't scrub; you missed several parts. What about all those folds there and the hole? You don't open it to wash inside?" and he said "That'd burn; what I did was enough. I've been doing it like that most of my penis's adult life and never had a rash or sore or anything like that on it and no smell or smegma ever," and she said "Will you permit me?" and grabbed it and he thought she was going to play with it and he lay back and rested his head on the top of the tub and shut his eyes and she washed it hard with a soapy washrag—"Hey, take it easy!"—seemed to get at almost every part but the eye, and then she said "What about the balls?" and he said "Leave them alone," and she said "Do you ever wash them? Because silky and clean as they might feel, they're just as liable to be dirty. And though they don't go in me they do often sleep against me or at least roll around on the sheet and there's hair on them and hair collects germs like nothing does," and he said "I do wash them, but in my own way: very gently. I know just the places where if I washed them even a little less than very gently, it'd hurt like mad. So never touch them, or if you do, then very lightly, but never the balls parts—only the top of the scrotum without the balls, okay? No, best you never touch them at all; a woman could never know how sensitive they are," and just with her hand this time she washed his penis but the way she was doing it with the soap it seemed more to get him hard and then tried putting it in her but it didn't work and the two or three other times they tried doing it in the tub like this it didn't work and she said one of those times "I wonder why men can't keep it stiff in water," and he said "What about women, not that I've truthfully ever tried doing it in a tub with anyone else, but are you so slick and open inside?" and she said "I think so," and raised her rear above the water and he felt her and she was. "Well then I'm sorry, it must be the warm water," and she said "Cold would make it worse even," and he said "Then maybe we should try something in-between," and they let the cold water run till the tub was lukewarm and then tried doing it and it still didn't work and then let the water get cool and it didn't work and he said "I'm sure there are some men who can do it in any temperature or some who are better at hot than cool and so on, but I'm just not one."

The tiger outfit she liked to wear and wore it till it was threadbare. It went from her neck to her ankles, one piece, long-sleeved, fastened with a couple of hooks near the neck in back, black and faded orange stripes, some material like muslin, bought for a buck at Goodwill. She never knew what to put on her feet with it—"Tiger in sneakers? Sandals, socks? Better I go barefoot," but she only did around the yard or house. When she wore it to the local supermarket or in town people would occasionally stare and a few times she quickly mussed up her hair till it was like a mane and raised her hands into tiger's paws and growled at them and once snapped. "Listen," he said, "people just haven't seen an outfit like this, so what are you doing that to them for? It's embarrassing, unpleasant; not like you," and she said "It's the skin that's making me do it. Anyway, nobody really minds. A pretty girl, you once said, can get away with almost anything like that, and a pretty tiger, but a small domesticated one, well maybe even more so," and he said "I find the scene ugly. Just don't ever bitch at me when I get stupid and rude," and she said "Oh brother, you sure have a nice way of putting it," and slid her nails across his cheek. She usually wore nothing underneath it, at the most a bikini brief, and she liked saying to him when they got home, if Brons was at someone else's house or sleeping in the car seat, something about how tiger and man should mate, and she continued pretending to be the tiger in bed, moving around on all fours, bounding over him, landing with her hands on his chest, scratching, hissing, snarling, rolling over playfully, ending up on her back with her arms and legs in the air and saying something like "Now's the optimum time, tiger's in extreme heat, take it any vaginal way you like, it won't bite off your head, whatever interdictions it had to the other customary positions are temporarily suspended."

For the first month after they left his parents' apartment they couldn't find any other place to live in New York but a single room in a halfway house. To pay for their room and board he did odd jobs for the woman who owned it: washed dishes, bussed tables, painted rooms, applied some sulfuric acid solution to the five flights of marble steps to take out the stains in them from about fifty years. Then they got an apartment and the woman claimed they owed her eighty dollars in back rent and he said he'd worked off the entire four weeks' room and board and she even owed him some dough for all the hours he put in at minimum wage and the woman said she'd take him to small claims court if he didn't pay and he said "Okay, I don't want any trouble or bad feelings between us, I think you're wrong but I'll come up with the money some way," and back in the room Evangeline said "Like hell we'll pay. What do I have to do, teach you how to talk back and get what's due you? Your father, for all his ugliness to Brons and me and his cheap picayune ways, would have known what to say: 'Eat pig meat, you bloodsucking bastard, and all the junk carts you rolled in on.' Because she's cheating you blind. You worked hard, at slave wages, scarred your fingers through the gloves on that lethal acid and maybe your lungs too, when she could have got a much safer but more expensive cleaner. She knew a jellyfish when she caught one but she's not going to bulldoze me," and he said

"Better we go along with it than risk a court case and have to pay double, is what I heard those judgments against you can be," and she said "Horsecrap. This is what we do," and they told the woman they'd pay the day they left, "Say around eleven or noon we should be all finished," he said, and Evangeline asked an actor friend to drive by at six that morning, there was a blizzard going, ten or so inches already and the actor was an hour and a half late and could barely get his car down the street through the snow, the woman was shoveling a path on the sidewalk and she said "Mr. Bookbinder?" when she saw him carrying some things to the car and he said "Just loading up for the first trip, Mrs. M. I'll see you when I get back, if I can make it in this snow," and she said "No funny business now. I've seen all kinds, you know," and he said "Don't worry, I'm leaving my family behind as collateral," and after the car was packed and the actor was at the wheel and the motor was running he went back to the room and said "This is terrible, and really bad for the kid to see, let's just pay her," and Evangeline said "No, we're going. Just keep walking and I swear, if she tries stopping us I'm going to push that woman, I don't care if she slips and breaks a leg," and he said "No pushing," and they left the building and started down the long stoop, which Mrs. M. had just cleared but it already had what seemed like a half inch on it; she was at the second-story window and threw it open and yelled "You come back here, Bookbinders; I'll have the police after you by the time you get there," and as they drove away he said "Let's go back; I'll write her a check. It'll be my money, not yours. She'll find us through our new phone number and we can be thrown in jail for beating out on the rent. Or I can—you, they'll say you've got to take care of your boy," and she said "She'll never chase after us for eighty smelly bucks. And serves the greedy yid right—I wish she had come at me and broken a leg," and he said "She isn't Jewish; what is it always with you? This is New York; you're not in the foothills. And she's Irish or something, maybe Welsh or Scottish, judging by her name. What's Macreedy?" he asked the actor and the actor said "Could be anything like you said but not Italian," and she said "Jewish, don't tell me. Maybe not the name, but she is. Macreedy's probably her husband who ran away from her like us, and in a hateful snowstorm also, but thirty years ago. Or she took the name out of a phonebook so she wouldn't be known as Jewish. But who can't see what she is by that big flabby nose and the Shylock way she treats people, pound of your foreskin or half pound of your balls," and he said "I don't know who I dislike more now, you or her. . . . I'm sorry, Brons, and I'm sorry, whatever your name is, driver, actor," and the actor said "Go ahead, say your spiel, don't mind me. What I'm doing today's a favor I owe Ev, so what's between you's between you," and he said "Why, what'd she do for you?" and the actor said "Another favor, friend to friend, but enough for me to stick my car's neck out in this blitz. . . . Gray," and shook Gould's hand and Gould said "Gould," and to Evangeline in back "Anyway, you're going to have to tell me you know how wrong it is what you said about Mrs. M. and that particular religious thing in general," and she said "You don't know what you're talking about now, so why should I?" and he said "You mean you're saying you don't know what I'm talking about," and she said "Yes, subject closed."

Books he read and then gave her that she got more out of than him. When friends seemed to intimate to him she was pretty or beautiful but not too smart he said "She's a much better reader than I. You should see her. Books I had trouble with, sometimes had to work hard to finish, she winged through and had insights into I never approached. Her intelligence is natural; she's shortchanged herself in not going through and past high school, but you can't say she doesn't speak well." She said she couldn't stand poetry, it wasn't that she didn't get it, though some of it no one could get; it was that most of it was useless and precious and made for fairies or textbooks and she was ashamed whenever he took a book of poems along with him when they went out, except the ones in both English and German or French or Spanish, because then people would think he was just trying to learn the language. "As for the others—keep them in your pocket, read them in the car in secret or when you're alone on the bus or just at home, but don't take them out in restaurants while we're waiting for a table or on the movie line. If you have to read anything at those places, why not history or stick with your good fiction, though to really please me I wish you'd take to books on investing money or how to repair my house."

Brons wanted a dry cereal the New York halfway house didn't provide and Evangeline said they were out of toothpaste and dental floss and while she was at it they could also all use new toothbrushes and he said he'd go out to buy them and she said "I didn't mean you had to do it tonight," and he said "Ah, I want to take a walk, this house is sometimes like a prison." At the market he got the cereal and a box of animal crackers for

Brons, went to the drug section and saw that except for the floss the dental stuff was expensive. He held three toothbrushes, put back the one he'd chosen for himself, dropped the floss into the basket with the cereal and crackers and then thought Screw it, do it, you just don't have the cash and Evangeline will like you got everything she needed, and after quickly looking up and down the aisle and only seeing an old lady facing the other way, slipped the brushes and toothpaste into his side coat pocket. Oy, God, what'd he do? why'd he do it? and looked up and saw the woman staring at him, hand to her mouth as if horrified at what she'd just seen, or maybe not and she was only staring that way because of how he looked: messed-up hair, rather shabby clothes, face which for a few moments must have gone pale and looked sick and frenetic—but she seemed to have seen him, he was almost sure of it—now she was turned away, facing shelves with cleaning and diaper things for babies and feminine hygiene—the look one has when catching someone in the act like that but one you'd never do yourself, but if she did see him he didn't think she'd tell anyone in the store while he was still there, she was old, frail-looking, very thin and short, she'd be afraid, for instance, she'd by chance bump into him on the street one day and he'd recognize her and knock her down, something he'd never do but maybe his appearance to her said he might. Should he put the brushes and toothpaste back? "Oh look at me," he could say to himself aloud, hoping she'd turn around so he could say it half to her too, "I'm so absentminded, I don't know where my head is today, excuse me," putting the brushes and toothpaste back in the racks, "I don't know if you saw them with me before but if you did I hope you didn't get the wrong idea, it was just a stupid mistake," or say all this but first look befuddled and slap his pocket and say "Holy shit—excuse me," and take the things out and put them in the basket and then walk around casually for a while, get one more thing—cheap bag of chips—and pay for all of it. No—something about what she was doing now, keenly interested in a row of different shampoos on the top shelf—she didn't see him and he had an idea and said "May I help you, ma'am?" and she turned to him and looked a bit startled but didn't back away, which he should take as a good sign—it was just his appearance; he also needed a shave—and he smiled and said "Sorry, didn't mean to startle you, but I was just thinking, you need any help there . . . reaching?" and she said "No thanks, I was only comparison shopping," and he said "Prices better here? Where else do you shop? I thought this was the only large market in ten blocks," and she said "Associated, on Ninth Avenue, two blocks west, but they're much more expensive on almost everything and the quality isn't as good," and he said "Oh yeah? That's good to know; I'll tell my wife," and from the way she smiled and said good-bye—neither seemed fake—he was almost sure she hadn't seen him but he'll still, just in case she did and only tells them after he leaves, not go by the front of the store for a week or in it for two or three, or he might never have to go in again, since by then he and Evangeline will have their own place uptown. He got a bag of chips, two oranges on sale and went to the shortest checkout line, one with only one person on it. Everything seemed all right, business as usual, till he noticed the checkout man eyeing him sort of suspiciously while bagging the groceries of the customer who'd just paid, and turned around and saw a man behind him without a coat and holding two loaves of bread—what was the man doing coatless when it was so cold out? . . . snow was predicted tonight, temperatures dipping into the teens and there were already freezing winds. Maybe he worked in the café a few doors down, or the one on the next block and he didn't bother with a coat because he was so close and was buying the loaves because they'd run out of the bread they had delivered early each day—Gould had seen the tall bags of them lying up against the café doors at seven or so when he went out for the paper or a run . . . or else they got him, and his stomach went cold. Well, shit, Jesus, too late if they did have him, for what could he do now, take the stuff out of his pocket and drop them into the basket? But wasn't he only imagining the worst again, which he often did, for he already explained the suspicious looks: his clothes, appearance, and he wasn't a regular here—had only been in the store three times in two weeks and always for just a couple of small items, and in this city, or just this kind of poorer neighborhood, if they don't know you they don't trust you, or something like that, but nobody's going to jump him just because he might fit the profile of what they think's a potential thief. He was fine, so long as nothing dropped out of his pocket or the pocket flap didn't open and someone could see right inside, and once out of here and around the corner he'll stick the stuff into his supermarket bag and go home, maybe even run with the bag he'd be so relieved, and in the room have a glass of wine or shot of scotch, even if

Evangeline complained about him drinking late at night—said it did something to his stomach, made him toss around in bed, keeping her up. "Next," the checkout man said, and he put the things in the basket onto that rubber runway, man rang everything up, wasn't looking suspiciously at him anymore, guy behind him was looking at the clock above the front window, the old woman was now on the next checkout line, three customers away from being taken—his would have been the best line to get on: just he and the guy with his two identical loaves, and he was almost done, and one of the people in front of her had a shopping cart of maybe fifteen items. She didn't look at him when he looked her way, maybe that was why she didn't get on his line: didn't want to talk to him anymore, felt their conversation—attention he gave her in the health-and-body-care aisle—was too much or had gone far enough or else she didn't want to be on his line because of the trouble she expected on it . . . but then she wouldn't have gone on any line, right? She would have stayed away from the checkout area, wouldn't have wanted to be seen and eventually blamed by him. The checkout man said what Gould owed, he paid, his stuff was bagged and handed to him, he said "Thanks," man said nothing and looked hard at the guy behind Gould in a way that suggested "What do we do next?" and Gould thought "Oh shit, get out of here," and started for the door and just as he had his hand on it to push it open, someone grabbed him from behind—the coatless man— the checkout guy ran around the counter and shoved his hands down both Gould's coat pockets and Gould said "Hey, what the hell you doing?—get off me, get off," and tried slapping the man's hand away from the pocket with the things in it but his arms were held tight, tried wriggling out of the grip and got one arm loose, checkout man yelled "Cliff . . . Hugo," and two young men with store aprons on ran to help the coatless man hold him, and he started dragging them all through the front door, wanted to get outside, once on the street they couldn't touch him, or was it the other way around, they couldn't grab you inside?—but he wrenched and tugged and grunted and lunged them along with him till he was past the door, on the street, still holding the bag, he suddenly realized, and dropped it and got his other arm free and slashed his hands in the air, whirling round and round as he did till there was nobody within fifteen feet of him, then felt his pocket—wait, the guy already took the stuff, but one of the brushes was still in it—and the checkout man said "You bum, you thief, these what you looking for?" and held up a toothbrush and the toothpaste. "You're lucky we don't hold you for the cops. Don't ever come back here, you creep, and take what you paid for," pushing the bag of groceries toward Gould with his foot, "that's the last you'll ever get from us," and Gould kicked the bag and said "Stick it you know where," and the coatless man said "Up our asses? Up yours, you dope. Feel good we didn't bash the bejesus out of you, which we could have—we'd the legal right to—defending ourselves against a bona fide thief. You're worse than a fucking street hooker," and Gould said "That so? I am? Well you forgot this, mister," and took out the other toothbrush and threw it on the ground to them and the checkout man said "Oh, bravado, or bravo—whatever they call those heroics—but just what we needed from the jerk. Forget him, we got work to do," and picked up the brush: "Every little bit appreciated," and laughed and they all went in, the two young men laying dirty looks on Gould before they went through the door. People on the street had stopped and were looking at him but keeping their distance and he said to a group of them "It was for my kids . . . I didn't hardly have the money for everything," in an Irish brogue and what he thought were the words and the way the Irish would use them, though why he went into it he didn't know. "The big store's gotta make its extortionate profit, that it? So what's a poor father to do? And three kids, not two, and I wanted them to have clean teeth after they finished their over-priced store cereal, they'd have to be sharing a single toothbrush between them anyway, but have you seen what even the cheapest toothbrush and toothpaste cost today? An arm and a leg it is, an arm and a leg." By now everyone but what looked like a bum had walked away, some shaking their heads at him and giving him that expression and he yelled "Where you going? Why you running? It's the godawful truth that I've been telling ya, but what am I wasting my breath on you for?" and started down the street to the house—maybe so they'd have more trouble point-ing him out some day later: "No, couldn't be the shoplifter; that one was dressed like a beggar and was loony as they come and had this thick Irish accent"—a few large flat snowflakes were now slowly falling and he thought "Perfect, just what the scene called for," and slapped at the flakes and said "Fuck it, I don't care if any of the store people are there, what's mine's mine and like they said I paid good money for," and ran back for the bag.

The bum was standing over it and Gould said "That's mine, sorry," and picked it up. It was wet and torn, an orange had rolled out of it to the curb and he stuck it into his side coat pocket, put the other orange into the other pocket, folded up the bag best he could with the rest of the things he bought, had to hold it from the bottom so it wouldn't split apart. When he got back to the room Brons was asleep in his cot, Evangeline was sitting up in bed drinking tea and reading, he wasn't going to say anything about what happened but she said "My goodness, look at you, you're a mess," and he said "It's beginning to snow, flakes falling so lazily, but sort of a cross between snow and rain—more like a floating slush, if that's possible—so I suppose my hair got a little wet," and she said "It's not that. The collar of your coat's torn, you have a scratch on your forehead that's still bleeding, you look roughed up—what did you do, get mugged, fall?" and he said "No," patting his forehead with a tissue, "but do I have those?" and looked at the tissue and said "Ah, it's more slush than blood. I didn't even know. Though I actually got close to being mugged, but didn't want to say anything," and told her what happened, didn't embellish or hold back, right down to the Irish brogue: "Don't ask me why; maybe to get them off my trail and so they wouldn't think the thief was Jewish," and she said "Oh stop. And the whole thing's horrible. Why'd you ever do it?" and he said "I could make up a lot of excuses but I just didn't think I could afford all the things you wanted or that I'd get caught, even if I knew how dumb it was," and she said "Was it ever. Suppose they had reported you or held you for the cops? You'd

252

have gone to jail. It would have disrupted our lives so much that I'm sure I would have had to quit school for a few weeks. And we would have been thrown out of here, since the landlady has this rule about that kind of behavior—it's written right up there on the common dining room wall—and then where would we have lived till we get our place? I couldn't have slunked back to your parents; and also think what it would have done to them and to Brons," and put her finger over her lips. "If we needed toothpaste that bad," she whispered, "we could have borrowed someone's here, though we still have enough in the tube to roll it up and get a couple more brushings from it. And I only said we needed new toothbrushes, not that we were out of them," and he said "This will sound stupid too, and I'm not saying it to elicit any sympathy, but I thought you'd like that I brought everything back that you asked for," and she said "I would have if you had paid for it. And a brogue. You're not an actor. You can't even tell a story in two different voices. Let me hear it," and he whispered in what he thought was close to the same brogue "For my poor kids I did it, my three little dear ones and their sweet mother, whose teeth are rotting to the quick because they've no toothpaste to use and I can't afford a proper dentist," and she said "It stinks. You were probably as bad at fooling them with it as you were at taking their goods. Please, I beg of you, for Brons and me and yourself too, and because shoplifting's wrong, all wrong, no matter how bad the situation gets— don't ever do it again," and he said "I hate this life—here, this freaking craphole and so little money. But you're right; I'm a flop at everything I do—I know, you didn't say that—and I never want to be forgiven for it. And whatever you do don't tell Brons till he's all grown up, and only if you have to, for some reason," and Brons said from the cot "I already know, Gould. That was real dumb what you did. It's the only good store around here. Now I won't be let in because of you," and he said "Yes you will. I'll just have to stay outside."

She had orgasms where she said she saw heaven. In one she said she met up with her dead brother on a cloud and there was a great light all around them and he put out his hand and she looked surprised at it at first but then shook it and he grinned as if he was in total bliss and then the scene ended and Gould said "Was his arm straight out when you shook it?" and she said "Yes, the way people shake," and he said "What could it mean then, except for the immediate obvious? Anyway, I'd be suspicious of it," and she said "How, suspicious? And what do you mean 'the immediate obvious'?" and he said "I don't want to talk about your brother in regard to it. He's dead, and that, if what I'm saying about the dream's right—'dream is right,' I mean—" and she said "It wasn't a dream. I wasn't asleep. I was in ecstasy here, mentally removed, yes, but not unconscious," and he said "Well, it was like a dream—you were put into this almost otherworldly or immaterial state—so I'm looking at it as one. And to me it was just typical dreamlike projection, innocent because you were in this state, of what any sibling, same sex or different, but especially the opposite sex, would dream of if it was a dream or have images of if you're in this ecstatic displaced condition," and she said "What, though, what? You started it, so say, and not just that I-don't-want-to-go-into-it gibberishness and then more unintelligibleness piled onto it," and he said "Okay. Did your brother—you know—do certain things physical to you when you were a girl, like get you to masturbate him or try to or fingerfuck you or hint at one of those or both with the hope you'd do it or allow him to or even just expose his erect penis to you or just expose himself, erect or not, but where you knew it was just for exposing?" and she said "I'm sure he didn't on most of those. The hints, naturally, I wouldn't remember, but I don't think any of what you said happened. Though he was two years older, he was sickly almost from birth, so always, once I was seven or so, around six inches shorter than me and then, when I was twelve and he was fourteen, which is when he died, almost a foot shorter. And he was always very immature for his age, not only physically but emotionally— that's what my folks have said and sort of what I recall—my younger brother, I used to think of him as, starting when I was around eight—that he might have died long before he was old enough to get erections he was conscious of or know what to do with one to get relief, though I could be wrong. Maybe, in the secret of his room, it was his only pleasure; I'd like to think he at least had that, but I doubt it because I don't even know if he was strong enough to do it. No, I guess anyone could, if the hands aren't paralyzed and the genitals are developed and the nervous system's working, but what I'm saying is I don't think the last two were for him. He barely had hair under his arms and no little sprouts on his chest and face. And once I saw him getting out of this special sitz bath installed for him in the bathroom and when he was . . . well, this might have been a few months before he died and there was only the littlest of mustaches there and his prick, if it hadn't been tremendously shrunk by the heat of the bath, was more like a boy's half his age," and he said "That bathroom scene—" and she said "Don't make anything more out of it. I walked in by mistake. He was as embarrassed as I was and quickly covered himself up with his hands. Do me a favor and don't refer to him in that way again or try to analyze my orgasm making something like mystical experiences right after we've had sex. Your judgment's impaired because your mind's still fixed on the sex subject. Also because he was the dearest person there ever was to me, always so sweet and mild-mannered and shy and self-insulting and so on. But the most loving of boys—he used to clean up my room for me when I was at school and he was home getting special ed, take my dinner dishes to the sink, follow me around whenever he could—so the person I miss most and feel worst about and appreciate meeting up with any way I can. And if you put too unseemly a meaning to my encounters with him it might do something to my head where I never see him again, not even in my dreams," and he said "Okay, will do, but one more thing, if you don't mind, and this may be way off . . . in fact, maybe I shouldn't say it," and she said "Better you don't then, if it concerns him," and he said "It's mostly about you. Did you, maybe, ever try to fool around with him? . . . oh, that was dumb, wasn't it, you already said how embarrassed you both were at that sitz bath scene. But you've also said you've been sexually aware since you were eight and active since you were thirteen, so I thought there might be a slight possibility—is this really too off the mark?" and she said "Yes, but it's not one of your worst questions, given what I've said about myself and the reasonableness of looking at this sex thing from both sides. But I told you: after awhile he was like my younger brother, to be protected and not taken advantage of, besides that I'd never do anything that perverse, even then when my morality code wasn't quite formed. All right? But enough," and he nodded and after about a minute she said "So what do you think, you're rested yet? Because I feel I could reach that plateau again, or come near. I'd like to at least try to and then who can say what I'll see if I get there. Maybe my brother again who I can apologize to for my little chat with you before," and he said "Honestly, I must have turned some irrecuperable corner in my sex life, if that makes any sense, but I've been feeling the last few weeks I need more time between them and now with this one that maybe what we did could be my limit for the day," and she said "Don't tell me; all any girl has to do is wait fifteen minutes and then play with you," and he said "I don't know, and certainly not that soon, but that's how I feel now." She screamed during some orgasms, even when Brons was home though asleep, and cried after about every fourth one of them and then usually clung to him, sometimes all night, face burrowed into his neck or armpit till he had to force it out if he wanted to get some sleep. "I don't know what it is with sex and us," she once said, "but it sure is a major plus in our arrangement and it could be the thing that keeps us together most along with your love for Brons. I don't like that but I'll take it for the time being. I got off with lots of other guys, of course, or did till you moved in and will no doubt do again once you're gone from here. But with you, I don't know what it is but like with no one else I actually see things like the birth of the universe or a disconnected star field forming into a constellation I can recognize like a dog or crab and other phenomenal or historical occurrences. Whole Mayan or Aztecan villages—I forget which culture was the one in Mexico and which not—with ceremonial dances and drum-beatings and men in spooky headdresses and codpieces and women with their big boobs showing and kids at their teats and huge beautiful buildings and entrance gates and those things they call ziggurats, I think, but no one on top of them getting his head chopped off. Sea creatures, for instance, one time, a pair of them slithering out of the sea and in quicktime develop-ing teeny legs to walk on land with. And a couple of times—all right, once—I touched but just barely the hand of what seemed like a gentle God, though He had a twinkle in his eye, the old geezer, knew what we'd just done and what I was still in the midst of and that He might even be interested in having a turn with me Himself, so maybe He was only one of God's more trusted helpers—I was going to say 'advisors,' but God wouldn't have that—a couple of seats down from the ones who sit on either side of God's throne. It could be that our genitals are a perfect match, in spite of the differences in your length and my depth. And maybe also something about our respective ages and health and the area we live in and this great California air and that my house sits next to an enormous church and the feelings we have for each other at the time, like the last one—I felt very good about you before and during it. And where we both are in our general all-around erotic development, or just I am, since you never seem to have these incredible comes and highs after, unless you've been muting them and controlling the body quakes. It's possible I'm at my absolute peak in all this, that the last one or one of the near future ones will be the highest I'll ever reach and then they'll slowly start peaking lower, though I'd hate to believe it. But I'm even worse at figuring these things out than you are, my dear dummy, so why should we try?"

So it could have been that small thin bony body that had as much to do as anything in keeping them together, that's what he now thinks. Ninety-six pounds, sometimes up to ninety-eight, but evenly distributed, nicely proportioned, and muscular from the waist down. That he could lift her body up as he would a kid's, hold it in the air by the buttocks and thighs and set it down on top of him, the few times she let them do it in that position, turn it around even when he was on his back and she was completely off the ground, lift it up and down on him repeatedly and without her moving on her own once till they came and if she did first, then still bob her up and down till he came, and if he did first, then he couldn't go on and she bounced up and down on him but it didn't work and after he flopped out she complained, but his arms hardly getting tired during any of it, and it wasn't that he was a strong guy, though his shoulders were pretty big. Also that her body was so limber, hard and quick. Meaning, what he liked about it. And what she wore in the bedroom sometimes—he's saying what also got him excited: sheerest of outfits, tiniest of briefs, rarely any socks, stockings or bra and never a watch, and all he had to do was see the small line of pubic hair on top—was she lying when she said she never razored it to get it that way? He didn't think so, since she also said she wished it was bushier so at least in that area she didn't look like a pubey girl—and he'd make a move. He also liked picking her up, cradling her in his arms and carrying her to bed that way or to a chair or wherever they'd do it, once on a covered toilet seat, she sitting facing him and flushing the toilet when she started making noises or before she sat on him would turn the sink faucet on and let it run, because her son was playing in his room down the hall. And he never had to suggest twice that they make love. He'd raise an eyebrow a certain way—cock it like a fop; she knew the signal—or would only have to say "So, what do you say?" or give a particular smile, more like a dumb grin, that only meant one thing to them and she usually said "Sure, I'm game, give me a minute," or "I'm ready, are you?" for he mostly said it or gave these signs when he thought she'd be interested, since she often gave little hints herself: smile more seductive than her others, brushing past him making sure their hips touched when it was obvious she could have more easily gone around—and she'd whip all her clothes off, sometimes letting the underpants dangle on the end of her raised foot before she flipped it into the air and caught it, get under the covers and pull them down on his side, maybe plump his pillow in the middle, say "How much time we have?" if it was before he was going to work or they had people coming over or one of them had to pick up her son at nursery or he was returning from school on the bus or expected back soon from a friend's home.

She used to say that most of the jokes he made were coarse, foolish and old or just made no sense but certainly weren't funny except perhaps to an immature twelve-year-old boy who also wasn't too bright, which was why she seldom laughed at them. That most of the books he read were written not to be read but only to be written about they were so obscure, pedantic, longwinded and dull. That all his tedious hard work at the typewriter was going to go for nothing because he wrote about people he hadn't the clearest idea of, like what went on in their heads or how they felt or what their jobs or home life or history were about, besides that she was sick of him stinking up her sewing room all day with his body sweat when he typed. That almost all the so-called suggestions and advice he gave her son were the opposite of what she wanted the boy to know or do. That he was the worst driver she'd ever seen and every time she got in a car with him she took her life in her hands as well as her son's if she was dumb or desperate enough to bring him with them. That he ought to grow a mustache to make his bland face more interesting, and when he did, that he should grow a beard to wipe out the devastating effects of the mustache, because he now looked a little like Hitler or Groucho Marx or someone else she didn't like—anyway, awful, much worse than before and she was sorry she first encouraged him to grow it and now that he'd got to like that bush. That he was getting a big pot belly and also seemed out of breath half the time and he ought to run or exercise more and also dance a lot if he didn't want to keep looking ten years older than he was and ridiculous in pants and shirts that were now four sizes too small for him. That he had to find a better-paying job or just two of the same-paying ones if he wanted to continue living with them, because she just couldn't take any more, always being so close to broke. That the only thing he was really good for now was sex and more sex and that for sure wasn't enough for what she wanted in a man and in fact was probably the easiest thing for her to find. That she did appreciate that he'd been there for her son at a time when he most needed a man and for the music he listened to sometimes that she occasionally liked and the dishes he'd concocted and introduced her to, like a simple vinaigrette dressing and slicing up raw mushrooms into the salad and beef Strogonoff and that vegetable curry with all the extras, things she never knew existed not that she couldn't have lived without them. That he was a terrible baby sometimes, jumping back when a mouse darted across the room and being too afraid to chase after it with a broom, not jogging through certain streets because dogs there once ran after him and snarled. That he drank too much, talked too much and was so damn opinionated, as if nobody on the West Coast ever had a brainy idea but him or did anything with any taste, and he wore clothes that were completely wrong for this area and climate, railed against petty things that other people would just say "That's life, what can you do?" to and swallow. Talked and made noises in his sleep to the point where she wanted to wear earplugs when she went to bed, but if she did who'd hear Brons if there was some kind of emergency and he needed them, since he also slept as if nothing in the world could awake him. His voice and choice of phrases and words sometimes were so vedy English that he sounded like the classic closet pansy. All the coffee he spilled on her rugs that he'd never in a year have the money to get professionally cleaned. His smelly bowel movements, the urine drops he left on the toilet seat, his body and head hair all over the bathroom floor and stuck in the shower soap. Why'd he stay with her for years? he thought. Why didn't he leave after a few months or go those times she asked him to rather than cajole her to let him stay? She was right, a little into their relationship, when she said he only continued to live with her and claim he loved her and wanted to marry her because of her son. He took Brons to nursery most times, picked him up whenever he could too, had snacks with him after, made him lunch every day for school, got him up for school and made him breakfast while she slept and stayed with him at the corner till the school bus came, helped him with his spelling words for the weekly first-grade spelling tests, read books or told stories to him almost every night, played board games or cards with him when he was too tired to and wanted only to lie on his bed and read a book or had important other work to do but just because the boy asked him to. Did whatever he could for Brons. It was true the kid had him around his little finger, as Evangeline liked to say, but he didn't think he ever did anything that was wrong or bad for him. Spoiled him, Evangeline said, but so much that Brons might never be the same after Gould finally left, because no one would ever give in to him that way again. Sat with him and the humidifier under a makeshift tent on the bed when Brons had a bad respiratory infection and trouble breathing. Spent the night on a mattress on the floor in Brons's hospital room when he had his tonsils removed. Hoisted him onto his shoulders, hoisted him onto his back, ran or bounced around with him like that, the two of them pretending they were all sorts of things, cowboy on a bucking bronco, desert warrior on a camel, Bellerophon on Pegasus when he killed the Chimera, but mostly knight errant on his obedient horse, till they both dropped. Stayed by his bed most nights till Brons was very sleepy or asleep and a couple of times said to him because he liked to hear the answer to it— "Tell me," "Tell you what?" "You know, what I am to you," "You're in my head forever and wherever and ever, so help my heart."

One night she threw a glass of wine in his face. It was his wine, he'd been holding it, but he'd put it down to make a call on the kitchen phone. The wine sprayed all around him— cabinets, ceiling, floor; glass flew out of her hand by mistake, she later said, and hit his face and cut him but smashed against the wall. She'd overheard him making the call. He was telling a woman he'd known before he'd met Evangeline that he was going to pack his essential things right away and somehow get to her place in Berkeley, and if the buses weren't running this late along El Camino and then from San Francisco or no friend would drive him to the Greyhound in Redwood City or all the way, he'd even splurge his last buck on a cab, for that was how much he wanted to get away. He and Evangeline had had a terrific fight that night, he then said he was leaving; she said "Shut up, you'll wake the kid," he said "What do you think our row was doing, and don't you think he should know by now how we really feel about each other?" she said "Great, couldn't be better, what a deal I won't pass up: get your ass out of my house, you filthy bastard; disappear for good." The woman said she could put him up for a few days, or more if it worked out between them, but they'd see. He said he should be there in a couple of hours if he made good connections, less if he got a ride right to her. "Anyway, don't wait up; put the key behind that brick, if you still use it and it's still a safe spot. I have your address and I think I remember where it is. Just tell me, does the key turn to the left or right?" Then the wine came and next the glass and then the threat not to use the phone again to call a friend or she'd get the cops. Knapsack and typewriter packed, he'd wiped the wine off the cabinets, ceiling and floor, looked in on Brons but didn't bend down to kiss him or touch his head, knocked on her bedroom door and said "Just want you to know, I'm going now. I'll try to catch the last bus at the stop. If I don't make it, don't worry, I'm not coming back. I'll slide the keys under the front door after I lock it, and tell Brons I'll call him tomorrow afternoon or night and of course that he had nothing to do with my going and that I absolutely love him," and she said "Why are you telling me all this?" and he said "I thought it was important, especially that I wasn't leaving the front door unlocked; so, I'll see ya," and she said "Hold it, will you?" and opened the door and she was crying and he said "What the hell are you crying for?" and she said "Please don't be obtuse," and he said "Okay, and I didn't mean it that way," and he cried and then, maybe the tenth time since he started living with her—about to go, his things on his shoulder and in his hands, his things by the door, his things on the other side of the door and once on the sidewalk while he waited for a cab he'd called to take him to a friend's place—they made up and went to bed. He called the woman first and said he was staying, Evangeline and he had worked it out, and she said she was disappointed but understood and probably it was for the best—"No doubt it was, if you patched it up so fast; though after what you said happened tonight and what I could make out from her in the background in our first call, who can say if you're not risking your life by staying another night—excuse me, because you probably love her." "Do you think we get into these uncontrolled howling brawls just to have the greatest times in bed?" Evangeline said after and he said "I don't think so; I hope not. They're real, unfortunately, at least on my part; I truly hated you and wanted to flee," and she said "Then flee, nothing's holding you: no kids or contract or dues," and he said "That what you want?" and she said "You can see that right now it's not, but who can say for later if we have another mad brawl. We should try to work out what causes them. I know we've said that before, but this time to really work at it: therapy together, speaking to people whose judgments we trust, reading about it; whatever helps. Even if it doesn't result in any long-standing arrangement for us with the whole caboodle kit of wedding rings and children thrown in, we'd find out for future relationships, and some perhaps of longer standing than ours, what bugs us about living with someone. And for the time being just to make it better for each other and Brons, since our fights damage him." She'll change her mind, he thought; if he just does his best to keep things smooth between them for a year and goes along with everything she says about helping them stay together and learning why they're at each other so much, she'll want to get married and have a kid with him and then maybe a second one, when she sees how helpful a husband and good a father he is with the first one, and even three kids if her body can take it. Three's the number he wanted for years, he thought, but of his own. "What I'd love," he said in bed that same night, "is just to have one good solid no-great-spats year," and she said "That'd suit me. But I have to admit that another side of me says it wouldn't be altogether healthy, or right for our natures, not getting things out fast and furiously that way, and think of those terrific screws we'd be missing right after we made up again. But we'll work toward it. More than anything, there's Brons to consider, as I said. You're my dear."

They drove to Washington State to visit her folks. Another of his old cars, this one a station wagon he bought for a hundred dollars and had to keep filling up with oil, backseat down, she and Brons sleeping most of the way on a double-bed mattress. "Where'd you ever find that goof?" he overheard her father say to Evangeline. They were in the kitchen, he was upstairs in the guest room just for him—her parents had given them separate rooms—and heard it through the floor. "The nose, the jug ears, the beefy lips and he's half bald; he'll be hairless as an egg in five years, and he looks like a bath is an on-and-off thing with him, or maybe that's because his clothes are so old and unkempt and the half-assed way he shaves. Not at all attractive. If I was a girl and had to face that face every day, I'd puke," and she said "Some people would disagree with you." "Who? He's also got no personality or bite. He's all brains, I'll give you that, but of the useless kind—clever remarks and bon mots and facts and dates no one else cares a zig for. He's a full-fledged dud as far as I can tell; nothing compared to the men you used to date here and even the shitheel you married," and she said "Gould and I knew you wouldn't like him that much, which is why I didn't ask. Let's say I don't want to discuss it and it'd be too futile to defend his good qualities to you. I only wanted you two to meet, even if just once—Mom already has—and for Brons and I to see you both again, and I couldn't afford the plane," and her father said "You should have told me. If I knew what you were bringing, I would have come up with the fare gladly if you had left him behind." "Is he fey?" he overheard her father ask her mother from the same room. "She leads such a crazy life in California, who can say what she goes after these days. The new kick down there might be to try and get a homo to do it to you, and they're supposed to be plenty sensitive, aren't they? So maybe that's it too: they know a woman's needs and aren't demanding and rough," and her mother said "He's good to our grandson and that's something. And they seem to get along together, and she says they have a good time in bed—don't you breathe a word of this to anyone—so it can't be that fey silliness you say. And when I stayed with them he was all over her house doing nice things for her, besides being attentive and considerate to me: getting her coffee, even heating up the milk for it because she liked it in the morning café au lait. Cooking good dinners from scratch and working hard at his own job but tending a lot to Bronson too." "That's all she probably thinks of," her father said, "—sex, and hooking up with another man who's worth a million, which this dud will never have. It won't last, that's my prediction, but if it does then she's more lost than I thought," and her mother said "I hope you're right, because I also know—remember, not a word of this!—that there'll be no tears from her once he's gone, not even the onion kind." Evangeline introduced him to her cousins and friends still living in the area. Friendly but uninformed people, he thought, and unsophisticated and dull and a couple of them fairly dumb and with not a single funny thing said by any of them and not one interested in anything he was. "I fart on art," one guy said and she laughed and the guy said "Should I make one, to emphasize my point?" and lifted his leg and this really cracked her up and later Gould said "How could you laugh so hard at that idiotic art-fart remark?" and she said "Because it was hysterically funny, why else?—I'm no phony. Not only what was said and the way he combined those words to make a rhyme and then with his leg like he was about to lay one, but also because I knew how it'd annoy you. They're great fun, my old chums. Fun and real people, earthy, homey, plain-speaking, unheld-back and direct, and you can't tolerate anyone who doesn't babble on about high culture and character and ethics and farty art and all that and who also isn't a gasbag and cryptic nitpicker to go with it. I'm sorry, but to me this is humor. What you pass off for it is intellectual chitty chatchat told to tickle and riddle," and he said "God, what am I doing with you? And stuck in this nowhere land no less," and she said "That's what I've been asking myself too. If you want, Brons and I can stay a few extra days and take the plane back and you can set out early tomorrow morning," and he said "Yeah, I heard, your big daddy will come up with the fare and there won't even be any onion tears from you when I'm finally gone. Won't he be glad to see me go, but I'll be ecstatic. Your mother, I'll admit, I like a lot and have from the first time I met her; a real mensch," and she said "Oh, aren't you nice; she'll be so happy to hear what you said, and the particular word you used."

The summer before he knew her she was on a two-month bus trip to almost the northern tip of Alaska and back where just about every new hallucinogenic drug known at the time was used aboard. Brons was left with her parents, her ex-husband was the driver and paid most of the costs of the trip, some West Coast writers and artists and a couple of well-known beatniks from the East joined the bus for a few days at a time, "I think I banged every guy on the bus at least twice, including my husband, though I didn't know it was him both times till after we woke up. That's the kind of adventure it was, free and fun and powerful and out-and-out unpredictable and outrageous and the most lovingly communal of moving communes, where you made peace and even sweetly balled the ones you once loathed. You would have freaked out in a day if you were on it, no matter how many chickies you could have laid, and pissed everyone off with your stodgy worries and complaints and morning regimens and needs like exercise and a newspaper and coffee and if you didn't shit by ten A.M. every day you'd get frantic," and he said "I wouldn't have minded the sex with the different women, if they were clean. But I doubt I could have done it with anyone else if you were along, maybe because I wouldn't have even needed to—would that be the same with you?" and she said "Of course not. That's what the trip was about. To lose it for a week or month or however long you're aboard; but all the conventional ways of living, I'm saying, which are okay for when you're home," and he said "Anyway, the drugs, since I've a predisposition to bad trips—I blame it on my hyperactive imagination— would have driven me close to insane if I'd taken them. So I never would have chanced going on it and you would have had the bus to yourself, not that any of your friends would have invited me." A twelve-hour psychedelic movie was made of the trip, a great deal of it financed by her ex-husband, and they occasionally went to parties where parts of it were shown, once with a group in the room accompanying it with flute, drum, bell and saxophone music and another time where a woman did shadow puppet theater against the images on the screen, and each excerpt was so slow, set-up and preachy about the delights of various drugs and their individual medical, therapeutic and dietary uses and incompetently shot and edited that even though she was in a lot of it, mostly high and looking silly and acting amateurishly and dressed in costumes and paper hats and masks and things but a couple of times in a more somber, natural mood and just holding a lit cigarette or iced tea and talking normally about how she enjoyed the long trip and being with her friends and seeing the interesting and dramatic scenery but missed her kid, that he usually, without popping any pills or smoking pot like the rest of the people watching it from mattresses and pillows on the floor, soon fell asleep.

He once awoke in the morning to her going down on him.

He once awoke late at night to her and some guy he'd never seen humping on the rug by his bed. He loved seeing her standing on the heat register outside their bedroom during some of the colder winter days, her light nightgown billowing above her knees from the air coming up, hugging herself. That smile of hers then, the little girl again, when she caught him looking at her. "I'd say come, come to me," she once said, "but that'd mean taking my arms from around me to open them to you and I'm just *too* cold." She could balance herself over a sink and pee in it without any threat of collapsing the washstand, when their one toilet was taken or clogged. She was the fastest woman he'd ever known, dashing to the store a mile away for a single item and racing back in a total of something like twelve minutes. She beat him in races and he was fast, and she was also a terrific swimmer and could do lap after lap for an hour straight and come out of the pool breathing evenly. She taught him the butterfly stroke, the scissor kick, the butterfly kiss, how to part his hair with his fingers but where it stayed parted the whole day, to blow into a leaf's seedcase and get a loud toot and a few times a quick tune, to fix a wall switch, replace a pane of glass, unstop a toilet, and once, something he could never do and when the plunger he used wouldn't budge it, she shoved her hand into the toilet bowl hole and pulled out her son's shit-smeared toy seal, and also insisted that when they drove together or when he was alone with Brons that he keep his hands in the ten-to-two position on the steering wheel, something she said her ex-husband insisted she do "and he used to race cars at Indianapolis and was so skilled at the wheel that I once saw him drive blindfolded for half a mile." One of the front wheels blew on the car she was driving and the car spun around, ripped through a fence on the right side of the highway and flipped over and landed on its roof, and neither of them was hurt though they both couldn't sleep or slept very little for weeks. "We got out alive," she said the next day, "because I steered into the spin rather than away from it, which is what I want you to learn to do for slick roads or something like what happened to us, till it becomes automatic," and he said "But we ran off the road, car was completely out of control, and landed on our heads and were lucky we didn't get killed, so why do you say your way's better than any other?" and she said "If I had tried correcting the skid the way most people instinctively do we'd have ended up in oncoming traffic and got creamed for life." Every other month or so she'd put on garageman's overalls her father had given her and change the oil in her car and lube it more thoroughly, she said, than any service station ever would. She had a cat she trained to sit up and beg and jump on and off stools and run down piano keys and ring, she swore, to get someone to come to the door to let it in, though he always thought it was by accident, since there was a ledge right under the bell so all the cat had to do was touch it when it wanted to rub against something. She had an art show at a reputable gallery in San Francisco just for the framings she did of old etchings and prints and some of them where there was no picture of any sort inside and one reviewer called it the rarest and most rewarding of exhibits to witness: the start of a new art form the artist invented and another reviewer said her work amounted to little more than a simple pastime she'd become as accomplished at as a hundred other hobbyists in the Bay Area and would her next project involve putting together ribbons, pine cones, juniper berries and leaves into charming seasonal wreaths? She became so depressed by the second review that she quit making and selling the framings, dismantled the remaining ones and gave the frames to Goodwill and converted her art studio into a sewing room. She also succeeded in getting him to say "Excuse me" and "Thank you" and "You're welcome" and "God bless you" or "Gesundheit" and expressions like that to people at the appropriate times, which he must have been taught to do as a boy and possibly even practiced for years but only when she pointed it out did he realize he hadn't done it for a long time before he met her, or not as a rule, and to answer the phone with a hello rather than a "yeah?" or "yuh?" or grunt. She was always planting flower bulbs, rearranging flower beds, cutting flowers and turning them into bouquets and placing them in vases and jars around the house, and when some of the petals fell to the floor or table, putting them in a saucer of water on the kitchen windowsill. And other things and glimpses, but does any of this explain, once it was clear to them they should break up, why he did everything he could not to? He was doing relatively little during the time he was with her—odd jobs, full-time jobs, but none of them paying much—and had no idea what he'd do in the future, and living with her in her comfortable home in a pleasant community and with an interesting enough group of friends around her and for the first year having her car to drive till he was able to afford his own, gave him some stability, he could call it, or permanence of some sort, or grounding in a way, even if he had to work hard at all those jobs to keep it going, or just a place to sleep and eat and a woman to be with and lay and whom he truly loved for a while, and her child. Finally she said "I want to start seeing other men in a more serious vein, not simply a night here and escapade there when I'm fed up with you or want to take revenge because of something you did or said or am just turned on for a day or two to another guy, so I want you out of here for good and that's the last time I'm going to say it," and he said "Maybe things can still work out between us, they always have, and if they really work out you won't feel you need to see anyone else, just as I never have, and I won't have to leave," and she said "We've tried and tried and for the most part it's been wretched year after wretched year and it's never going to work and you know it, besides that you didn't hear much of what I said," and he said "I heard, I was listening, and you're right, of course, about almost everything, so why am I acting so desperately now? But what about Brons—won't my going hurt him?" and she said "He's of the age where it'll hurt for a short time and then, with all his other interests and activities and because I'm here for him and I'll make sure his father calls and shows up more, he'll get over it quicker than you think. It's also possible, because you can be so cloistering—" and he said "You probably mean 'cloying,' " and she said "I probably mean both, but what are you implying, that I'm not good with words? Anyway, what I was saying is that Brons will ultimately feel, because of your way of engulfing anyone you love, immensely relieved," and he said "Is that what you think I was with you, *engulfing?* And also that 'relief' business; you'll feel that way about me too once I'm out of here?" and she said "I wasn't even thinking of them for myself." So he left, drove to New York in a U-Drive-It car, later saw them and her new boyfriend in Spain, felt he went crazy there for a few days, maybe over her, maybe it was other things—he forgets now—but quickly recovered, and that was the last he saw of them except for brief visits to California because Brons asked him to come—two? three?—and a business trip when he only saw them for a day. And now he didn't even have a photo of her, though when he was living with her he had a few, including a topless shot of her and several other women from the bus trip she took to Alaska, and one with her, Brons and him mugging four times in a New York City photo machine, but he did have several of Brons, one a newspaper photo, which the *Chronicle* photographer sent him the original of when he wrote to him for it: Brons on his shoulders: "Father and Son, Gould and Bronson Bookbinder, Enjoying the First Spring Day in Golden Gate Park"—"Why didn't you tell them his real last name and that he was my son, instead of claiming he was your own?" and he said "I thought it'd be too much trouble getting that across to the photographer and that the paper wouldn't run the photo if they thought Brons and I weren't related and I was living with his mom. But I guess also because I liked the idea of it written that way"—others of Brons at his birthday party three years straight, graduating nursery school, entering first grade, on Stimson Beach making a huge sand sculpture of some sea animal with a shovel and pail, he and Brons in a rowboat on the

Stanford University lake, the two of them fishing off a cliff near Tarragona, Brons sitting in the driver's seat of his father's sports car and pretending to steer, and which Gould occasionally looked at if he didn't mind getting up on a chair in front of his open bedroom closet and taking out the shoebox of them and most of his other photos, some dating back to the time he was a boy himself.